Theatre and Drama

Other Subjects

THE MAGIC MIRROR

LOUIS FAURER

The Magic Mirror

SELECTED WRITINGS ON
THE THEATRE BY

George Jean Nathan

EDITED, TOGETHER WITH
AN INTRODUCTION, BY
THOMAS QUINN CURTISS

New York: Alfred · A · Knopf

1960

L. C. Catalog card number: 60–11316

THIS IS A BORZOI BOOK,
PUBLISHED BY ALFRED A. KNOPF, INC.

Copyright © 1960 by Alfred A. Knopf, Inc. All rights reserved. No part of this book may be reproduced in any form without permission in writing from the publisher, except by a reviewer who may quote brief passages in a review to be printed in a magazine or newspaper. Manufactured in the United States of America. Published simultaneously in Canada by McClelland & Stewart, Ltd.

FIRST EDITION

The selection on pages 23–6 is reprinted from I BELIEVE, *edited by Clifton Fadiman, by permission of Simon and Schuster, Inc. Copyright 1938, 1939 by Simon and Schuster, Inc.*

INTRODUCTION

A RT," DECLARED ZOLA, "is life seen through a temperament." Criticism, then, might be defined as art seen
through a temperament, and this description explains very
aptly the technique and interpretation of George Jean
Nathan.

Nathan held up his mirror to the drama, but the reflections it caught unfailingly included a glimpse of the critic
himself. His mirror was a magic instrument that tinted,
lent dazzle to, and sometimes distorted the object on which
it played. Nathan, in short, was a literary illusionist, a
dexterous practitioner of transformation and an untiring
prophet of change. One of his books is entitled *The Autobiography of an Attitude,* and indeed all his work is a form
of public confession. In reading him we see the stage
through his temperament, a strong and unique one, and
there is the bold stamp of his personality on almost every
paragraph to have come from his pen.

George Jean Nathan was born at Fort Wayne, Indiana,
at midnight on February 14, 1882. His father, Charles
Naret Nathan, was from Alsace-Lorraine and owned vine-
yards in France and a large coffee plantation near Bahia,
Brazil. Nathan père was a graduate of Heidelberg and one
of the best fencers of his time. An excellent linguist and
an insatiable traveler, he had spent six years in Buenos

Introduction

Aires, eight in Brazil, two in India, and three in Pekin. His father was one of the leading criminal lawyers of Paris, and his father's brother, Paul Duchelle Nathan, was professor of history at the University of Brussels.

George Jean's mother, Ella Nirdlinger Nathan, was born in Fort Wayne, and her parents came from Nordlingen, Germany. Her father, Frederick Nirdlinger, and her mother, the former Hannah Mysorson, were among the first settlers in Fort Wayne, then still a fort in Indian territory. Nirdlinger and his wife had come west by covered wagon from Chambersburg, Pennsylvania, where they had first settled on arriving in America. A cattleman and a frontier trader, Nirdlinger did his share in building up Fort Wayne as a Midwestern trading post.

Nathan's mother was educated at a convent in Notre Dame, Indiana. As a child Nathan often heard her speak of the quiet beauty and religious devotion of a certain classmate, Ella Quinlan, who came from Cleveland. Miss Quinlan, who in her schooldays considered becoming a nun, later married James O'Neill, the popular actor. Their second son was Eugene O'Neill.

When George Jean was six the family moved to Cleveland, where he was tutored privately and attended school. In the late 1890's he spent summers abroad with his father, and in 1898 he studied at the University of Bologna and in 1899 at Heidelberg. He entered Cornell in 1900 and was graduated in 1904. At college he became an expert fencer and took part in matches in France and Italy. He showed a flair for journalism in his undergraduate days and became editor of both the campus publications. In 1904 he came to New York to begin his professional career.

The theatre was very close to Nathan in his childhood. One of his uncles, S. F. Nixon, was an impresario who managed theatres in Philadelphia and Cleveland. When

Introduction

Sarah Bernhardt came to play an engagement at Nixon's playhouse in Cleveland she was a guest at the family home. As a souvenir of her visit she placed a ring on the finger of the ten-year-old George Jean. He wore it the rest of his life, a symbol perhaps of his devotion to the stage.

Another uncle, Charles Frederic Nirdlinger, was a dramatic critic and a translator whose adaptation of Echegaray's *El gran Galeoto* William Faversham acted with considerable success as *The World and His Wife*. It was Nirdlinger who guided the young Nathan, advising him to acquaint himself with the Continental drama and to adopt journalism as a profession. Nirdlinger had served as dramatic critic and foreign correspondent for the *New York Herald* and was a friend of that paper's owner, James Gordon Bennett. He secured his nephew his first newspaper post on the *Herald* as a thirty-dollar-a-week reporter.

Nathan was set to covering the police courts and several important murder trials. His first theatrical reporting was a short account of a Lincoln J. Carter melodrama, *Bedford's Hope*, which was considered unworthy of the attention of the first-string reviewer.

Nathan had developed a lively, bizarre style at a very early age, as may be observed by reading his acid, adolescent essay "Love: A Scientific Analysis," written when he was sixteen. He was soon contributing to the magazines, in addition to his newspaper reporting. Lynn G. Wright, a Cornell alumnus, was editing the Knapp magazines *Outing* and *The Bohemian*, and he suggested that Nathan take over their dramatic departments.

His bright, impudent articles, already marked by his original outlook, attracted other editors. Soon he had retired from the *New York Herald* and was writing for the *Burr McIntosh Monthly* and *Munsey's*, and in 1908 he became associated with *Harper's Monthly*. It was here that

Introduction

his reviews came to the attention of Norman Boyer, managing editor of *The Smart Set*, who engaged him as that periodical's dramatic critic. A month earlier Boyer had taken on a young man from Baltimore, H. L. Mencken, as book reviewer, and Mencken and Nathan first met in Boyer's office.

When Nathan began evaluating the American theatre in *The Smart Set*, David Belasco, Charles Klein, Augustus Thomas, and Clyde Fitch were the gods of the Rialto. No echo of the evolution that had been taking place in the European theatre since the 1880's had disturbed the stubborn slumber of Broadway. Even such Continental plays as were imported—the farces of Feydeau, the problem plays of Brieux, Bataille, and Bernstein, *Zaza* and Sardou —were emasculated by their American adaptors, for the public of that day would have thought the original versions "not quite nice." As recently as 1905 a play by Bernard Shaw had been banned in New York by the police.

The dreary octogenarian William Winter, who had been in command as an authority since the end of the Civil War, was dean of the native critical fraternity, and in his pompous essays prudery and pedantry were combined. He had denounced Ibsen and Shaw as spawn of the devil and referred to leading Continental actresses who came to tour the United States as "brazen strumpets."

Nathan's friend and mentor, James Huneker, steeplejack of all the arts, who in his books had written much about the dramatic renaissance in Europe, regarded the American stage as beneath critical comment, and Nathan's other great friend, H. L. Mencken, restricted his theatregoing to burlesque shows. The Broadway theatre of that era seemed a dull, despised, and barren field for a young man of talent, taste, and new ideas.

The theatre, however, amused Nathan even when it was

Introduction

very bad. Criticizing it served him as a flexible springboard for expressing his views on many matters, from literature to human conduct. Then, too, he found in this seeming wilderness some promising signs that his colleagues had loftily overlooked. He detected the shrewd craftsmanship of George M. Cohan's plays when Cohan was still being dismissed as a crass vaudeville vulgarian. He cited as an innovation George Ade's clever knack of catching the flavor of breezy American slang in his comedies. He hailed Ziegfeld as an artist for the suave production of his revues. He found in Arthur Hopkins a young producer of adventuresome spirit and budding style, and in Avery Hopwood a concocter of farces not inferior to those of the Paris boulevards.

But praise was a minor motif in his monthly concert. There was too much demolition work to be accomplished first.

The spectacular dynamiting must have been fun, and Nathan went at it with the gusto of a boy igniting the Fourth of July skyrockets. It shook the established producers and professors into an alarmed awakening and won him his spurs as a feared iconoclast. Later he wrote: "There are two kinds of dramatic critics: destructive and constructive. I am destructive. There are two kinds of guns: Krupp and pop."

It was a performance similar to the one Bernard Shaw had given in London in the 1890's when, taking over the drama columns of the *Saturday Review* at Frank Harris's request, he blasted the complacent British theatre and its vainglorious actor-managers into the vaulted blue. Like the Shavian performance, Nathan's had a salutary effect.

To the pre-1914 period of *The Smart Set* belong his daring onslaughts on the sacred idols of the era, his debunking of Augustus Thomas as the Great American Drama-

Introduction

tist, of Mrs. Fiske's pose as an intellectual, of Belasco as a metteur en scène comparable to Stanislavsky, Antoine, Reinhardt, and Meyerhold, and his dismissal of native dramatic criticism as the tiresome and unenlightening ramblings of senile graybeards and rather backward, sentimental sophomores.

Puritanism, academicism, and commercialism were strongly entrenched as the guardians of the American stage, and to attack them was to court disfavor in many circles. In the independent *Smart Set* Nathan could have his full and devastating say, but elsewhere such outspoken criticism with its witty bite was not always welcome. A lighthearted, irreverent spoofing of a "Biblical" spectacle aroused the ire of the influencial theatre manager, Abraham Erlanger, and Nathan lost, from his list of syndicates, the Philadelphia *North American* and the Cleveland *Leader* and was relieved of his duties as dramatic critic of *Puck*.

Meanwhile, in addition to clearing the path for the American dramatists of the future by sweeping away the stupidities that had been accepted as tradition, Nathan— who became co-editor with H. L. Mencken of *The Smart Set* in 1914—was sounding a new note in American letters.

In the pages of this saucy, unorthodox magazine—a wicked, scarlet devil smiled knowingly on its cover—were published poetry, short stories, and short plays by such distinguished European authors as Yeats, Lord Dunsany, Aldous Huxley, Frank Wedekind, Arthur Schnitzler, Leonid Andreyev, and Hermann Bahr, none of whom were very familiar to the American reader at that time. The first work of James Joyce to appear in the United States—a story from *Dubliners*—was published in *The Smart Set*, as were the first of Joseph Conrad's two plays and W. Somerset Maugham's short story "Miss Thompson," later dramatized as *Rain*.

As editors, Mencken and Nathan gave space to many of the young American writers who were still struggling for recognition, and the magazine became a showcase for new talents, as *The New Yorker* was to become later on. Among the contributors were Theodore Dreiser, James Branch Cabell, Joseph Hergesheimer, Thomas Beer, Ruth Suckow, Carl Van Vechten, F. Scott Fitzgerald, John McClure, George Sterling, Jim Tully, Edgar Lee Masters, and Sherwood Anderson. Here were kindled the fires of the literary revolt that was to burst into full flame during the 1920's.

Nathan's long and relentless battle on the old-fashioned standards of the American theatre ended in victory about the time the Great War was drawing to a close in Europe. Belasco, Thomas, and the other idols were by then considered passé even by their former admirers. There was a new and daring spirit in the air, an exhilarating breath of spring, and the public was ripe for the rush of fresh ideas.

Many of the authors who had made their debut in *The Smart Set* were being widely read. Dreiser and Cabell, after bouts with the censors, had become best-sellers. The better plays from Europe were being imported intact. Hauptmann, Shaw, Porto-Riche, Molnar, Hermann Bahr, and Sacha Guitry were being presented by the commercial Broadway managers. The Washington Square Players moved uptown to the Garrick Theatre and founded the Theatre Guild. Zona Gale's realistic folk comedy, *Miss Lulu Bett*, was awarded the Pulitzer Prize. Zoë Akins and Susan Glaspell had their first plays produced, and Clare Kummer was introducing the Continental technique into native farce-writing.

In 1918 Eugene O'Neill, still unknown and living in Provincetown, sent a batch of his plays to *The Smart Set*.

Introduction

"I sent three of my one-acters to 'The Smart Set,' " he wrote Barrett H. Clark, the first of his biographers. "They were all three fo'c'sle plays, not at all the kind of thing 'The Smart Set' prints. I wrote Mencken that I knew this, but that I merely wanted his opinion of them. I had a fine letter from him, saying that he liked them and was passing them on to George Jean Nathan. I received a letter from Nathan also, and to my surprise the three plays were published in 'The Smart Set.' That was my first ray of recognition."

When O'Neill came to New York shortly after this to attend the performances of his cycle of sea plays in Greenwich Village, he and Nathan met and a firm friendship was formed. It would be difficult to overestimate the importance of their close association during the years that followed, the years that marked O'Neill's full development as a dramatist.

It was Nathan who had conditioned the American playgoer to accept such a dramatist as O'Neill. It was Nathan who persuaded John D. Williams to stage the first full-length O'Neill play, *Beyond the Horizon*, and it was Nathan again who urged Arthur Hopkins to produce *Anna Christie* when Hopkins became reluctant about the project.

It is supposed that O'Neill was a favorite of the critics from the beginning, but every one of his major plays— *The Great God Brown, Desire under the Elms, Strange Interlude*, and *Mourning Becomes Electra*—encountered all sorts of ridiculous objections from the reviewers. Even in 1947, after he had been honored with the Nobel Prize, one finds the New York Critics' Circle voting Arthur Miller's *All My Sons* the best play of the season over his *The Iceman Cometh*, now believed by many to be O'Neill's finest drama.

In O'Neill, Nathan saw an American playwright potentially capable of taking a lasting place in world drama. He criticized certain of O'Neill's plays severely, but he never lost sight of O'Neill's stature. Nathan led the campaign for O'Neill as America's foremost dramatist, and he often found that he was fighting alone.

With the publication of his books (his first, *Another Book about the Theatre*, appeared in 1915) Nathan's fame spread abroad. Reviewing Nathan's *The Popular Theatre* in his magazine, *The Mask*, in 1919, Gordon Craig wrote: "It would be a mistake to say that Mr. Nathan is as clever as Bernard Shaw—as a critic he is twice as clever—he sees —Shaw tries to see. He feels—Shaw thinks—that is the difference, and to us it seems so clever to be born with eyes with some sight in them. To say that Mr. Nathan possesses a clearness of vision, a breadth of horizon and vigour of ideas seldom found in present-day dramatic criticism would be to miss the target. Change the 'seldom' to 'never' and you hit the bull's eye."

William Archer, A. B. Walkley, Arnold Bennett, Arthur Symons, Max Beerbohm, Alfred Kerr, and Frank Harris were but a few of the European literary elite to echo the Craig verdict. Later Bernard Shaw hailed Nathan as "Intelligent Play-goer Number One." His books were translated into a dozen languages, and wherever there was theatre his name was known.

By 1925 Nathan was probably the most famous dramatic critic in the world and certainly the highest-paid. Aside from his magazine articles, his editorial chores, and his books (he published a book—usually one on the theatre— almost annually between 1915 and 1954) he wrote a weekly review for national syndication.

By 1925, too, Mencken and Nathan had left *The Smart Set* to found *The American Mercury,* of which they were at first again co-editors. But these two veterans who had done so much to bring about a new order in national literature were suddenly at odds. Mencken believed the new magazine should take on a different tone, discussing politics and American sociology at length and avoiding the purely literary, while Nathan reiterated his indifference to the world outside the arts. In 1926 Nathan withdrew from *The American Mercury* as co-editor, though he remained a contributing editor and dramatic critic until 1929, when he joined the staff of *Vanity Fair*.

In 1932—with Theodore Dreiser, Eugene O'Neill, Sherwood Anderson, James Branch Cabell, and Ernest Boyd—Nathan launched a magazine known as *The American Spectator*. A monthly newspaper devoted to the arts, it recalled in policy *The Smart Set*. Much worthy material by its editors and by contributors—among these were Sean O'Casey, Ivor Brown, Jim Tully, Thomas Beer, and Ben Hecht—appeared in its columns, but the time—the United States was in the midst of the Depression—was inopportune for such an exclusively literary venture, and in 1935 it ceased publication.

Thereafter Nathan became dramatic critic for *Newsweek* and *Scribner's*, and later for the New York *Journal-American* and the King Features syndicate, assignments he held until he was stricken with arteriosclerosis in 1956.

For over five decades Nathan was a prominent and picturesque figure of the New York scene and one who held the imagination of the public. He had an aristocratic manner and an aristocratic viewpoint that were in striking contrast to the background against which he moved, the background of democratic, happy-go-lucky Broadway. He was feared for his humorous sarcasm, his staggering erudition, and his delight in deriding pretense, and he was admired for his lordly comportment, his elegant dress, and his lasting good looks. He had a close circle of friends and did

Introduction

not seem anxious to enlarge it. From 1907 until the day of his death, April 8, 1958, his residence was the same book-lined studio apartment in the Hotel Royalton on 44th Street, just a step from Times Square.

About his achievements and influence as a critic there are no longer doubts. At first his merry fashion of telling the truth, his brilliant but informal style, and his ever-ready audacity disconcerted the ponderous just as the Shavian fireworks had startled them in the nineties. Nathan, like Shaw, could be profound without being heavy. He could be serious without being dull.

He helped in destroying the American theatre of old, and he aided enormously in keeping the values of the new American theatre high. After heralding O'Neill as a dramatist of heroic size, he encouraged William Saroyan, Maxwell Anderson, S. N. Behrman, Zoë Akins, Vincent Lawrence, George Kelly, Arthur Richman, and Arthur Miller. He was a staunch supporter of Sean O'Casey, Jean Giraudoux, Christopher Fry, and countless European play-wrights from Hauptmann to Ludwig Thoma and from the Capeks to the Quinteros. He demanded an appreciation of the musical show as an art, and he was always an exacting judge of acting and production.

There has always been a widespread curiosity about the man behind the criticism—who was often in the criticism, too—and on different occasions Nathan sought to satisfy this interest by exposing the Autobiography of the Atti-tude. That attitude, however, was ever changing, as the reader may discover in the section called "Nathan on Na-than." The revelations of the man of forty, which were set forth in *The World in Falseface* and which have since been quoted in most attacks on Nathan—from those by the Ku Klux Klan to those by Alfred Kazin—differ from the stock-taking of the man of sixty.

Introduction

In one burst of self-explanation he wrote: "My code of life and conduct is simply this: work hard, play to the allowable limit, disregard equally the good and bad opinions of others, never do a friend a dirty trick, eat and drink what you feel like when you feel like it, never grow indignant over anything, trust to tobacco for calm and serenity, bathe twice a day, modify the aesthetic philosophy of Croce but slightly with that of Santayana and achieve for one's self a pragmatic sufficiency in the beauty of the aesthetic surface of life, learn to play one musical instrument and then play it in private, never allow one's self even a passing thought of death, never contradict anyone or seek to prove anything to anyone unless one gets paid for it in cold, hard coin, live the moment to the utmost of its possibilities, treat one's enemies with polite inconsideration, avoid persons who are chronically in need, and be satisfied with life always, but never with one's self."

In the last lines of this credo we may have the key to the complicated personality of the critic, for Nathan was never satisfied either with himself or wholly with his brand of playful, surface philosophy. "Every change is a change for the better," he once remarked, and he was always ready to change his mind.

At seventy-three, he ended his long, proud bachelorhood by marrying the actress Julie Haydon; and the worldly boulevardier, renowned for his cynicism, died a convert to Catholicism.

To Nathan both art and life were forms of metamorphosis, and in mirroring the drama in his work he demonstrated the rich development that transformation ever brings.

Contents

Contents

I

NATHAN ON NATHAN

Nathan on Nathan: I

No LESS THAN once a week I am asked by some otherwise amiable person why I, after all these years, persist still in consecrating my time and what measure of talent I may possess to a critical consideration of the theatre. "You have said your say," they tell me. "The theatre is too trivial for your later years. Why continue? Why not devote your effort to books on other and more important subjects?" I have been told this so often of late that it has begun to disturb me a bit. It is time, I conclude, to seek counsel with myself. Why, then, let me ask of myself, *do* I persist?

Performing, in the first volume of his *Prejudices*, a critical phlebotomy upon me, H. L. Mencken made the following observation: "At the brink of his forty years, he remains faithful to the theatre; of his books, only one does not deal with it, and that one is a very small one. In four or five years he has scarcely written of aught else. I doubt that anything properly describable as enthusiasm is at the bottom of this assiduity; perhaps the right word is curiosity. . . . I sometimes wonder what keeps such a man in the theatre, breathing bad air nightly, gaping at prancing imbeciles, sitting cheek by jowl with cads. Perhaps there is, at bottom, a secret romanticism—a lingering residuum of a boyish delight in pasteboard and spangles, gaudy colours and soothing sounds, preposterous heroes and appetizing wenches."

It is true that enthusiasm does not figure in my effort.

3

I am, constitutionally, given to enthusiasm about nothing. But it is not true that curiosity is at the bottom of my effort. While curiosity is an habitual impulse with me, it has no part—or at best a very small part—in my devotion to the theatre. To the final indictment, however, I offer a plea of guilty, though with reservations. The theatre is, to me, a great toy; and upon the toys of the world what Mr. Mencken alludes to as my lingering residuum of boyish delight concentrates itself. What interests me in life—and my years have since he wrote marched across the frontier of forty—is the surface of life; life's music and color, its charm and ease, its humor and its loveliness. The great problems of the world—social, political, economic, and theological—do not concern me in the slightest. I care not who writes the laws of a country so long as I may listen to its songs. I can live every bit as happily under a King, or even a Kaiser, as under a President. One church is as good as another to me; I never enter one anyway, save only to delight in some particularly beautiful stained-glass window, or in some fine specimen of architecture, or in the whiskers of the Twelve Apostles. If all the Armenians were to be killed tomorrow and if half of Russia were to starve to death the day after, it would not matter to me in the least. What concerns me alone is myself, and the interests of a few close friends. For all I care, the rest of the world may go to hell at today's sunset. I was born in America, and America is to me, at the time of writing, the most comfortable country to live in—and also, at the time of writing, the very pleasantest—in the world. This is why, at the time of writing, I am here, and not in France, or in England, or elsewhere. But if England became more comfortable and more pleasant than America tomorrow, I'd live in England. And if I lived in England I should be no more interested in the important problems of England than I am now interested in the important problems of America. My sole interest lies in writing, and I can write as well in one place as in another, whether it be Barcelona, Spain, or Coon Rapids, Iowa. Give me a quiet room, a pad of paper, eight or nine sharp lead pencils, a handful of thin, mild cigars, and enough to eat and drink—all of which, by the Grace of God, are happily within my means—and I do not care a tinker's dam whether Germany invades Belgium or Belgium Germany, whether Ireland is free or not free, whether the Stock Exchange is bombed or not bombed, or whether the nations of the earth arm, disarm, or conclude to fight their wars by limiting their armies to biting each other. . . . On that day during the World War when the most critical battle was being fought, I sat in my still, sunlit, cozy library composing a chapter on aesthetics for a new book on the drama. And at five o'clock, my day's work done, I shook and drank a half-dozen excellent apéritifs.

Such, I appreciate, are not the confessions that men usually make, for they are evil and unpopular confessions. My only apology for them is that they are true. That is the kind of dog I happen to be, and, I take it, a curse upon me for it! But if some tremendous event were breaking upon the world and men and women were shaking their heads in terrified foreboding, I know myself well enough to know that if I had an agreeable engagement for the same evening I should keep it, were the streets flowing with lava and the heavens thundering forth their feuersnot. I speak, of course, figuratively, for if it so much as rains I do not challenge my comfort to the point of going out and getting my hat wet. What I mean to say, in plain English, is that if it rested with me to decide the fate of the West Virginia coal miners or to hear Fritz Kreisler play the fiddle, the West Virginia coal miners would have to wait until the next day. The Soviet theory of government doesn't interest me one tenth as much as Gordon Craig's theory of the theatre. Whether the Methodists will go to heaven or to hell when they die doesn't interest me one twentieth so much as Adele Astaire's dancing. And whether the Japs will conquer Los Angeles or Los Angeles the Japs doesn't begin to interest me one hundredth so much as whether Anatole France's next novel will be as fine as his memorable *Revolt of the Angels.* I am not glibly posing myself here as an "artist," an aloof, exotic, and elegant fellow with a maroon bud in his lapel and his nose in the air. I am merely a man gifted, as I see it, with an admirable practicability; one who believes that the highest happiness in life comes from doing one's job in the world as thoroughly well as one knows how, from viewing the world as a charming, serio-comic, childish circus, from having a few good, moderately witty friends, from avoiding indignation, irritation, and homely women, and from letting the rest—the uplift, the downlift, the whole kit and caboodle—go hang. Selfish? To be sure. What of it?

But what has all this directly to do with the theatre? The theatre, as I have said, is to me one of the world's pleasures. On such occasions as it devotes itself to fine art it is one of the world's genuine pleasures. On such occasions as it devotes itself instead to the spectacle of Dutch comedians alternately kicking each other in the scrobiculus cordis and falling violently upon their amplitudina emphatica, it is a pleasure no less, albeit of a meaner species. It is, of course, not to be denied that for one evening of real pleasure in the theatre one often has to undergo a number of profound tortures, but the same thing holds true of the aesthetic satisfaction to be derived in an art gallery, where bogus art is often no less relatively in evidence than in the theatre. One reads a dozen new books before one encounters one that imparts a glow. One sits through a dozen new plays before one encounters a *White-Headed Boy*, or a *March Hares*, or a pas seul by George Bickel—and through nine or ten dozen before one encounters a *Caesar and Cleopatra*. To hold against the theatre on that score is to hold as well against most of the other sources of human gratification.

With all its faults, the theatre has amused and improved the spirit of man for centuries on end. Like the doll, it is the one toy that has outlived, and will continue to outlive, the horde of attacking years. It has now and then risen to greatness; it has now and then fallen to triviality—so have literature, and music, and sculpture, and painting. William Shakespeare and Owen Davis, Michelangelo and Paul Manship, Peter Paul Rubens and Penrhyn Stanlaws, Johann Sebastian Bach and Raymond Hubbell. There is no argument in contrasts; there are always contrasts. But aside from the question of the theatre's place in art, it remains that the theatre is good fun—and it is of good fun of one kind and another that I am, at the moment, speaking. My days are spent professionally in the channels of literature —my mornings with reading, my afternoons with writing. When evening comes, I am occasionally very glad to have done with literature. Dinner parties I can't abide; they bore me to death; I never accept an invitation to one if I can lie out of it. Drinking is amusing enough, but it is not easy to find sufficiently amusing persons to drink with. I am, furthermore, a bachelor and have no household duties to concern me, no wife to drive me crazy, no offspring to play peek-a-boo with. Clubs no longer interest me. Every time I enter one, some terrible wet-blanket, preposterously overjoyed at seeing me again after so long an absence, rushes up to me, invites me to dinner on Wednesday at the other end of Long Island, and asks me to tell him confidentially if it is really true that Irene Castle is in love with her husband. I lost my taste for card playing some years ago; if I want to go to a supper party, there are still four hours to kill; and the diversions that most persons favor in the intervening time do not especially quicken me. There is left, as Goethe agreed, the theatre. There is left, between the demitasse and the bedtime cigarette, this night *Romeo and Juliet,* that night Sam Bernard, this night *Electra,* that night Ann Pennington, this night a smash of beauty, and that, a smash of slapsticks. A farce by the younger Guitry, an operetta from the Kärntner-Ring, a burlesque show down in Fourteenth Street, the monkey-shines of Robert B. Mantell, a Eugene O'Neill play, a touch of double meaning from Budapest, an unintentionally jocose English "society play," a tune by Oskar Straus or Emmerich Kalman or Victor Herbert, a Ziegfeld show, something by Dunsany or Synge or Rostand or Thoma, a revival of some excellent comedy or merely, perhaps, a trim ankle, a sudden, surprising lightning flash of real poetry, a comedian with an allegorical nose—one pays one's money and takes one's choice. It is the grab-bag nature of the theatre that makes it what it is. It is not curiosity that takes me there, but hope.

But all this has to do with the theatre merely as a diversion, and not as the peg for a writing man on which to hang, as I have more or less hung, a career. Pleasure is one thing, serious work quite another thing. Well, let us see. The theatre, as I look at it, is one of the best subjects in the world from which to fashion a variegated assortment of predicates. It is almost impossible for the writer on politics to use politics as a hook whereon to hang his opinions, say, of music or cow diseases. The same thing holds true of writers on music itself, or painting, or architecture, or sports, or science, or archaeology, or economics, or religion, or almost anything save books. The theatre, to the contrary, by the very nature of its diverse constituent elements and its peculiar ramifications offers to the man who writes about it a hundred convenient opportunities to air his views con sordino on nearly everything under the sun, and what a writer craves is such opportunities. What is more, these digressions from the main theme are not, in dramatic and theatrical criticism, so patently or objectionably out of key as they would be in other forms of critical exposition. Furthermore, if Mr. H. G. Wells is justified in using the history of the whole world to work off his implied opinion of Lloyd George, I see no reason why objection should be made to me for using a single line in a play by Mr. Samuel Shipman to work off my opinion of unipolar induction, sex hygiene, the political situation in central Siam, or anything else.

For such meditations, the theatre provides an admirably provocative field. One of the best ideas I ever got for a digressive essay on humor came to me while I was watching the characters in a Strindberg play go crazy. The best essay on Shakespeare that I ever composed was inspired by a play written by the Hattons. My most valuable sardonic ideas on the labor problem came to me while a two-hundred-pound blonde in strip tights was being chased around the stage of a fifty-cent burlesque theatre by an Irish comedian, as the soundest theory I ever achieved on the flaw in Regulus' African campaign in the first Punic war was inspired by a shapely leg in a Gaiety show. This is why my critical writings deal at times with trivial and obscure plays and playwrights. The trivial is often the inspiration of something that is not trivial. Shakespeare so engrosses the mind that it cannot wander, cannot stray into other meadows. It is in the tensest moment of a Broadway crook play that one philosophizes upon the initiative and referendum, the life and habits of the bee, the condition of the babies in the southern provinces of Russia, the art of Henri Emmanuel Félix Philippoteaux, and the battle of Bull Run.

I am, of course, not so vainglorious as to imply that what I personally am able to derive from the trivial is always unfortunately also not trivial; I address myself simply to the theory, which is, at least in the instance of others more talented than I, sound enough. The common notion that only great art can inspire and produce great criticism does not entirely convince me. Great criticism often from little acorns grows. Dryden's "Defence of an Essay of Dramatic Poesy" grew out of a third-rate preface to his brother-in-law's book of fourth-rate plays, as his "Of Heroic Plays" and "Defence of the Epilogue" grew out of Buckingham's inconsiderable *The Rehearsal*. Some of the greatest criticism in Lessing's *Hamburg Dramaturgy* grew out of completely negligible theatrical performances. Goethe wrote imperishable criticism that grew out of plays by Kotzebue, Raupach, and Iffland, and some of Zola's finest critical writing (vide "Our Dramatic Authors" and, more particularly, "Naturalism in the Theatre") was inspired, during the years of his service as dramatic critic, by the trifling exhibitions that he was forced to sit through. Some of Hazlitt's most pointed criticism in his celebrated "On the Comic Writers of the Last Century" was derived from such artistic immaterialities as Mrs. Centlivre, the actor Liston, and Cibber's feeble *Love in a Riddle*, together with such mediocrities in playwriting as Bickerstaff, Arthur Murphy, Mrs. Cowley, Charles Macklin, and John O'Keefe. And half of George Bernard Shaw's admirable critical essays are founded upon such things as *Trilby*, *The Girl I Left Behind Me*, *The Sign of the Cross*, *The Colleen Bawn*, *True Blue*, *The Sin of St. Hulda*, *A Night Out*, *Under the Red Robe*, *The Sorrows of Satan*, *The White Heather*, *The*

Nathan on Nathan: I

Heart of Maryland—plays by Sydney Grundy, Stanley Weyman, Marie Corelli, Herman Merivale, Paul Potter, and David Belasco—French bedroom farces by Antony Mars, Drury Lane melodramas by Cecil Raleigh, and leg shows. . . . A thousand trivialities are placed in the test tubes of aesthetics that a single piece of sound criticism may endure. Ten thousand unknown men die in battle that history shall record—and the human race take inspiration from—the name of a hill.

This, then, is one way in which I, hopeful of worthy critical accomplishment on some future day, look on the theatre. I do not deny, plainly enough, that I might perhaps more profitably devote my efforts to writing on a subject or subjects of conceivably graver importance to the world we live in; some such subject, say, as a theory for the improvement of the condition of the working classes, or birth control, or civil-service reform, or international peace, or Peggy Hopkins; but I know nothing about such things, and, as I have already said, care less. What interests me are not the troubles or problems of the world, but its joys. Art, the thrill of beauty, and the aesthetic happiness of the minority are among these joys. And in so far as the theatre can provide them, the theatre engages me.

Life, as I see it, is for the fortunate few—life with all its Chinese lanterns, and sudden lovely tunes, and gay sadness. In so far as I have any philosophy at all, it is founded upon that theory. For the Nietzschean "Be hard!" I have no use, however. It savors too much of cannon, thong, and overly intense purpose. For myself I substitute "Be indifferent." I was born indifferent; and at forty I find myself unchanged in attitude. When I read some enkindled yogi's indignations over the slaughter of eight thousand Polish Jews, or over the corrupt administration in this or that country, state, or city, or over the Ku Klux Klan, the absence of true culture in Kansas, the riots in Dublin, or the political machinations of the American Legion, I only smile, and wonder. Indignation does not make, and never has made, the world any better than has my own objectionable philosophy of contentful laissez-faire. No great man from Jesus Christ to Stonewall Jackson has, in his effort to make the world better, been fired by philosophical asperity and spleen. Rome, the greatest nation in history, was never indignant about anything. Nor has been or is the nation of tomorrow, Japan. The chronic indignation of France is rapidly driving her onto the rocks.

It is in this spirit that I seek the theatre as an outlet for my ideas. An idea, on whatever subject, seems to me to be more in key with my attitude toward life if it is predicated upon an art. I like the notion of that kind of ideational genealogy. Art is, in the view of nine tenths of the human race, bootless, "unpractical." Thus, whether good or bad, art provides an admirable postulate for my philosophical snobberies. Life, to me, is artificial; all my criticism of drama is based upon the theory that drama is artificial life. There isn't so much difference, in my way of looking at things, between life as it actually is and life as it is shown in the theatre. I have often been accused of this attitude by critics of my criticism, and often been lambasted for it; I plead guilty to the charge. The theory that drama, while admittedly mimicking life, yet in some esoteric way departs violently and absurdly from life is maintained chiefly by persons whose life departs violently and absurdly from drama. "That isn't true to life," said the Harlem shoe dealer, as he watched *Lord and Lady Algy*. "That isn't true to life," echoed the flapper, as she watched *Rosmersholm*. . . .

Artificiality is often a premise from which one may draw

sound and ponderable conclusions. There is no more logical reason why a sound philosophy may not be extracted
from such variably factitious a thing as a play by Björnson
than there is why a sound philosophy may not be extracted
from such equally variable and factitious a thing as the
naturalist transcendentalism of Lorenz Oken or the Kirk-
caldyan gospel of unscrupulous Mammonism. If there is in
all this an air of what Mr. Burton Rascoe alludes to as the
intellectual practical joke that I frequently play whereby
I may have my little laugh on the reader, I hasten to make
assurance that it is the fault of my defective writing alone,
and not of my convictions. That I am not always able, alas,
to make the most of the opportunities that the theatre and
its drama offer in this direction, that the ideas I am able to
develop from the artificiality of the theatre are not often
notable or even remotely interesting, is nothing against the
doctrine and everything against the meagerness of my
talents.

Drama, to come more intimately to cases, is—to me—
one of the most interesting of the seven arts. With music
and literature, it appeals to me more than all the others in
combination. Unlike sculpture and painting, it is alive. It
is quick, electric; genius in flame. It *is* literature; they are
Siamese twins. It *is,* in Shakespeare and even in such as
Rostand, music: music on the violins of metaphor, on the
cellos of phrase, on the drums of rumbling adjectives and
verbs. There is for me a greater aesthetic thrill in the second scene of Act II of *Midsummer Night's Dream* alone
than in all the sculpture in the whole of Italy.

But, the argument goes, the theatre does not always, or
even often, vouchsafe such agreeable and tonic reactions.
Well, neither does the printed book page in literature nor
the concert hall in music. If the theatre gives us a new Roi
Cooper Megrue more often than it gives us a new Haupt-

mann, so the printed book page gives a new E. Phillips Oppenheim more often than it gives us a new Joseph Conrad. And the concert hall gives us many more Vincent d'Indys and Tschaikowskys than it gives us Liszts. What man is there who wouldn't sit through fifty compositions by Erik Satie, Walter Braunfels, Harry von Tilzer, Tosti, Josef Suk, Rudolf Friml, Hans Pfitzner, Zdenko Fibich, Othmar Schoeck, Elgar, and Ravel if that were the price for hearing Chopin's scherzo in E major? And what man is there who wouldn't sit through fifty plays by Horace Annesley Vachell, Jules Eckert Goodman, Charlotte Chisholm Cushing, the Rev. Thomas Dixon, Wilson Collison, George Scarborough, Cosmo Hamilton, and the Hattons if that were the penalty for seeing, on the fifty-first evening, Rostand's *Last Night of Don Juan?* Art, whatever her platform, is sparing, even miserly, with her genuine gifts.

But, unlike in the instance of the other arts where it is a case of art or nothing, a case either of aesthetic satisfaction or aesthetic irritation and disgust, the theatre is often immensely agreeable in an obscene way when it is not concerning itself with art of any size, shape, or color. When it is concerning itself with art, the theatre is at once great, noble, and hugely delightful. When it is not concerning itself with art, the theatre is neither great nor noble, but it is often hugely delightful just the same. I have made bold to hint as much on a previous page. Mr. Charles Judels's lengthy description of his brother's prowess as an architect of superhumanly toothsome omelets in the show called *For Goodness Sake* has no more relation to art than it has to pleuro-pneumonia in horses, but it would take a peculiar idiot to deny that it is tremendously enjoyable for all that. August Wilhelm Schlegel would have laughed himself sick over it. And so would any other serious and important critic and art lover either before or since his time. W. C. Fields's golf game, Fred Karno's night in an English music hall, Harry Tate's aeroplane flight, Frisco's derby hat and cigar acrobatics, *Krausmeyer's Alley,* the old Russell Brothers' act, Bert Savoy's Margie, Collin's and Hart's muscular nonsense, George Robey's painted nose, Ben-Ami's serious acting—of a thousand and one such things is the gaiety of the non-art theatre composed. There is, in the theatre, a surprise ever around the corner. It may be a great performance of *Hamlet,* or it may be a good new blackface comedian—or it may be a memorable night of superb awfulness such as that provided by the play called *Survival of the Fittest* down in the Greenwich Village Theatre. Each, in its different way, is excellent diversion.

If one goes to a concert hall and hears a bad performance or to an art exhibition and sees only bad paintings, one's disappointment is complete. In the theatre, contrariwise, the worst play and performance of the year may provide the greatest hilarity. I have been going to the theatre professionally now for more than eighteen years, and the four most thoroughly amusing evenings I have engaged during that period were provided by as many exhibitions so excessively bad that they baffle description, to wit, the play named above, the showing of *The London Follies* at Weber's Theatre about a dozen years ago, the play called *The Sacrifice* written, produced, and financed by a Brooklyn baker with his fat daughter in the star role, and the late Charles Frohman's production of Bataille's *The Foolish Virgin.* Nor do I set down merely a personal experience. There is not a man who saw any of these who will not wholeheartedly agree with me. For the theatre is never more entertaining than when its effort to entertain skids, and when the species of amusement that it provides is not strictly of the species that it has intended to provide. James K. Hackett's Macbeth with the fresh shave, talcum powder, and round Milwaukee haircut, Mrs. Fiske as the sixteen-year-old cutie in the first part of Edward Sheldon's *The High Road*, Robert Edeson's glisteningly new patent-leather pumps in the African jungle scene of a Rida Johnson Young masterpiece, Louis Mann's professorial curtain speeches expatiating upon the great literary properties of the gimcrack in which he is at the moment appearing, Jane Cowl's society play in which the Knickerbocker Club, the Ritz Hotel, and the Rolls-Royce motor car are mentioned every few minutes and in which the male guests at a fashionable town house appear at breakfast—if my memory doesn't err—in tennis flannels, the child actress as Mielchen in the production of *The Weavers* at the Irving Place Theatre who drops a piece of extremely intimate lingerie in a particularly tense dramatic situation, the Belasco adaptation of a Picard farce-comedy in which a chorus girl lives with a theatrical manager for a month but modestly declines to let him kiss her—find their match for sheer low amusement if you can!

That, in essence, is the theatre as I see it; that the theatre to which I devote my pen, and with a pestiferous catholicity of taste that embraces *Medea* and *The Follies*, Eleonora Duse and Florence Mills. I do not take it very seriously, for I am of the sort that takes nothing very seriously; nor on the other hand do I take it too lightly, for one who takes nothing very seriously takes nothing too lightly. I take it simply as, night in and night out, it comes before my eyes: a painted toy with something of true gold inside it, And so it is that I write of it. I criticize it as a man criticizes his own cocktails and his own God.

The World in Falseface, 1923

Nathan on Nathan: II

A MAN'S PHILOSOPHY, his attitude toward the world, is very seldom found to be the result of carefully reasoned reflection, meditation, and deduction. It is, to the contrary, generally the largely fortuitous end-product and sum-product of a hundred and one extra-subjective occurrences, adventures, and phenomena that have figured in his life. A man's immediate philosophy thus has infinitely less relation to cold intellect and shrewd penetration than to how much money he happens to have in the bank, how thin his hair is on top, how biologically spry he is when he wakes up in the morning, how much he has swindled his partner out of, or vice versa, how his last girl treated him, and how much genuine Piesporter he has left in his cellar.

There may be, true enough, men whose philosophical attitudes toward the world are removed from such things, whose doctrines and views are direct descendants of the cerebral centers, uncontaminated by the passing humors and megrims of life or by personal triumphs and despairs. But they are surely few and far between. Even the worldly philosophy of the greatest of our rationalists has doubtless been conditioned much more than we suspect by extra-metaphysical eventualities. To penetrate to the genesis of the divers philosophies of these presumably august and secluded fellows, we should, as I have hinted in the past, first ferret out their immediate state and condition of life, mind, health, heart, and finance at the time when they conceived and recorded their contributions to the wisdom of the world. What, in other words, were the provoking causes, the psychological bricks, the personal influences that figured in the rearing of their attitudes toward the cosmos? For example, what was Nietzsche's blood pressure and how hard was his tailor pressing him when he wrote *Human—All Too Human*? What had Schopenhauer's pet chambermaid, Gusti, just done to him when he sat down to his essay on women? What—I have often speculated—was the exact relationship of John Stuart Mill and his wife at the time he composed his celebrated paper on the subjection of the female of the species? What did Spencer eat and drink, and did his physician compel him to wear flannel underwear, and, if so, did it tickle? What—as I have asked a thousand times, with no satisfactory answer forthcoming—did Darwin's mother-in-law look like at the time he first thought of his theory of evolution?

The generality of men, indeed, great and small, are not so much the fathers of their worldly philosophy as the children. Their attitude toward life and their fellow men is not born in them, it is thrust upon them. If a man hasn't a cent in the world one day and suddenly comes into twenty thousand dollars the next, he is not the same man, and his philosophy is not the same philosophy. If a man's wife runs away with the family osteopath at five fifteen one afternoon, the man's five-ten philosophical attitude toward the globe we inhabit is as dead as a wet tennis ball. Man in the mass derives his view of the world from what the world does to him. His mind is not a free agent, but one in thrall to a thousand external happenings. Cleopatra's nose changed the history of the world no more than a defective sinus frequently changes the history of men's attitudes toward the world. If Walt Whitman had owned an extra pair of pants, he would have been a royalist.

. . .

Nathan on Nathan: II

What is my own philosophy of life? It is, in simple, merely this: to forget the miseries of the past and remember only its charms, to live the present to the limit of its utmost possibilities, and to view the future as one who has traveled romantically in a colorful far country views the skyline of his nearing homeland—with a sense of great content and slightly sad resignation.

The older I grow, the more I am persuaded that hedonism is the only sound and practical doctrine of faith for the intelligent man. I doubt, indeed, if there has ever lived an intelligent man whose end in life was not the achievement of a large and selfish pleasure. This latter is often shrewdly swathed in the deceptive silks of altruism or what not, but brush the silks aside and the truth of self-gratification is visible in all its nudity. Mohammed's altruism was as completely hedonistic as Charlemagne's frank hedonism. The greater the idealist, the greater the hedonist behind the whiskers.

Altruism, it seems to me, is the highest flowering of selfishness. In the heart of the greatest altruist one will always find the largest mirror. The history of altruism is a long series of self-engraved, adultatory epitaphs.

I find, upon honest reflection, that I am uplifted not by my virtues, but by my vices. They cheer me, make me happy and contented, make life seem worth while when my day's work is done, send the blood of tonic joy shooting through my veins, banish blueness and self-doubt and worry and despond.

I am not what is generally known as the popular type of man. That is, I am not the sort of man who is liked by the majority of persons with whom he comes into contact. I have a number of very good friends, among both men and women; but, aside from these, the general run of people whose paths cross my own are of as little personal interest to me as I am, assuredly, to them. I am not interesting to these persons because I prefer their disinterest, and am at no pains to conceal it. I know and always feel that it would be the simplest thing in the world to provoke their interest, at least to a degree, a technique grantedly not occult—but I am not able to persuade myself that their interest in me, the one way or the other, is worth concerning myself with. If I like a person, he or she knows it; I show my interest at once. If I don't care for a person, he or she knows it just as quickly; the lack of interest on my part is at once obvious.

All this makes for unpopularity. To be popular, one must show interest in persons and things that do not interest one and simultaneously conceal the interest that one has in persons and things that do interest one. One must always side with the prejudices and emotions of the person one happens to be with, however idiotic. One must laugh when one doesn't feel like it; be quiet when one would be gay. One must tell old women one loves them, and young women one doesn't. One must be humorous but never witty, interested but never enthusiastic, complacently bored but never tired. When one is with one's intellectual inferiors, one must agreeably reduce one's self not to the level of these others, but below that level, that they may have the comfortable feeling of being at complete conversational ease. One must be privy to the trick of flattering another person's vanity by contradicting what he says and then allowing him to convince one that he is right. One must pretend to take lightly what one feels about most profoundly. One may be original in manner, but never in thought.

I am able to negotiate all these things, but I decline to do so. Among the many millions of persons in this fair land, there are not more than a dozen at the very outside who, known to me personally, interest me personally in the slightest. The rest, so far as I am concerned, can go chase themselves.

Nothing is so challengeful as a defense of one's self. Nothing is so disarming as the custom of admitting everything.

Every time I hear a man pound a table with his fist and loudly endorse common sense I permit myself a pianissimo hiccup. What, I ask myself, is this much lauded common sense? Is it the absolute thing it is believed to be? Has the phrase, indeed, any common sense in it? The answer is no. Common sense is what any man, however doltish, believes it to be. What one man regards as common sense, further, another man, equally intelligent, does not regard as common sense. The common sense of one generation is often found to be the nonsense of the next generation. It is as variable as the wind. Common sense, in short, is frequently nothing more than a name for man's foolish conviction that what he thinks is right. Is there such a thing as absolute truth? Is there such a thing as absolute common sense? No prize is offered for the correct answer.

Common sense, in so far as it exists at all, is for the bourgeoisie. Nonsense is the privilege of the aristocracy. The worries of the world are for the common people. Meanwhile the elect may amuse and divert itself with tzigane philosophies and Puckish metaphysics. Only the cultivated, the well-to-do, and the secure are safe and free to indulge themselves in holidays from acumen.

I am a relatively happy and contented man. Therefore, I often act in ways and do things that others less fortunate than I consider unseemly and foolish.

Nathan on Nathan

Of all human emotions, this one of contentment is, however, the most puzzling. The contentment of other people I can often understand no better than I can understand my own. Why should contentment, the glorious harbor of the wearied mind and soul and heart of mortal man which should be reached only with the very greatest difficulty—why should this contentment so often be achieved, as it is achieved, through means of such childish simplicity and with such apparent ease? Is it because of all emotions contentment is the most transitory, that it is comparatively only of the moment, for the moment, and by the moment? Consider. There is no person who, for all his travail, does not achieve contentment many, many times during his life. It is, in point of fact, the one emotion, the one sensation, that he experiences the least trouble with. He may never achieve a woman's love, or a worth-while man's bracing hate, or a sweet grief, or supreme happiness, or the sense of power—any of the emotional satisfactions or paradoxically satisfactory dissatisfactions of life on earth, but contentment is none the less periodically his. In this lies the secret of man's smiling acceptance and endurance of his fate, whatever its nature. In his many little contentments rests life's apologia to him. A letter of pleasant promise that is destined never to be fulfilled, a decent meal with a cigar that burns evenly, the passing smile of a pretty girl, a successful petty swindle, the failure of an anticipated embarrassment to materialize, the mellifluous effect of a couple of whiskies and soda, a pair of surprisingly comfortable new shoes, the first well day after an illness—in such things, most of them of an obvious triviality, lies the seed of man's temporary complacency and happiness. For the moment he is reconciled with life; for the moment the rags of his ache and worldly disappointment are concealed beneath the ermine of a refulgent mirage.

As for happiness, on the other hand, the trouble with it is that it generally comes to one too early in life. I speak, of course, of the sensation of happiness, not happiness in its permanence, which, equally of course, is a bird so rare as to be almost nonexistent. In youth there are many more moments of happiness than there are in later years; youth is made happy by things that age is not; it is more easily tickled and satisfied by those phenomena of life that produce what passes for happiness. To be made happy, age demanded phenomena increasingly novel and vastly more complex. As sensations decrease in power with repetition, happiness thus becomes a weaker and weaker emotion as life goes on. It suffers a discounting; the warmth that it leaves as its residuum becomes less and less warm. The happiness of a little boy over a Christmas stocking filled with peppermint candy, tangerine oranges, and pretty tissue-paper cornucopias, were it susceptible of psychological laboratory analysis, would be found to be of six times the voltage of the happiness of the same little boy, now arrived at the age of fifty, who had just achieved his millionth dollar.

The Autobiography of an Attitude, 1925

Nathan on Nathan: III

Aᴌᴛʜᴏᴜɢʜ, with the passing of the years and the changing of the world we live in, certain convictions which I entertained in other and younger days have undergone some alteration, I find that the body and the essence of my beliefs remain, for good or ill, very much what they were. There are some things which I no longer believe, but they are of relatively lesser importance in the general fabric, and it may even happen that as time again passes and as the world again changes I may revert to my earlier hold with them. So the qualifications and amendments may be accepted as being possibly temporary.

No man can live through the upset and agony of our time and remain insensible to it. The sounds of barbaric cannon, the cries of starving and helpless masses of men, the tears and curses of humanity reach to even the remotest ivory tower. And the human mind, however independent and self-frontiered, must find its aloof contemplation invaded and shattered by them, as the pounding G minor chords and roaring drum invade and shatter the air-drawn mood of the Requiem. It is thus that philosophy is emotionalized out of some of its steel; it is thus that that eternally greatest enemy of cold, hard meditation, the heart, beats its sympathetic tune into the toughest and most gasconading brain.

Once—and still to a considerable extent—content to let the rest of the world manage its own concerns and to devote myself humbly to an attempt to manage my own, I accordingly find myself touched by the whirlpool that touches us all. In the midst of death, we are in life; and the mortal wounds of civilization fleck us with their blood. Ivory towers show red stains.

Although conceivably not all, as the indignant sentimentalists proclaim, in Fascism is bad, I am against Fascism in any of its phases, whether good or bad. Although not all in Communism, as the rashly arbitrary contend, is conceivably bad, I am equally against Communism, whether good or bad. Believing more fully than ever in individualism and autonomy, I compromise with my philosophy to the degree of persuading myself that, of all present forms of government, what goes roughly by the name of democracy is the least discommodious and the most satisfactory. There may be a better form in one's philosophical imagination, but this is a pragmatic age and we are not privileged to dwell in a land of our philosophical imagination. Its flag is too brilliantly hued for these harsh, drab days. It isn't that we must take the world as we find it. That we must never do. It is rather that we must try, vainly or successfully, to devote our efforts to make the world one day take us as we find ourselves. A lovely job, that!

With honor and decency to so appalling an extent forgotten and contemptuously dismissed on every hand, with so many of the nations of the world breaking their faith, their promise, and their word to one another, and with men in high office and position the world over turning traitor, welcher, thief, and poltroon, anyone who holds with honor and decency is likely to be looked upon today as either something of an eccentric or something of a dubious poseur. For there are fashions, paradoxically enough, in honor and decency, and they change with the changing times like fashions in clothes, dances, the lighter therapeutics, and anatomical morality. Yet I cannot believe in a world that does not accept and adhere to the old, unchanging concepts of honor and decency, and have only an acute disrelish for one that seeks apologetically to live by paraphrases.

I am no pacifist; far from it. To be a pacifist in today's world is akin to looking under the bed at night for Bérylune. This is an age of swords and guns, whether we like it or not, and swords and guns are not to be too happily met with sentimentalized logic and prayers. A cannon a day keeps the undertaker away. Let us be prepared to the teeth, and when the time comes, as it is sure to come, let us make further certain that our teeth are in good, sharp, biting condition. Diplomacy is simply procrastination. History, despite Henry Ford and H. G. Wells, is not a liar.

But under and beyond all such matters, it remains my conviction that in one's own work, whatever it may be, lie one's only salvation, one's only true purpose on earth, and one's only measure of self-justification and happiness. That there is in such a conviction a deplorable selfishness and an even more deplorable taint of vanity I duly appreciate, but I believe it still today as I believed it yesterday. There may come irresistible and necessary interruptions; there may be times when extrinsic phenomena for the moment cast doubt upon the integrity of one's convictions; but as God created man in His own image so man in turn creates his work in his own image—and that is the least reciprocity that he may humbly vouchsafe to his Maker.

Nor, as I have suggested, have the majority of my other earlier credences and conclusions altered. Some of my opinions on minor matters have experienced minor changes, obviously enough in view of internal changes in those matters themselves. But by and large I am what I have been and shall doubtless continue to be. For I persist in believing that men do not, basically, much change. Suddenly and for a spell they may now and again veer from the straight line of their imposed or self-imposed destiny, but soon thereafter you will generally discover them once again following their ingrained, traditional, and established paths, whether mental, emotional, physical, or spiritual—or all four together.

I Believe, 1939

II

CRITICAL THEORY

Aesthetic Jurisprudence
Dramatic Criticism

Aesthetic Jurisprudence

ART IS A REACHING OUT into the ugliness of the world for vagrant beauty and the imprisoning of it in a tangible dream. Criticism is the dream book. All art is a kind of subconscious madness expressed in terms of sanity; criticism is essential to the interpretation of its mysteries, for about everything truly beautiful there is ever something mysterious and disconcerting. Beauty is not always immediately recognizable as beauty; what often passes for beauty is mere infatuation; living beauty is like a love that has outlasted the middle years of life and has met triumphantly the test of time, and faith, and cynic meditation. For beauty is a sleepwalker in the endless corridors of the wakeful world, uncertain, groping, and not a little strange. And criticism is its tender guide.

Art is a partnership between the artist and the artist-critic. The former creates, the latter re-creates. Without criticism, art would of course still be art, and so with its windows walled in and with its lights extinguished would the Louvre still be the Louvre. Criticism is the windows and chandeliers of art; it illuminates the enveloping darkness in which art might otherwise rest only vaguely discernible, and perhaps altogether unseen.

Criticism, at its best, is a great, tall candle on the altar of art; at its worst, which is to say in its general run, a campaign torch flaring red in behalf of aesthetic ward-heelers. This campaign-torch motif in criticism, with its drunken enthusiasm and raucous hollering born of ignorance, together with what may be called the Prince Albert motif, with its sober, statue-like reserve born of ignorance that, being well-mannered, is not so bumptious as the other, has contributed largely to the common estimate of criticism as a profession but slightly more exalted than Second Avenue auctioneering if somewhat less than Fifth. Yet criticism is itself an art. It might, indeed, be well defined as an art within an art, since every work of art is the result of a struggle between the heart that is the artist himself and his mind that is the critic. Once his work is done, the artist's mind, tired from the bitterness of the struggle, takes the form of a second artist, puts on this second artist's strange hat, coat, and checkered trousers, and goes forth with refreshed vigor to gossip abroad how much of the first artist's work was the result of its original splendid vitality and how much the result of its original gradually diminished vitality and sad weariness. The wrangling that occurs at times between art and criticism is, at bottom, merely a fraternal discord, one in which Cain and Abel belabor each other with stuffed clubs. Criticism is often most sympathetic when it is apparently most cruel: the propounder of the sternest, hardest philosophy that the civilized world has known never failed sentimentally to kiss and embrace his sister, Therese Elisabeth Alexandra Nietzsche, every night at bedtime. "It is not possible," Cabell has written, "to drag inspiration from a woman's beauty unless you comprehend how easy it would be to murder her." And "Only those who have firmness may be really tender-hearted," said Rochefoucauld. One may sometimes even throw mud to tonic purpose. Consider Karlsbad.

Art is the haven wherein the disillusioned may find illusion. Truth is no part of art. Nor is the mission of art simple beauty, as the textbooks tell us. The mission of art is the magnification of simple beauty to proportions so heroic as to be almost overpowering. Art is a gross exaggeration of natural beauty; there was never a woman so beautiful as the Venus di Milo, or a man so beautiful as the Apollo Belvedere of the Vatican, or a sky so beautiful as Monet's, or a human speech so beautiful as Shakespeare's, or the song of a nightingale so beautiful as Ludwig van Beethoven's. But as art is a process of magnification, so criticism is a process of reduction. Its purpose is the reducing of the magnifications of art to the basic classic and aesthetic principles, and the subsequent interplay of fundamental skill and overtopping imagination.

The most general fault of criticism lies in a confusion of its own internal processes with those of art; it is in the habit of regarding the business of art as a reduction of life to its essence of beauty, and the business of criticism as an expansion of that essence to its fullest flow. The opposite is more reasonable. Art is a beautiful, swollen lie; criticism, a cold compass. The concern of art is with beauty; the concern of criticism is with truth. And truth and beauty, despite the Sunday school, are often strangers. This confusion of the business of art and that of criticism has given birth to the so-called "contagious," or inspirational, criticism, than which nothing is more mongrel and absurd. Criticism is designed to state facts—charmingly, gracefully, if possible, but still facts. It is not designed to exhort, enlist, convert. This is the business not of the critic, but of those readers of the critic whom the facts succeed in convincing and galvanizing. Contagious criticism is merely a vainglorious critic's essay at popularity; facts heated up to a degree where they melt into caressing nothingness.

But if this "criticism with a glow" is not to be given countenance, even less is to be suffered the criticism that, in its effort at a fastidious and elegant reserve, leans so far backward that it freezes its ears. This species of criticism fails not only to enkindle the reader, but fails also—and this is more important—to enkindle the critic himself. The ideal critic is perhaps much like a thermos bottle; full of warmth, he suggests the presence of the heat within him without radiating. This inner warmth is essential to a critic. But this inner warmth, where it exists, is automatically chilled and banished from a critic by a protracted indulgence in excessive critical reserve. Just as the professional frown assumed by a much photographed public magnifico often becomes stubbornly fixed upon his hitherto gentle brow, so does the prolonged spurious constraint of a critic in due time psychologically hoist him on his own petard. A writer's work does not grow more and more like him; a writer grows more and more like his work. The best writing that a man produces is always just a little superior to himself. There never was a literary artist who did not appreciate the difficulty of keeping up to the pace of his writings. A writer is dominated by the standard of his own writings; he is a slave in transitu, lashed, tormented, and miserable. The weak and inferior literary artist, such a critic as the one alluded to, soon becomes the helpless victim of his own writings; like a vampire of his own creation, they turn upon him and suck from him the warm blood that was erstwhile his. A pose in time becomes natural; a man with a good left eye cannot affect a monocle for years without eventually coming to need it. A critic cannot write ice without becoming in time himself at least partly frosted.

Paraphrasing Pascal, to little minds all things are great. Great art is in constant conflict with the awe of little minds. Art is something like a wonderful trapeze performer swinging high above the heads of the bewildered multitude and nervous lest it be made to lose its balance and to slip by the periodic sudden loud marvelings of the folks below. The little mind and its little criticism are the flattering foes of sound art. Such art demands for its training and triumph the countless preliminary body blows of muscular criticism guided by a muscular mind. Art and the artist cannot be developed by mere back-slapping. If art, according to Beulé, is the intervention of the human mind in the elements furnished by experience, criticism is the intervention of the human mind in the elements furnished by aesthetic passion. Art and the artist are ever youthful lovers; criticism is their chaperon.

I do not believe finally in this or that "theory" of criticism. There are as many sound and apt species of criticism as there are works to be criticized. To say that art must be criticized only after this formula or after that, is to say that art must be contrived only out of this formula or out of that. As every work of art is an entity, a thing in itself, so is every piece of criticism an entity, a thing in itself. That *Thus Spake Zarathustra* must inevitably be criticized by the canons of the identical theory with which one criticizes *Tristan and Isolde* is surely difficult of reasoning.

To the Goethe-Carlyle doctrine that the critic's duty lies alone in discerning the artist's aim, his point of view, and, finally, his execution of the task before him, it is easy enough to subscribe, but certainly this is not a "theory" of criticism so much as it is a foundation for a theory. To advance it as a theory, full-grown, full-fledged, and flapping, as it has been advanced by the Italian Croce and his admirers, is to publish the preface of a book without the book itself. Accepted as a theory complete in itself, it fails by virtue of its several undeveloped intrinsic problems, chief among which is its neglect to consider the undeniable fact that, though each work of art is indubitably an entity and so to be considered, there is yet in creative art what may be termed an aesthetic genealogy that bears heavily upon comprehensive criticism and that renders the artist's aim, his point of view, and his execution of the task before him susceptible to a criticism predicated in a measure upon the work of the sound artist who has just preceded him.

The Goethe-Carlyle hypothesis is a little too liberal. It calls for qualifications. It gives the artist too much ground, and the critic too little. To discern the artist's aim, to discern the artist's point of view, are phrases that require an amount of plumbing, and not a few footnotes. It is entirely possible, for example, that the immediate point of view of an artist be faulty, yet the execution of his immediate task exceedingly fine. If carefully planned triumph in art is an entity, so also may be undesigned triumph. I do not say that any such latter phenomenon is usual, but it is conceivable, and hence may be employed as a test of the critical hypothesis in point. Unschooled, without aim or point of view in the sense of this hypothesis, Schumann's compositions at the age of eleven for chorus and orchestra offer the quasi-theory some resistance. The question of the comparative merit of these compositions and the artist's subsequent work may not strictly be brought into the argument, since the point at issue is merely a theory and since theory is properly to be tested by theory.

Intent and achievement are not necessarily twins. I have always perversely thought it likely that there is often a greater degree of accident in fine art than one is permitted to believe. The aim and point of view of a bad artist are often admirable; the execution of a fine artist may sometimes be founded upon a point of view that is, from an apparently sound critical estimate, at striking odds with it. One of the finest performances in all modern dramatic writing, upon its critical reception as such, came as a great surprise to the author who almost unwittingly had achieved. Art is often unconscious of itself. Shakespeare, writing popular plays to order, wrote the greatest plays that dramatic art has known. Mark Twain, in a disgusted moment, threw off a practical joke, and it turned out to be literature.

A strict adherence to the principles enunciated in the Goethe-Carlyle theory would result in a confinement of art, for all the theory's bold aim in exactly the opposite direction. For all the critic may accurately say, the aim and point of view of, say, Richard Strauss in *Don Quixote* and *A Hero's Life* may be imperfect, yet the one critical fact persists that the executions are remarkably fine. All things considered, it were perhaps better that the critical theory under discussion, if it be accepted at all, be turned end foremost; that the artist's execution of the task before him be considered either apart from his aim and point of view, or that it be considered first, and then—with not too much insistence upon them—his point of view and his aim. This would seem to be a more logical aesthetic and critical order. Tolstoy, with a sound, intelligent, and technically perfect aim and point of view, composed second-rate drama. So, too, Maeterlinck. Synge, by his own admission adjudged critically and dramatically guilty on both counts, composed one of the truly first-rate dramas of the Anglo-Saxon stage.

In its very effort to avoid pigeonholing, the Goethe-Carlyle theory pigeonholes itself. In its commendable essay at catholicity, it is like a garter so elastic that it fails to hold itself up. That there may not be contradictions in the contentions here set forth, I am not sure. But I advance no fixed, definite theory of my own; I advance merely contradictions of certain of the phases of the theories held by others, and contradictions are ever in the habit of begetting contradictions. Yet such contradictions are in themselves apposite and soundly critical, since any theory susceptible of contradictions must itself be contradictory and insecure. If I suggest any theory on my part, it is a variable one: a theory that, in this instance, is one thing and in that, another. Criticism, as I see it—and I share the common opinion—is simply a sensitive, experienced, and thoroughbred artist's effort to interpret, in terms of aesthetic doctrine and his own peculiar soul, the work of another artist reciprocally to that artist and thus, as with a reflecting mirror, to his public. But to state merely what criticism is is not to state the doctrine of its application. And herein, as I see it, is where the theorists fail to cover full ground. The anatomy of criticism is composed not of one theory, but of a theory—more or less generally agreed upon—upon which are reared in turn other theories that are not so generally agreed upon. The Goethe-Carlyle theory is thus like a three-story building on which the constructor has left off work after finishing only the first story. What certain aspects of these other stories may be like, I have already tried to suggest.

I have said that, if I have any theory of my own, it is a theory susceptible in practice of numerous surface changes. These surface changes often disturb in a measure this or that phase of what lies at the bottom. Thus, speaking as a critic of the theatre, I find it impossible to reconcile myself to criticizing acting and drama from the vantage point of the same theory, say, for example, the Goethe-Carlyle theory. This theory fits criticism of drama much better than it fits criticism of acting, just as it fits criticism of painting and sculpture much more snugly than criticism of music. The means whereby the emotions are directly affected, and soundly affected, may at times be critically meretricious, yet the accomplishment itself may be, paradoxically, artistic. Perhaps the finest acting performance of our generation is Bernhardt's Camille: its final effect is tremendous: yet the means whereby it is contrived are obviously inartistic. Again, *King Lear*, searched into with critical chill, is artistically a poor instance of playmaking, yet its effect is precisely the effect striven for. Surely, in cases like these, criticism founded strictly upon an inflexible theory is futile criticism, and not only futile but eminently unfair.

Here, of course, I exhibit still more contradictions, but through contradictions we may conceivably gain more secure ground. When his book is once opened, the author's mouth is shut. (Wilde, I believe, said that; and though for some reason it is today regarded as suicidal to quote the often profound Wilde in any serious argument, I risk the danger.) But when a dramatist's play or a composer's symphony is opened, the author has only begun to open his mouth. What results, an emotional art within an intellectual art, calls for a critical theory within a critical theory. To this composite end, I offer a suggestion: blend with the Goethe-Carlyle theory that of the aforementioned Wilde, to wit, that beauty is uncriticizable, since it has as many meanings as man has moods, since it is the symbol of symbols, and since it reveals everything because it expresses nothing. The trouble with criticism—again to pose a contradiction—is that, in certain instances, it is often too cerebral. Feeling a great thrill of beauty, it turns to its somewhat puzzled mind and is apprised that the thrill which it has unquestionably enjoyed from the work of art might conceivably be of pathological origin, a fremitus or vibration felt upon percussion of a hydatoid tumor.

The Goethe-Caryle theory, properly rigid and unyielding so far as emotional groundlings are concerned, may, I believe, at times safely be chucked under the chin and offered a communication of gypsy ardor by the critic whose emotions are the residuum of trial, test, and experience.

Coquelin put it that the footlights exaggerate everything: they modify the laws of space and of time; they put miles in a few square feet; they make minutes appear to be hours. Of this exaggeration, dramatic criticism—which is the branch of criticism of which I treat in particular— has caught something. Of all the branches of criticism it is intrinsically the least sober and the least accurately balanced. It always reminds me somehow of the lash in the hands of Oeacus, in *The Frogs*, falling upon Bacchus and Xanthus to discover which of the two is divine, the latter meantime endeavoring to conceal the pain that would betray their mortality by various transparent dodges. Drama is a two-souled art: half divine, half clownish. Shakespeare is the greatest dramatist who ever lived because he alone, of all dramatists, most accurately sensed the mongrel nature of his art. Criticism of drama, it follows, is similarly a two-souled art: half sober, half mad. Drama is a deliberate intoxicant; dramatic criticism, aromatic spirits of ammonia; the re-creation is never perfect; there is always a trace of tipsiness left. Even the best dramatic criticism is always just a little dramatic. It indulges, a trifle, in acting. It can never be as impersonal, however much certain of its practitioners may try, as criticism of painting or of sculpture or of literature. This is why the best criticism of the theatre must inevitably be personal criticism. The theatre itself is distinctly personal; its address is directly personal. It holds up the mirror not to nature, but to the spectator's individual idea of nature. If it doesn't, it fails. The spectator, if he is a critic, merely holds his own mirror up to the drama's mirror; a reflection of the first reflection is the result. Dramatic criticism is this second reflection. And so the best dramatic criticism has about it a flavor of the unconscious, grotesque and unpremeditated. "When Lewes was at his business," Shaw has said, "he seldom remembered that he was a gentleman or a scholar." (Shaw was speaking of Lewes's free use of vulgarity and impudence whenever they happened to be the proper tools for his job.) "In this he showed himself a true craftsman, intent on making the measurements and analyses of his criticism as accurate, and their expression as clear and vivid as possible, instead of allowing himself to be distracted by the vanity of playing the elegant man of letters, or writing with perfect good taste, or hinting in every line that he was above his work. In exacting all this from himself, and taking his revenge by expressing his most laboured conclusions with a levity that gave them the air of being the unpremeditated whimsicalities of a man who had perversely taken to writing about the theatre for the sake of the jest latent in his own outrageous unfitness for it, Lewes rolled his stone up the hill quite in the modern manner of Mr. Walkley, dissembling its huge weight, and apparently kicking it at random hither and thither in pure wantonness."

Mr. Spingarn, in his exceptionally interesting, if somewhat overly indignant, treatise on "Creative Criticism," provides, it seems to me, a particularly clear illustration of the manner in which the proponents of the more modern theories of criticism imprison themselves in the extravagance of their freedom. While liberating art from all the old rules of criticism, they simultaneously confine criticism with the new rules—or ghosts of rules—wherewith they free art. If each work of art is a unit, a thing in itself, as is commonly agreed, why should not each work of criticism be similarly a unit, a thing in itself? If art is, in each and every case, a matter of individual expression, why should not criticism, in each and every case, be similarly and relevantly a matter of individual expression? In freeing art of definitions, has not criticism been too severely defined? I believe that it has been. I believe that there may be as many kinds of criticism as there are kinds of art. I believe that there may be sound analytical, sound emotional, sound cerebral, sound impressionistic, sound destructive, sound constructive, and other sound species of criticism. If art knows no rules, criticism knows no rules—or, at least, none save those that are obvious. If Brahms's scherzo in E flat minor, op. 4, is an entity, a work in and of itself, why shouldn't Huneker's criticism of it be regarded as an entity, a work in and of itself? If there is in Huneker's work inspiration from without, so, too, is there in Brahms's; if Brahms may be held a unit in this particular instance with no consideration of Chopin, why may not Huneker with no consideration of Brahms?

If this is pushing things pretty far, it is the Spingarns who have made the pushing necessary. "Taste," says Mr. Spingarn, "must reproduce the work of art within itself in order to understand and judge it; and at that moment aesthetic judgement becomes nothing more or less than creative art itself." This rings true. But, granting the perfection of the taste, why define and limit the critical creative art thus born of reproduction? No sooner has a law been enunciated, writes Mr. Spingarn, than it has been broken by an artist impatient or ignorant of its restraints, and the critics have been obliged to explain away these violations of their laws or gradually to change the laws themselves. If art, he continues, is organic expression, and every work of art is to be interrogated with the question, "What has it expressed and how completely?", there is no place for the question whether it has conformed to

Aesthetic Jurisprudence

some convenient classification of critics or to some law derived from this classification. Once again, truly put. But so, too, no sooner have laws been enunciated than they have been broken by critics impatient or ignorant of their restraints, and the critics of critics have been obliged to explain away these violations of the laws, or gradually to change the laws themselves. And so, too, have these works of criticism provided no place for the question whether they have conformed to some convenient classification of the critics of criticism or to some law derived from this classification.

"Criticism," said Carlyle, his theories apart, "stands like an interpreter between the inspired and the uninspired, between the prophet and those who hear the melody of his words, and catch some glimpse of their material meaning, but understand not their deeper import." This is the best definition that I know of. It defines without defining; it gives into the keeping of the interpreter the hundred languages of art and merely urges him, with whatever means may best and properly suit his ends, to translate them clearly to those that do not understand; it sets him free from the very shackles which Carlyle himself, removing from art, wound in turn about him.

The Critic and the Drama, 1922

Dramatic Criticism

ARTHUR BINGHAM WALKLEY begins one of the best books ever written on the subject thus: "It is not to be gainsaid that the word criticism has gradually acquired a certain connotation of contempt. . . . Every one who expresses opinions, however imbecile, in print calls himself a 'critic.' The greater the ignoramus, the greater the likelihood of his posing as a 'critic.' " An excellent book, as I have said, with a wealth of sharp talk in it, but Mr. Walkley seems to me to err somewhat in his preliminary assumption. Criticism has acquired a connotation of contempt less because it is practiced by a majority of ignoramuses than because it is accepted at full face value by an infinitely greater majority of ignoramuses. It is not the mob that curls a lip—the mob accepts the lesser ignoramus at his own estimate of himself; it is the lonely and negligible minority man who, pausing musefully in the field that is the world, contemplates the jackasses eating the daisies.

No man is so contemptuous of criticism as the well-stocked critic, just as there is no man so contemptuous of clothes as the man with the well-stocked wardrobe. It is as impossible to imagine a critic like Shaw not chuckling derisively at criticism as it is to imagine a regular subscriber to the *Weekly Review* not swallowing it whole. The experienced critic, being on the inside, is in a position to look into the heads of the less experienced, and to see the wheels go round. He is privy to all their monkey-shines, since he is privy to his own. Having graduated from quackery, he now smilingly regards others still at the trade of seriously advancing sure cures for aesthetic baldness, cancer, acne, and trifacial neuralgia. And while the yokels rub in the lotions and swallow the pills, he permits himself a small, but eminently sardonic, hiccup.

It is commonly believed that the first virtue of a critic is honesty. As a matter of fact, in four cases out of five, honesty is the last virtue of a critic. As criticism is practiced in America, honesty presents itself as the leading fault. There is altogether too much honesty. The greater the blockhead, the more honest he is. And as a consequence the criticism of these blockheads, founded upon their honest convictions, is worthless. There is some hope for an imbecile if he is dishonest, but none if he is resolute in sticking to his idiocies. If the average American critic were to cease writing what he honestly believes and dishonestly set down what he doesn't believe, the bulk of the native criticism would gain some common sense and take on much of the sound value that it presently lacks. Honesty is a toy for first-rate men; when lesser men seek to play with it and lick off the paint, they come down with colic.

It is further maintained that enthusiasm is a supplementary desideratum in a critic, that unless he is possessed of enthusiasm he cannot impart a warm love for fine things to his reader. Surely this, too, is nonsense. Enthusiasm is a virtue not in the critic, but in the critic's reader. And such desired enthusiasm can be directly generated by enthusiasm no more than a glycerol-nitrate explosion can be generated by sulfuric acid. Enthusiasm may be made so contagious as to elect a man president of the United States or to raise an army large enough to win a world war, but it has never yet been made sufficiently contagious to persuade one American out of a hundred thousand that Michelangelo's David of the Signoria is a better piece of work than the Barnard statue of Lincoln. Enthusiasm is an attribute of the uncritical, the defectively educated; stump speakers, clergymen, young girls, opera-goers, Socialists, Italians, such like. And not only an attribute, but a weapon. But the cultivated and experienced man has as little use for enthusiasm as for indignation. He appreciates that while it may convert a pack of ignoble doodles, it can't convert anyone worth converting. The latter must be persuaded, not inflamed. He realizes that where a double brass band playing "Columbia, the Gem of the Ocean" may leave a civilized Englishman cold to the virtues of the United States, proof that the United States has the best bathroom plumbing in the world may warm him up a bit. The sound critic is not a cheerleader, but a referee. Art is hot, criticism cold. Aristotle's criticism of Euripides is as placid and reserved as Mr. William Archer's criticism of the latest drama at the St. James's Theatre. Brunetière is as calm over his likes as Mr. H. T. Parker of the Boston *Transcript*. There is no more enthusiasm in Lessing than there is indignation in Walkley. Hazlitt, at a hundred degrees emotional Fahrenheit, remains critically cool as a cucumber. To find enthusiasm, you will have to read *The New York Times*.

Enthusiasm, in short, is the endowment of immaturity. The greater the critic, the greater his disinclination to communicate aesthetic heat. Such comunication savors of propaganda and, however worthy that propaganda, he will have nought to do with its trafficking. If the ability to possess and communicate enthusiasm is the mark of the true critic, then the theatrical page of the New York *Journal* is the greatest critical literature in America.

44

Dramatic Criticism

A third contention has it that aloofness and detachment
are no less valuable to the dramatic critic than honesty
and enthusiasm. Unless I am seriously mistaken, also bosh.
Dramatic criticism is fundamentally the critic's art of appraising himself in terms of various forms of drama. Or,
as I some time ago put it, the only sound dramatic critic
is the one who reports less the impression that this or that
play makes upon him than the impression he makes upon
this or that play. Of all the forms of criticism, dramatic
criticism is essentially, and perhaps correctly, the most
personal. Tell me what a dramatic critic eats and drinks,
how far north of Ninetieth Street he lives, what he considers a pleasant evening when he is not in the theatre,
and what kind of lingerie his wife wears, and I'll tell you
with very few misses what kind of critic he is. I'll tell you
whether he is fit to appreciate Schnitzler, or whether he is
fit only for Augustus Thomas. I'll tell you in advance what
he will think about, and how he will react to, Hauptmann,
Sacha Guitry, or George V. Hobart. I'll tell you whether
he is the sort that makes a great to-do when his eagle eye
spots Sir Nigel Waterhouse, M. P., in Act II fingering a
copy of the Philadelphia *Public Ledger* instead of the
London *Times*, and whether he is the sort that writes:
"Mr. John Cort has staged the play in his customary
lavish manner" when the rise of the curtain discloses to
him a room elaborately decorated in the latest Macy
mode. To talk about the value of detachment in a dramatic critic is to talk about the value of detachment in a
Swiss mountain guide. The criticism is the man, the man
the criticism.

Of all forms of criticism, dramatic criticism is the most
purely biological. Were the genii to put the mind of Max
Beerbohm into the head of Mr. J. Ranken Towse, and vice
versa, their criticisms would still remain exactly as they

45

are. But, on the contrary, were the head of Mr. J. Ranken Towse to be placed on the body of Max Beerbohm, and vice versa, their criticisms would take on points of view diametrically opposed to their present. Max would begin admiring the Rev. Dr. Charles Rann Kennedy and Towse would promptly proceed to put on his glasses to get a better view of the girl on the end. Every book of dramatic criticism—every single piece of dramatic criticism—is a searching, illuminating autobiography. The dramatic critic performs a clinic upon himself every time he takes his pen in his hand. He may try, as Walkley puts it, to substitute for the capital I's "nouns of multitude signifying many," or some of those well-worn stereotypes—"It is thought," "One may be pardoned for hinting," "Will anyone deny?" etc., etc.—by which criticism keeps up the pretense that it is not a man but a corporation, but he fools no one.

To ask the dramatic critic to keep himself out of his criticism, to detach himself, is thus a trifle like asking an actor to keep himself out of his role. Dramatic critics and actors are much alike. The only essential difference is that the actor does his acting on a platform. But, platform or no platform, the actor and the dramatic critic best serve their roles when they filter them through their own personalities. A dramatic critic who is told to keep his personality out of his criticism is in the position of an actor who, being physically and temperamentally like Mr. John Barrymore, is peremptorily directed by a producer to stick a sofa pillow under his belt, put on six extra heel-lifts, acquire a whisky voice, and play Falstaff like the late Sir Herbert Tree. The best dramatic critics from the time of Quintus Horatius Flaccus (vide the *Epistola*) have sunk their vivid personalities into their work right up to the knees. Not only have they described the adventures of

their souls among masterpieces, but the adventures of
their kidneys, spleens, and caeca as well. Each has held the
mirror of drama up to his own nature, with all its idiosyncrasies. And in it have been sharply reflected not the
cut and dried features of the professor, but the vital features of a red-alive man. The other critics have merely
held up the mirror to these red-alive men, and have reflected not themselves but the latter. Then, in their vainglory, they have looked again into the handglass, and have
mistaken the reflection of the parrot for an eagle.

A third rubber stamp: the critic must have sympathy.
As properly contend that a surgeon must have sympathy.
The word is misused. What the critic must have is not
sympathy, which in its common usage bespeaks a measure
of sentimental concern, but interest. If a dramatic critic,
for example, has sympathy for an actress, he can no more
criticize her with poise than a surgeon can operate on his
own wife. The critic may on occasion have sympathy as
the judge in a court of law may on occasion have it, but
if he is a fair critic, or a fair judge, he can't do anything
about it, however much he would like to. Between the
fair defendant in the lace baby collar and a soft heart,
Article X, Section 128, page 416, absurdly interposes itself. (In example, being a human being with a human
being's weaknesses before a critic, I would often rather
praise a lovely one when she is bad than an unlovely one
when she is good, and, alas, I fear that I sometimes do—
but in the general run I try to remember my business and
behave myself. It isn't always easy. But I do my best, and
angels and Lewes could do no more.) The word *sympathy*
is further mishandled, as in the similar case of the word
enthusiasm. What a critic should have is not, as is common, sympathy and enthusiasm before the fact, but after
it. The critic who enters a theatre bubblingly certain that

he is going to have a good time is no critic. The critic is he who leaves a theatre cheerfully certain that he has had a good time. Sympathy and enthusiasm, unless they are ex post facto, are precisely like prevenient prejudice and hostility. Sympathy has no more preliminary place in the equipment of an ambulance driver or a manufacturer of bird cages. It is the caboose of criticism, not the engine.

The trouble with dramatic criticism in America, speaking generally, is that where it is not frankly reportorial it too often seeks to exhibit a personality when there exists no personality to exhibit. Himself perhaps conscious of this lack, the critic indulges in heroic makeshifts to inject into his writings a note of individuality, and the only individualty that comes out of his perspirations is of a piece with that of the bearded lady or the dog-faced boy. Individuality of this freak species is the bane of the native criticism. The college professor who, having nothing to say, tries to give his criticism an august air by figuratively attaching to it a pair of whiskers and horn glasses, the suburban college professor who sedulously practices an aloofness from the madding crowd that his soul longs to be part of, the college professor who postures as a man of the world, the newspaper reporter who postures as a college professor, the journalist who performs in terms of Art between the Saks and Gimbel advertisements—these and others like them are the sad comedians in the tragical crew. In their heavy attempts to live up to their fancy-dress costumes, in their laborious efforts to conceal their humdrum personalities in the uncomfortable gauds of Petruchio and Gobbo, they betray themselves even to the bus boys. The same performer cannot occupy the roles of Polonius and Hamlet, even in a tank-town troupe.

Dramatic Criticism

No less damaging to American dramatic criticism is the dominant notion that criticism, to be valuable, must be constructive. That is, that it must, as the phrase has it, "build up" rather than "tear down." As a result of this conviction we have an endless repertoire of architectonic advice from critics wholly without the structural faculty, advice which, were it followed, would produce a drama twice as poor as that which they criticize. Obsessed with the idea that they must be constructive, the critics know no lengths to which they will not go in their sweat to dredge up cures of one sort or another. They constructively point out that Shaw's plays would be better plays if Shaw understood the punctual technique of Pinero, thus destroying a *Caesar and Cleopatra* to construct a *Second Mrs. Tanqueray*. They constructively point out the trashy aspect of some Samuel Shipman's *Friendly Enemies,* suggest more serious enterprises to him, and get the poor soul to write a *The Unwritten Chapter* which is ten times as bad. They are not content to be critics; they must also be playwrights. They stand in mortal fear of the old recrimination, "He who can, does; he who can't, criticizes," not pausing to realize that the names of Mr. Octavus Roy Cohen and Matthew Arnold may be taken as somewhat confounding respective examples. They note with some irritation that the critic for the Wentzville, Mo., Beacon is a destructive critic, but are conveniently ignorant of the fact—which may conceivably prove something more— that so was George Farquhar. If destructive criticism, in their meaning, is criticism which pulls down without building up in return, three fourths of the best dramatic criticism written since the time of Boileau, fully filling the definition, is worthless. One can't cure a yellow-fever patient by pointing out to him that he should have caught the measles. One can't improve the sanitary condition of a neighborhood merely by giving the outhouse a different coat of paint. The foe of destructive criticism is the pro-German of American art.

Our native criticism suffers further from the commercial Puritanism of its mediums. What is often mistaken for the Puritanism of the critic is actually the commercial Puritanism forced upon him by the owner and publisher of the journal in which his writings appear, and upon which he has to depend for a livelihood. Although this owner and publisher is often not personally the Puritan, he is yet shrewdly aware that the readers of his journal are, and out of this awareness he becomes what may be termed a circulation blue-nose. Since circulation and advertising revenue are twins, he must see to it that the sensibilities of the former are not offended. And his circumspection, conveyed to the critic by the copyreader or perhaps only sensed, brings about the Puritan play-acting by the critic. This accounts to no little degree for the hostile and uncritical reviews of even the most finished risqué farces, and of the best efforts of American and European playwrights to depict truthfully and fairly the more unpleasant phases of sex. "I agree with you that this last naughty farce of Avery Hopwood's is awfully funny stuff," a New York newspaper reviewer once said to me. "I laughed at it until my ribs ached; but I don't dare write as much. One can't praise such things in a paper with the kind of circulation that ours has." It is criticism bred from this commercial Puritanism that has held back farce-writing in America, and I venture to say much serious dramatic writing as well. The best farce of a Guitry or a Dieudonné, produced in America today without childish excisions, would receive unfavorable notices from nine

newspapers out of ten. The best sex drama of a Porto-
Riche or a Wedekind would suffer—indeed, already has
suffered—a similar fate. I predicted to Eugene O'Neill,
the moment I laid down the manuscript of his pathological play *Diff'rent*, the exact manner in which, two months
later, the axes fell upon him.

For one critic like Mr. J. Ranken Towse, who is a Puritan by tradition and training, there are a dozen who are
Puritans by proxy. One can no more imagine a dramatic
critic on a newspaper owned by Mr. Cyrus H. K. Curtis
praising Schnitzler's *Reigen* or Rip's and Gignoux's *Scan-
dale de Deauville* than one can imagine the same critic
denouncing *Ben-Hur*. What thus holds true in journalistic criticism holds true in precisely the same way in the
criticism written by a majority of college professors. I
doubt that there is a college professor in America today
who, however much he admired a gay, reprobate farce
like *Le Rubicon* or *L'Illusioniste*, would dare state his admiration in print. Puritan or no Puritan, it is professionally necessary for him to comport himself as one. His university demands it, silently, sternly, idiotically. He is the
helpless victim of its aesthetic Ku Klux. Behind any drama
dealing unconventionally with sex, there hovers a specter
that vaguely resembles Professor Scott Nearing. He sees
it . . . he reflects . . . he works up a safe indignation.

Dramatic criticism travels, in America, carefully laid
tracks. Signal lights, semaphores, and one-legged old men
with red flags are stationed along the way to protect it at
the crossings, to make it safe, and to guard it from danger.
It elaborately steams, pulls, puffs, chugs, toots, whistles,
grinds, and rumbles for some three hundred miles—and
brings up at something like Hinkletown, Pa. It is eager,
but futile. It is honest, but so is Dr. Frank Crane. It is

fearless, but so is the actor who plays the hero strapped to the papier-mâché buzz saw. It is constructive, but so is an embalmer. It is detached, but so is the man in the Fiji Islands. It is sympathetic, but so is a quack prostatician.

The Critic and the Drama, 1922

III

SOME THEATRICAL PERSONALITIES

Belasco · Alexander Woollcott

Max Reinhardt · A. B. Walkley

Ziegfeld · The Censor · Eugene O'Neill

as a Character in Fiction

Belasco

To APPLAUD the practice of Mr. David Belasco in expending infinite care and time in perfecting the production of so empty and bootless a play as *Little Lady in Blue* is akin to an admiration for the sort of adult who triumphantly expends painstaking effort and time in putting together the several hundred little pieces of a jigsaw puzzle. That such veneration is as without foundation as a tent is probably perfectly well appreciated by the folk who participate in it, yet the Belasco tradition dies hard, and of that tradition this particular veneration is, one may believe, something in the nature of a death rattle. It is as if they who stand by the bedside, at a bit of a loss what nice to say, murmur gently: "But anyway—he had a good heart."

It is perhaps now a dozen years since the Belasco legend slid off the well-oiled ways and sailed gaudily forth, with flags flying and guns booming, into the gullibilities of the American public—a public already celebrated for having swallowed in high clover Mme Janauschek as a great artist, Richmond Pearson Hobson as a great naval strategist, Hamlin Garland as a great novelist, Tom Sharkey as a great prize fighter, and May Yohe as a great beauty. Nurtured by the gentleman himself with an even more scrupulous cunning than Barnum exercised in the exploitation of Jenny Lind, the Russian press bureau in preliminary missa cantata of the genius of Admiral Rodjestvenski or Mr. Ziegfeld in the glorification of Lillian Lorraine, the tradition fattened with the years and, fattening, established its creator in the American mind as a leading figure in the world's theatre.

To the fattening of this tradition, Mr. Belasco was tireless in contributing albumenoids of various and succulent genres. First, by way of bequeathing to himself an air of aloof austerity and monastic meditation, he discarded the ordinary habiliments of commerce and, by the simple device of turning his collar hind end foremost, made of himself a sort of Broadway Rasputin, a creature for awe and pointings and whisperings. Arrayed so, he strode as a messiah among the peasants and, by putting on a show in a barn in El Paso, Texas, brought down the wrath of these aesthetes upon the sack-suited infidels of the Syndicate, who, very probably because his show wasn't so good or so much of a drawing card in El Paso as the Byrne Brothers' *Eight Bells*, denied him their El Paso mosque on the theory that if Mrs. Leslie Carter was a great artist then the whole darned artist business was Greek to them and they would just as lief take their chances on getting simultaneously into the Hall of Fame and the First National Bank with Nellie McHenry.

But this Belasco, a sapient fellow withal, knew well what he was about. The thing worked like a charm. And the yokelry, egged on by the ever naïve and infatuated St. William Winter and other such credulous emotionals, raised cries of persecution, and Belasco became, overnight, the martyred Dreyfus of the American drama. High-salaried press agents who knew how suavely to soulé and roget and bartlett were commissioned now to fashion compositions to be signed by Belasco and spread discreetly in the more literary gazettes. And by way of augmenting the aloofness, the mystery, the remote melancholy, and the artistic temperament of him, the monsignor sold now his old swivel chair, his old desk light with the green shade, and the chromo of Ned Harrigan that hung on the wall and bought to take their places a Ming dais, an altar candlestick, and a copy of the *Mona Lisa*. Carpets ankle-deep were laid upon the floor, the blinds were drawn, and Vantine's entire stock of joss sticks set to smell up the place with a passionate Oriental effluvium. In that corner a single wax taper, inserted artistically in a Limoges seidel, illumined the chamber with its ecclesiastic glow, and in that was glimpsed a single narcissus in a wistful pot. Upon the inlaid onyx commode that served as a desk rested carelessly a framed photograph of Dante, with the inscription "To my warm friend, Dave, in token of his services in the cause of art"—and duly autographed by the poet in that peculiar and unmistakable flowing hand of his. Outside the heavy bird's-eye maple door studded with big brass thumbtacks, two small colored bellboys, impressed into service from a nearby hostelry and outfitted with green turbans and yellow togas, were made to sit cross-legged like twin gods of the mountain. And atop the door, to be set melodiously ringing at appropriate moments by a pushbutton neighborly to Mr. Belasco's great toe, was arranged a set of chimes.

This restful chamber was christened a "studio," and, so was the news given out, it was here, amid these classic inspirations, that the Belasco withdrew from the sordid, workaday world to woo the muse. Among the muses that Belasco wooed in these surroundings was the muse of dramatic criticism, for here were bidden from time to time, with much flourish and ado, much subtle greasing and tony flimflam, the newspaper theatrical writers. One at a time, and after much stunning hocus-pocus, were these gentlemen received. When they entered, Mr. Belasco was invariably seen to be seated on the Ming dais, forefinger to brow, in attitude of profound and impressive meditation. All was still as the tomb and dim, and but the thin spirals of the burning joss sticks disturbed the solemn lull. Presently, as from a distance, though in reality hidden under the dais, a music box began a sweet and mellow lay. And as the music died away, a press agent, secreted behind a heavy purple Baluchistan portiere at R1, made sweet sounds on a small whistle filled with water as of a canary singing.

Suddenly then, as if startled out of deep reverie, would the surprised Belasco become aware of his guest's presence. As some kindly and generous emperor, the Belasco would deign now bid the fellow near his throne and, putting the fellow at his ease, would express to the fellow his vast admiration for the fellow's critical and literary abilities and beseech his advice on how best to end the second act of the play he was even then working on. Allowing ample time for the grease to sink in good and deep, the Belasco would then descend in queenly abandon from the dais and sink wearily into the tufts of the Louis XIV chaise before the Louis XV table, meanwhile adroitly pressing the button under the table with his toe and setting the chimes over the door to dulcet playing. Followed now, penseroso, a lament on the crass commercialism of the theatre, ending up, allegro, with a quotation from Shakespeare and another from a recent article written by the visitor. . . . An hour later the newspaper writer might be seen on the highway cutting one of his old friends dead. . . . And the following Sunday might be seen in his gazette a six-column article attesting to the extraordinary intelligence, learning, discernment, taste, artistry, and genius generally of David Belasco, maître and wizard extraordinaire of the American theatre.

Gradually the legend, nursed and coddled now by an affectionately inscribed card at Yuletide, now it may be by a rarebit à deux, now mayhap by an irresistibly polite note of thanks for a favorable bit of written comment, spread its wings in Forty-fourth Street and flew with loud flutter far and wide across the countryside. Did the tradition perchance periodically show signs of drooping, then were apéritifs hustled to its reviving in the shape of a couple of recherché lamps hoisted in the aisles during the intermissions, or in the shape of one of Gorham's country-house dinner gongs to signal the curtain's rise, or in the shape of Reinhardt's old trick of sackcloth hangings for the boxes and proscenium during the presentation of a play of pious countenance, or, more recently, in the shape of a series of profound essays on artistic stage illumination and like subjects (signed by Mr. Belasco but written by Mr. Louis DeFoe) and in the shape of a legend-boosting autobiography written for the Belasco signature by a needy member of the Drama League.

As has been said, this ingenuous bait worked like magic and the yokelry swallowed it hook and sinker. For this Belasco was a clever man—the cleverest, and by all odds, in the native theatre—and, doubtless chuckling up his sleeve, for it is impossible to imagine him deceived by his own tin-pantaloonery, he witnessed the canonization of his simple humbug and through that simple humbug the canonization of himself by the absorbent rhapsodists. But this was yesterday.

Already there is considerable evidence, even in the newspapers, of a grievous lèse-majesté. One observes a profane grinning and head-shaking. And the Belasco legend shows signs of soon going to the foot of the class to join its comrades, the stork and Santa Claus, Friedmann the tuberculosis curer and Eusapia Palladino, Dr. Cook and Granville-Barker, Augustus Thomas the Dean and the Mann Act, black hose with white feet and Swiss vermouth, eugenics and neutrality, Rabindranath Tagore and the Russian Army.

What now is becoming belatedly apparent to the hoaxed Hazlittry and its proselytes has of course been familiar these many years to everyone else. The facts, bereft of Ming sofas and perfumed punk sticks, are these. During his activity as a producer, Mr. Belasco has produced not one fifteenth so many worthy plays as the late Charles Frohman produced during a precisely corresponding period. Mr. Belasco has produced *The Easiest Way*, *The Concert*, and *The Phantom Rival*—three meritorious plays: so much and no more. As against these lonely three, he has presented an astounding procession of show-shop piffle including such things as *The Governor's Lady*, *The Woman*, *Seven Chances*, *The Fighting Hope*, *Alias*, *The Rose of the Rancho*, *Adrea*, *The Warrens of Virginia*, *A Good Little Devil*, *The Heart of Maryland*, *May Blossom*, *Peter Grimm*, *The Music Master*, *The Case of Becky*, *The Heart of Wetona*, *Men and Women*, *The Grand Army Man*, *The Wife*, *The Very Minute*, *Little Lady in Blue*. . . . A show-shop peg higher, but certainly of not authentic stature, have been his presentations such as *The Darling of the Gods*, shilling melodrama in Morocco binding; *The Lily*, one of the least interesting specimens of the modern French problem play; *The Boomerang*, a pleasant but unimportant trifle; *The Auctioneer*, not to be compared with the Montague Glass dramaturgy. . . . The financial success of most of these plays has, of course, no more relevance to the question of their artistic status than the financial success of the novels of A. N. and C. M. Williamson has to theirs.

During a like and parallel period of managerial activity, Charles Frohman, on the other hand, produced any number of plays of the order of *Peter Pan*, *Mid-Channel*, *The Legend of Leonora*, *L'Aiglon*, *The Silver Box*, *Alice-Sit-by-the-*

*Fire, Preserving Mr. Panmure, The Twelve Pound Look,
The Admirable Crichton, The Mollusc, The Hypocrites,
His House in Order, A Wife without a Smile, Trelawny of
the Wells, The Importance of Being Earnest, Chantecler,
The Tyranny of Tears*—the plays of such as Ibsen, Shake-
speare, Pinero, Rostand, Barrie, Fitch, Chambers, Gals-
worthy, Jones, Wilde, and Ade, as opposed to the Belasco
catalogue of William C. DeMilles, Roi Megrues, Edward
J. Lockes, John Meehans, Lee Arthurs, Wigney Percyvals,
Willard Macks, Richard Walton Tullys, and Victor
Mapeses.

And Charles Frohman was and is not the only one. Win-
throp Ames, who has been producing plays but a very
short time in comparison with the lengthy career of Belasco, has in that brief period achieved a vastly more important position for himself through the presentation of
such works as *Anatol, Strife, The Pigeon, Prunella, L'En-
fant prodigue, Old Heidelberg, Rutherford and Son, Sister
Beatrice, The Thunderbolt, The Piper.* . . . William
Faversham, during his few years as a producer, has done
*The World and His Wife, The Faun, Othello, Julius Cae-
sar, Herod,* and *Getting Married,* an honorable record
marred only by the flonflon called *The Hawk.* True
enough, these producers have also on occasion presented
plays quite as seedy as those presented by Mr. Belasco, yet
such plays have in their repertoire been the exception, certainly not, as with Mr. Belasco, the rule. . . .

To compare Belasco with such men afield as Antoine or
Stanislavsky or Reinhardt—a fruity frolic of the newspapers—is to compare Holbrook Blinn with Max Maurey,
Ned Wayburn with Meyerhold, or Butler Davenport with
Victor Barnowsky. (Indeed, I do Mr. Wayburn, at least,
something of an injustice. Mr. Wayburn has brought a
great deal more to the music-show stage than Mr. Belasco

has brought to the dramatic.) Such comparisons are of course altogether too absurd to call for serious notice. These producers are as far removed from Belasco as is Mr. Ziegfeld from Al Reeves, or as is Arthur Hopkins from Corse Payton. A mere glance at their records, records brave with the production of fine drama, development of fine acting, and successful research and innovation in stagecraft, is sufficient to shrivel to the vanishing point even the best of Belasco's achievements. Beside such men, beside even such second-rate producers as Granville-Barker or Von Fassmann or Roebbeling, Belasco is a schoolboy in the art of the theatre. And beside the inventiveness and imagination of such as Marstersteig, Gordon Craig, Adolph Linnebach, or Hagemann, his inventiveness and imagination seem so much chintz. . . . But these are facts to be found by the bad sailor in the most accessible books of reference and I pose as no apothecary of news.

Mr. Belasco has contributed one—only one—thing for judicious praise to the American theatre. He has brought to that theatre a standard of tidiness in production and maturation of manuscript, a standard that has discouraged to no little extent that theatre's erstwhile not uncommon frowzy hustle and slipshod manner of presentation. But what else? His plays, in the main, have been the sentimental vaporings of third- and fourth-rate writers. He has produced none of the classics; he has produced not a single modern first-rate British play or French play or German play; he has produced but two Austrian plays and one of these he deleted of its two most striking factors; he has encouraged no young American talent, and those young Americans whom he has encouraged, he has encouraged to write not dramatic literature but so-called sure-fire shows, lending to their manuscripts his fecund aid in devising superficial hokums and punches and other such stuffs of the two-dollar vaudevilles; he has developed, in all his career, but one actress, Miss Frances Starr; he has developed, in all his career, but a single actor, David Warfield—and this single actor he has long since stunted by casting him year in and year out in revivals of the lucrative trash of Lee Arthur and Charles Klein.

Upon what, then, does his eminence rest? The circusing, after the manner of Oscar Hammerstein, of an inferior actress who had come before the public notice through a sensational divorce case; the promulgation, as original, of a system of stage lighting that had been in use a long time before all over Germany and had already been borrowed by producers in the theatre in Russia; the promulgation, also as original, of a so-called ultra-realismus in stage settings which dates back to Charles Kean in the 1850's and which was elaborated to very nearly its present painful proportions by Otto Brahm in Berlin, if I am not mistaken, as far back as 1888 and carried even further two years later in the Moscow Art Theatre; the divulgation, also as original, in 1902, of a scenic treatment of such a play as *The Darling of the Gods*, already familiar to youthful students of a stage that years before had been occupied by Franz Ebert, Adolph Zink, and the other imported lilliputians in an extravaganza called *The Magic Doll*.

I have been Mr. Belasco's guest in his theatres these many years. He has, with unfailing courtesy, regularly invited me to review his efforts and, with an equal courtesy, has uniformly assigned to the reception of my tender upholstery a most comfortable and well-placed seat—unlike the rude Mr. John Cort, who always, with shrewd and uncanny precision, sits me in an ulterior pew without any stuffing in it and, to boot, directly behind a very fat gentleman guest who is given, particularly at tense dramatic moments, to stupendous and disconcerting nose-blowings. I admire Mr. Belasco as a showman—he is probably the best and certainly the most successful in the Anglo-American dramatic theatre. Indeed, if ever I write a bad play, I promise him the first refusal of it. I admire him for having gauged the American esthetik as probably no other showman since Adam Forepaugh and Barnum has gauged it. And I admire him, further, for having done several really good things really well. But, though he has been ever to me an urbane host and though ever he has subtly flattered my sense of humor by hesitating to bid me inspect his "studio" or his first-edition E. Phillips Oppenheims or his collection of Byzantine soup ladles, I cannot but believe, albeit unmannerly, that he has by his many counterfeits worked a vast and thorough ill to the American playhouse and its drama. And I cannot but further believe that his legend is ending, to the brightening of a new and more understanding dawn in the native theatre.

Mr. George Jean Nathan Presents, 1917

Alexander Woollcott

THE SEIDLITZ POWDER IN TIMES SQUARE

THAT NINE TENTHS of our American actors are not in insane asylums imagining themselves the Malay Archipelago, collecting photographs of Rupert Hughes, and playing "Deutschland Ueber Alles" on the lemonade glasses is perhaps due to an illiteracy so unsuspectedly great that it has made reading an accomplishment foreign to them. No other explanation seems reasonable, for, were they able to read, certainly a perusal of the criticisms of their performances which appear in the New York newspapers would soon or late contrive to dispatch the majority of them to the nearest chateau des noisettes. I for once speak authoritatively, for I have made concrete experiments upon my Negro, Waldo. This Waldo, erstwhile my valet de chambre, was once an actor with Martin's *Uncle Tom's Cabin* company. By way of testing my hypothesis, I recently clipped from the local gazettes the criticisms of the Yiddish actor Jacob Ben-Ami, carefully erased Jake's name and substituted Waldo's, and then bade the fellow imagine himself the star of *Samson and Delilah* and read them. My trousers are now being pressed by Waldo's cousin, Delmar.

I can speak even more authoritatively. Although I am not, and never have been, an actor—save once, in my university days, when I and fourteen other freshmen by lying on our stomachs behind a strip of brown canvas and rolling over in unison served as the treadmill in the chariot-race scene for the No. 3 *Ben-Hur* company playing the local opera house—although, as I say, I am not, with this qualification, a brother to Macready, Booth, and Salvini, I may say that a reading of the criticisms has almost driven *me* crazy. If George Cohan's *The Tavern* has played to less than $10,000 a week at the Cohan Theatre, it is simply because *The New York Times*, across the street, has proved too strong competition.

Having already reviewed Mr. Cohan's lampoon of reason, let us consider—by way of laboratory exercise—the attraction across the way.

At the outset it must be confessed that, as a comedian, as a confiseur of droll humor, nay, as a downright, first-rate laugh-getter, Mr. Ochs, the producer of this second show, is the superior of the hitherto pre-eminent Giorgio. Mr. Cohan, true enough, has a theatrical slyness, a cunning, that Mr. Ochs lacks—the latter goes after his laughs with a sledge-hammer—but when it comes to the good loud bull-roar, the kind of laugh that begins in the caecum, foments the undershirt, and ends by exploding the waistcoat and cracking the watch, the sagacity of this Ochs makes poor Mr. Cohan seem like the talent at an Elks smoker. After many years' labor Mr. Ochs contrived to make his Literary Supplement the George Bickel of its species in America. But though a lesser journalist would have been content with this coup—it surely requires something akin to genius to take literary criticism, drop it into a silk hat, and then, to the "oh's" and "ah's" of the onlookers, pull out a dime museum whose most favored figures are Marie Conway Oemler, T. M. Longstreth, Stella G. S. Perry, Katherine Newlin Burt, and Robert W. Chambers —M. de Ochs still pined for greater comedic glory. The merriment evoked by his literary criticism, enough to have satisfied all the Pixley and Luders comedians who ever wore zebra waistcoats with six-inch pearl buttons, was not sufficient for the insatiable régisseur of the *Times*, and he turned him to auxiliary fields. Finally, after much experimenting, he hit upon his dramatic department as a twin stage to his literary. And so amazing is the man's foresight, so signally expert his judgment, that *in less than three years* he brought this department or dramatic criticism to a point where it was as superior in a comic sense to the literary department as Eddie Cantor is to Lyman Abbott. And today Mr. Ochs has the satisfaction of knowing that there is perhaps not a schoolboy or schoolgirl in the eastern part of the United States who wouldn't rather read a single piece of his theatrical criticism than the entire works of Ezra Kendall, Irvin Cobb, and Daisy Ashford. To achieve this end, the good Ochs had, of course, to try out many fancy prancers, but he at last found the True Pumpkin in an effervescent young neo-Acton Davies from a small upstate college, and his reward was immediate. At first, true enough, the only response was faint chuckles, but presently these chuckles resolved themselves into hearty, old-fashioned laughs, and not long afterward the laughs swelled to the present bowel-rousing, intestinal thunders.

Not five minutes had this amiable young brunetière been transferred to the post of dramatic critic from his duties of chronicling the amount of change cabbaged from the cash register in August Minzmann's delicatessen store in West 167th Street by the absconding Schweitzer cheese cutter, Sig Bortsch, than he began to Lay Down The Law. With the instantaneity of Sal Hepatica, the erstwhile reporter of the fire in Flaherty and Klein's saloon up in East 98th Street became an Authority on acting, dramatic writing, scenic investiture, lighting, music, painting, the foreign drama, the art of stage direction—everything concerned with the theatre. And not only in the pages of the Ochs intelligencer, but in theatre lobbies, on the highway, in the coffee houses, in the nearby candy stores, wherever there was an uncreased buttonhole. There was no note of reserve nor of qualification, as one encounters, say, in the writings of such droll geese as Hazlitt, Symons, Walkley, et al., who never enjoyed the same experience and schooling in unraveling delicatessen intrigues and beer-saloon arsons: all was peremptory, decisive, that's that. And very soon M. de Ochs found his ambition realized, to the consternation of George Cohan and his burlesque show across the street.

So much for Chapter I of our hero's biography. Let us proceed now to his decisions on the mimes. These are, for the most part, stage-struck. The appraisals of Mrs. Fiske, estimable comedienne, of Ethel Barrymore, competent actress, and of Emily Stevens, dinner-party giver, read like a bewitched college boy writing to the Elsie Ferguson of *Liberty Belles* days and beseeching a lock of hair. Of a pleasant but not unusual young actress in a Clare Kummer play, is not the appended "criticism," for instance, like a valentine to one's best prep-school girl?

> This most beguiling role . . . is played to incredible perfection by Lotus Robb, the April charm of whose delicate performance seemed in the confusion of last evening a thing which only lyric verse could adequately describe. Etc. . . .

Miss Robb is probably an intelligent woman, and capable now and then of a self-grin. I should like to know what such a woman thinks when, after a good performance of a very incomplex and easy role, she reads such vanilla as this, with its irrelevant ravings about spring and its inability to describe in simple straightforward prose the performance of an ingenue, however pretty.

The Russian Ben-Ami, the superior of whom any critic who has looked into the Russian theatre during the last twenty years has found on innumerable stages—even in the old semi-mongrel Meyerhold companies, to say nothing of the often more carefully pruned troupes of Stanislavsky, Arbatoff, and Teliakovsky—actors like Dalmatoff, Glagolin, Massalitiniff, Rafael Adelheim, Katchaloff, Moskvin, and possibly Uraloff, to name a few—the profundo of the *Times*, all excited like a Seidlitz powder, has imperiously knighted a matchless world-genius. "It is," he announces with finality, "scarcely open to question," and adds, after some words on an appropriate ten-year repertory program for the Heaven-Kissed One, the crowning bathos: ". . . some of us would crawl on our hands and knees to

see it." Now, while I don't wish to use the *Times*'s young
man as a meat block to show off my own more momentous
knowledge of the business of acting—as a matter of fact,
criticizing acting has always seemed to me approximately
as important, and as efficacious, as criticizing mosquito
bites—it is still perhaps fair to set down that this Ben-Ami,
as any man who has ever studied the European theatre
will concur, is, save for sporadic flashes, the second-rate
kind of actor that you will encounter up the Petrograd,
Moscow, and Berlin side streets. Every once in so often
some clever manager hauls one of these exotic creatures
out of the East Side and exhibits him or her to a Broadway
audience, whereupon the Broadway audience promptly
mistakes a queer look, an accent, and red ears for high virtuosity, and the clever manager makes money.

There is no limit to the *Times*'s ecstasy. I have quoted
numerous examples of the fanaticism in the past, and have
incorporated several, for the edification of European joke-
lovers, in some of my own not entirely blameless treatises
on the theatre: such hysterics as the now celebrated explosion over Elsie Janis wherein so self-confessedly over-
wrought was the young man by the lady's vaudeville show
that he found himself rendered "incoherent" and unable
adequately to set down its wonders, and as the swelling
hymn to the obscure actor in an Arthur Hopkins company
who pronounced "human beings" as "youman beans," etc.,
etc., but was none the less entitled to sit on the right hand
of God. These grease spasms break out in the most unexpected quarters and surely must baffle the poor actors who
read them in the hope of guidance to the point where they
begin chasing their noses around the room. An actor like
Arnold Daly, for example, is given the disdainful pooh-
pooh, and one like the "bouncing Reggie Sheffield" (as the
Times phrase has it) bequeathed the diamond medal of

Some Theatrical Personalities

the first rank. Tom Powers, Gregory Kelly, Schuyler Ladd, and a half-dozen other striplings of indifferent talent—I offer not my own perhaps equally faulty appraisal, but that of the majority of competent newspaper and magazine reviewers—are hailed in terms of so many Edmund Keans. John Barrymore, grantedly a very able actor, is made the subject of countless feverish rhapsodies. Brandon Tynan, surely an actor of a not especially high kidney, if we are to believe the men who are accepted as able critics of acting, comes in regularly for the old frat grip and hot slap on the back. And a play cast with a young girl in a little boy's role brings forth the somewhat puzzling lachrymation that the aforesaid play "could have been made something memorably beautiful and exciting had it been possible to engage Gareth Hughes for the part." This Hughes is an adult male. Qu'est-ce que cela, "exciting"?

Gilda Varesi, the uptown Bertha Kalich, is the occasion for a delirious racket of Yale Bowl proportions, while Florence Reed is given the raspberry. Alice Delysia, a French music-hall singer the like of whom the rest of us have encountered time and again in Paris—who forgets, for example the migratory chanteuses of the old Rabelais in the Boulevard de Clichy, Stéphanie of Le Caveau de la République, Thérèse Arney and Marguerite Deval of the Boite-à-Fursy, Davrigny, who played on the same Marigny bills with Irene Bordoni, the best of the lot, and Pretty-Myrtill, as she was pleased to call herself, to say nothing of Alice de Tender, Jeanne Perriat, the admirable Régine Flory, Mado Minty, the lovely Djin d'Irroy and Yetta Rianza of the Moulin Rouge, and the black-eyed Gaby Benda, Claudie de Sivry, and Nelly Vignal?—this unexceptional boulevard performer is proclaimed the true Parisian nonesuch. . . . Too rich a bean feast to remain in the memory in all its details. A razzle-dazzle to blind the poor actor who attempts to get his bearings. He reads in the *Times*, this poor actor, that he is a seidel-bumper with Booth and Barrett, goes crazy, then reads in the other reviews that he is not fit to clean Lew Dockstader's galoshes, and goes crazier still.

I do not set myself bumptiously to say that the *Times* hazlitt's estimates are always wrong (it is not a question of their rightness nor wrongness; they may often be fully right) ; the style in which they are expressed is the particular bouquet that I invite you to sniff. This style presents an interesting study. It never strikes a mean; it is either a gravy bomb, a bursting gladiolus, a palpitating missa cantata, an attack of psychic hydrophobia, or a Roman denunciation, unequivocal, oracular, flat, and final. This actor or actress is pronounced a flawless ruby in terms of Meyerbeer's "Brautgeleite aus der Heimat" and Henry Wadsworth Longfellow; that actor or actress an unconscionable lemon in terms of a tack hammer and a Mystic Shriner pallbearer. Adultory frenzy over a certain cabotin sweats itself out in such verbiage as "one swoons at" the splendor of this or that performance; naïve sentimentality, in such passages as the following anent Fred Stone: "As the audience boomed its fond and genuine welcome to him last evening . . . it may be guessed he was thinking of Dave Montgomery, and it may be hoped that a good many of those out front had the same thought running through their minds"; and not less naïve indignation in such notations as: "This special arrangement, according to Mr. Kelly's drama [*The Phantom Legion*], was made by God in the interest of the allied arms—a notion so entirely Hohenzollern in its blasphemous egotism *as to make the mind dizzy in contemplation.*" A style, in brief, that is purely emotional, and without a trace of the cool reflectiveness and contagious common sense suited to criticism.

Some Theatrical Personalities

It is not that enthusiasm and impatience are not on occasion valuable critical attributes, but that the *Times*'s particular species of enthusiasm is less the enthusiasm of criticism supported by cultural background and experience than that of a small boy at his first circus, and that the *Times*'s species of abrupt impatience is less that of the same school of criticism than that of a fox-trot dancer who has had his toe stepped on. I am no psychochirographist and am, unfortunately, unable to plumb the mysteries underlying a style of this kind. It may be, for all I know, that the mysteries are simply pathological in origin: a too high blood pressure perhaps, an unfortunate chronic costiveness, something of the sort. But, whatever the reason, there it is; and one can easily imagine the effect of it upon the thespians who engage it.

A professional writer of any sound talent and with any sound faith in that talent reads the reviews of his work, however numskullish, but is no more influenced by them one way or another than he is influenced by the make of the socks that he wears. Actors, however, even the best of them, are children, and not only believe all that is written about them, be it from a William Archer or the police-court reporter on the Logansport *Whoop*, but are more or less influenced by it. One still recalls, indeed, the case of one of the most illustrious actresses on our stage who, some twelve or thirteen years ago, informed the management on the noon after her play opened in New York that she would not appear at the second-night performance unless the management made an obscure actor in an obscure role in the play get a haircut, the importance of which to the ensemble Acton Davies had pointed out in his review in the *Evening Sun*. And one further recalls the case of the actor in a Stuart Walker company who actually had to be put away in a sanatorium after he had read the inordinate praise of himself set down by the prankful Louis Sherwin, whom nothing delighted more than befuddling actors with deliberately extravagant criticism to the point where they didn't know where they were at. What Sherwin did with his tongue in his cheek, and what—if I am not mistaken —Mr. Broun of the *Tribune* does with a like roguish chuckle up his sleeve, Mr. Ochs's goldoni accomplishes as unconsciously and naturally as breathing. Let us watch the returns from Bloomingdale. Sport promises, messieurs!

Perhaps this is all a trotting out of artillery to shoot a clay pipe. Now that I have got this far, I conclude that it is, and that the joke is somewhat on me. All that I have written here—some two thousand words or so—was summed up much better in the instance of just such a local reviewer of the day by the late Maurice Barrymore in his now celebrated barroom story about the strictures of the press. But it still seems to me, or, I suppose, to anyone else whose heart is very close to the better and finer theatre, that a newspaper as influential and important as *The New York Times* should treat the theatre at least as dignifiedly as *Bruno's Weekly*. It is not a matter of differing with the opinions of Mr. Ochs's chosen one—one can't get anywhere arguing on that count—it is a matter of maintaining toward the theatre the dispassionate, irritable, and sober attitude of such a journal, say, as the New York *Evening Post*, for all the circumstance that the opinions of its reviews are actually more often not so substantial as those of this same *Times* reviewer. But, as it is, the *Times*, with its grotesquely uncritical partiality for the Actors' Union, its "lump in the throat" manner of play-reviewing, its wild ravings and equally wild improbations, and its general air of treating a première and its principals either as a boozy Quat-z-Arts Ball or a police raid on a sailors' boarding-house—but, as it is, the *Times* lacks only Everett Shinn and

Charles Withers to convert it into a first-rate satirical burlesque for Raymond Hitchcock's next edition of *Hitchy-Koo*.

The Smart Set, February 1921

Max Reinhardt

Preceded by that species of irrelevant and trumpery press-agency which, somewhat disconcertingly, he would seem fond of allowing to make him appear rather like German silver, Max Reinhardt, the foremost active producer in the world theatre, has lately come again across the Atlantic to display his wares. That this virtuoso of dramatic production should permit himself publicity devices that Peaches Browning and even Otto Kahn might balk at is gagging to those of his critics who peculiarly believe that art and dignity should have something in common and who have difficulty in determining just what connection there can be between some of the very finest dramatic presentations of the modern stage and a lot of free lunches at Salzburg, to say nothing of widely disseminated photographs showing the impresario and Miss Julia Hoyt posed against the façade of Schloss Leopoldskron eating sizable hunks of Wiener Lungenbäuscherl. For, while such stuff may be all right on the part of self-advertising vaudeville actors and pentecostal clergymen, it is hardly an admirable business for a man of Reinhardt's attainments. He may thus impress a senate of doodles, but in the minds of others he lowers himself considerably.

That Reinhardt is the most talented director and producer operating in the theatre in these years is certainly not news, except perhaps to a few Russians. With Craig, the greatest genius of them all, in forced retirement in Genoa, with Stanislavsky, a skillful fellow, calmly relying for eminence upon a few already ancient achievements, with Dantchenko, very little better than a second-rater, idiotically frittering away his time out in Hollywood, and with Pitoëff going in simply for a series of exaggerted imitations and caricatures in France, Reinhardt has the field pretty well to himself. He is an extraordinarily fertile and alive figure, indefatigable, imaginative, and resourceful; he works like a Trojan; he has, unlike these other producers, a sense of internationalism—all drama, whatever the land of its origin, is of interest to him; he has a mind that adapts itself to a diversity of drama and a fancy that filters it with a various force and beauty onto a fluid and galvanic stage. It is Reinhardt's outstanding characteristic, indeed, and the quality that has raised him to leadership among the active producing talents of the day, that he is, in a sense, a different man in the instance of each separate production which he makes. Where the majority of producers have a very definite and unmistakable personal label that sticks betrayingly to each of their presentations, however essentially different the dramas themselves may be, Reinhardt changes his directing personality according to the drama he happens to be dealing with. There is not one director Reinhardt—there are a dozen director Reinhardts. But there is only one Stanislavsky, one Gémier, one Granville-Barker, one Copeau, or one Sierra, be the play farce or comedy, tragedy or allegory, spectacle or what not. The signature is genuine, but the contents of the bottle are often spurious. For these directors and others like them are bent upon impressing their own idiosyncratic personalities on a variety of drama, where Reinhardt is concerned chiefly with so adjusting the many facets of his directorial personality that one of them that most patly suits the particular drama in hand shall not obscure the latter to his own vainglory and to its own infinite damage.

Going into the theatre of any outstanding director and producer save Reinhardt, one can discern the director's arbitrary method and technique, be the exhibit Shakespeare or Racine, Lenormand or Oscar Wilde. The label is there as flamboyantly—and as dubiously—as on the bottle of bootleg Scotch. Everything is sacrificed to make a Roman holiday for the producer himself, and for his personal kudos. The dramatist is simply a tool wherewith he seeks to fashion his own monument. Among directors both big and little the world over, one finds this vain adherence to and exposition of an inflexible technique or style, as set in each of its several ways as the writing tricks of the more celebrated popular fictioneers or the steps of the more celebrated colored hoofers. Thus, one need not refer to the playbill to know a Stanislavsky production, whether of Chekhov or Maeterlinck; the Stanislavsky idiosyncrasies periodically thrust themselves forward willy-nilly, and the devil take the dramatist. So, also, with Jessner—at times, like Stanislavsky, a praiseworthy craftsman—and his arbitrary stairways, with Copeau and his arbitrary salon method of staging, with Pitoëff and his arbitrary bolshevik hocus-pocus, with Gémier and his arbitrary portière nonsense, with Barker and his arbitrary gilt Oxonianism, with Arthur Hopkins and his arbitrary Barnowsky naturalism, or—to descend to the little fellows—with Belasco and his silk laboriously thrown over cotton, Basil Dean and his drugstore-window-lighting monkeyshines, and the relatively much superior André and his secondhand Reinhardt-isms out of Rapallo.

In Reinhardt's theatre, as I have noted, technique of production is no such more or less exactly pigeonholed business. For each separate drama a new technique is devised. For one, we have the Craig concepts visualized by the Reinhardt imagination; for another, the principles of the commedia dell'arte elaborated and edited; for still another, music and the spoken word deftly orchestrated; for still another, the sixteenth-century moralities beautified by a twentieth century looking imaginatively backward; for yet another, modernism plus modernism; and for yet another still, impressionism and expressionism enjoying a picnic of acutely critical production. In this lies the estimable and protean Max's directorial expertness and felicity: that all manner of drama is grist for his mill and that, more important, that mill revolves not to a single wind, as with the other producers, but to whatever wind the drama in point may blow. There are times, it may be, when Reinhardt plainly strains himself for effect, when a trace of illegitimacy insinuates itself into his work and causes one transiently to suspect the mountebank, when those snapshots of Max kneeling piously before a ten-foot crucifix in Schloss Leopoldskron with Fanny Brice, Morris Gest, and other such devout fellow Christians come to mind, but in the general run of things the honest artist is clearly to be felt and seen beneath and beyond the momentary posturer. Reinhardt, with Papa Craig peeping over his shoulder, has brought more actual life to the modern stage than any other practicing director and producer of his time. His influence has spread over all lands and seas. He has been Gordon Craig's Paul.

Art of the Night, 1928

77

A. B. Walkley

AMONG THE CRITICS of the drama in regular and active practice in the Anglo-Saxon yoshiwara today, it seems to me that there is one who stands out from all the others like a sprig of fresh green mint from a julep. That one is the Englishman, Walkley. Since the retirement of Shaw from the British circle some twenty-eight years ago, there has been no one to offer him serious challenge. Several vital and eloquent voices, true, have lifted themselves against the grisly routine: C. E. Montague and John Palmer among them; but the vitality and eloquence, admirable as they have been, have for one reason or another lacked staying power, and have died out, after a brief spell, from the scene. The voice of Walkley, on the other hand, has been consistently clear and resonant for something like three decades. And it has been a voice that has uniformly had in it, unless I am greatly mistaken, the most thorough theatrical and dramatic common sense that has been heard in England or America in its time.

I do not forget Walkley's late colleague, the estimable and engaging Archer. Archer was a cultivated and experienced critic; he did some excellent and valuable pioneering; his judgments were often sound and stimulating. But as between the two men, the choice presents little difficulty. Archer's attitude toward the theatre, due to the fundamental nature and disposition of the man himself, was ever

78

A. B. Walkley

that of the professor. (What was *The Green Goddess*, in
sooth, but a professor cracking a classroom joke?) He approached the theatre intelligently, but his intelligence was
largely set to a fixed pattern; it lacked the warmth and
fluidity so necessarily a part of the biology of dramatic
criticism. He looked into the theatre, in our colored
friends' phrase, from the outside in—like a university don
with his eye to the keyhole of a peepshow. He followed the
gypsy caravan in a dress suit. He understood, and understood well, the drama, but he did not understand so well,
because it was not in the soul of him to understand it, the
theatre. Walkley, gifted with all the qualities that Archer
had, has been gifted, to boot, with a cosmopolitanism of
psyche and a metropolitanism of taste that have given him
a roundness, a fullness, in the contemplation of drama and
the theatre not possessed by his late lamented associate.
Archer was a theory criticizing the theatre; Walkley is, in
a figurative manner of speaking, a theatre criticizing a theory. His mind is a stage, brightly illuminated and suavely
draped, whereon dance with sunny and lagerish smiles a
hundred comedians casting hither and thither their sagacious and penetrating banderillas into the flanks of whatever species of critical bull happens to be prancing around
the ring at the moment. There is ever the quality of the
theatre and the feel of the theatre in Walkley's criticism, as
there is and has been in the criticism of every man whose
writings on the theatre have been worth any attention. In
the criticism of Archer, one got this feel of the playhouse
all too seldom; one got the impression, rather, of a confusion of the theatre and the library.

It isn't that Walkley does not take the theatre seriously.
It is simply that, like a man with the woman he truly and
deeply loves, his very seriousness makes him lighthearted,
happy, and gay. Beauty makes idiots sad as it makes wise

men merry. Men laugh with the things and persons that are closest to their hearts. But because the rank and file of critics believe that there is something wrong with the kind of critic who, understanding thoroughly a thing that they themselves do not so thoroughly understand, takes that thing with a pleasantly careless whistle and the jaunty, sauntering swing of a cane, Walkley has often been looked on with disfavor, and favor been bestowed instead upon the kind of critic who would wear a long face at a Ladies' Day in a coon Turkish Bath. This is always the fate of a critic who knows his job so superlatively well that he can turn it inside out. The ideal critic of the multitude is not such a critic, but rather one who knows only half of his job and who conceals his lack of knowledge of the other half by taking seriously what he does not know, and writing of it even more seriously.

Walkley is not profound, in the common interpretation of the term, only in that he does not elect to be profound over matters that are intrinsically not profound. He senses the ridiculousness of sweating to build up complex theories that so little as twenty or thirty years later—thus fitful, since Aristotle lifted it out of its cradle, has the drama been —will be quite as empty and useless as an old tooth-powder can. He appreciates that the theatre and drama are as shifting as the sands of the sea and that in that very shifting lies the true secret of their golden, sunlit beauty. The basic laws, everyone knows; there is no need to write of them. But the bylaws change constantly; one may write of them interestingly, but, as of things that are ever in process of change, at best with an air of dubiety and evanescence, and perhaps the flicker of a snicker. *The Frogs* is a good play; *Hamlet* is a good play; *Seven Keys to Baldpate* is a good play. That's that. Try to fit them to the same, definite, positive, unvarying dramatic theory and go crazy

A. B. Walkley

in the attempt. Theories are for the classroom; drama is
for the theatre. Walkley is a critic of culture, experience,
and sensitiveness and, being such a critic, knows just two
sound standards of judgment, to wit: (1) whatever interests me is good; and (2) whatever doesn't interest me is
not good. The critical technique of critics of the Archer
school, on the other hand, runs thus: (1) whatever is good
interests me; and (2) whatever is not good does not interest me. The subtle difference between these criteria of appraisal is the signal difference between Walkley and his
contemporaries, both as critics and as men. Walkley is a
personality; his contemporaries are, most of them, just persons. Walkley is a positive agent; the others are positive-
negative. Walkley is a cool syllogism; the others are inde-
terminate symposiums of prejudice, prejudgment, and the
dusty critical bibles of the past.

Walkley's *Dramatic Criticism*, a slender little book made
up of lectures delivered at the Royal Institution about
twenty years ago, has more sober sense in it, to my way of
thinking, than any treatise or volume on the same subject
published in its time. (This statement includes Croce from
stem to stern.) His various collections of dramatic criticisms, *Playhouse Impressions, Drama and Life*, and certain
portions of his more recent books such as *Pastiche and
Prejudice, More Prejudice*, and *Still More Prejudice* contain, also to my way of thinking, the soundest criticism of
its kind that has been published in English since Shaw,
though, as I have said, Montague's and Palmer's work, on
a considerably smaller scale, is not to be sniffed at. The
criticism of Walkley is not only shrewdly discerning and
fundamentally common-sensible; it is, in addition, eminently readable and eminently charming. It also has its
own share of beauty. And this beauty that it has is the
genuine beauty of a tonic point of view and of a great love

of life and of an easy and gracious personality, not the spurious beauty of literary pretension with which certain other critics, both in England and America, seek vaingloriously to deck out their critical nonsense. There is more good sense and more delightful reading in a casual critical essay of Walkley's than in any half-dozen of the professorial flower pots. As a critic, he is the most convincing, persuasive, and attractive actor off the Anglo-Saxon stage.

He is not without his faults, of course. He has rolled a log or two in his time; he has now and again, for all his cosmopolitanism—and he is by all odds the most cosmopolitan critic in the England of his day—disclosed himself to be exceedingly insular (like most Englishmen, there is little in America that seems to him to be any good); he has been curiously anesthetic to some of the most noteworthy advances in the art of scenic design and stage production (he has never been able to judge accurately and fully the experiments of such men as Gordon Craig, for example); he has at times permitted politeness to stand in the way of sharp and forthright execution. And in later years he has periodically descended to the promiscuous and very awful present-day British habit of following up an excellent critical essay with one of those mild Lamb-like papers on the lark singing outside the bedroom window in the early morn or on the toothsome pasties one can find at the Sign of the Galloping Cuckoo. Thus, in *More Prejudice* we find much first-rate critical writing interspersed with the kind of essays on blackbirds, lipsticks, and letter-writing, to say nothing of a day at the zoo, that Englishmen have been writing ever since they laid poor Elia in his final resting place these ninety-odd years ago. There is only one compensating circumstance in Walkley's case. He can make even such gimcrack subjects interesting.

A.B.—as they call him across the pond—is personally

A. B. Walkley

perhaps best to be described as a British James Huneker. To the late Lord Jim add a measure of British reserve, picture a mind that resembles a placid hillside stream rather than a leaping, sparkling waterfall which splashes everybody for miles around, and substitute a filet of sole Bearnaise and sauterne for a platter of sauerkraut and Pilsner —and you have Walkley. Otherwise, the two have much in common. The same multiplicity of interests, the same genial raillery, the same easy familiarity with everything from what Beethoven said to Rochlitz to what Steve Donaghue said to his barber, the same intense and warming humanness, the same broad acquaintance with everything from the best Paris restaurant wherein to get snails cooked in absinthe to the best place in Constantinople to get a shoeshine, the same winking and humorous eye, the same simplicity, the same it's-all-beautiful-but-what-the-hell's-it-all-about quality—these are Walkley's as they were Huneker's. Like the latter—God rest his companionable and deeply missed bones—Walkley is interested in everything and gives a tinker's dam for nothing. He has found that greatest of all secrets to human happiness: the philosophy of indifference. And, like all indifferent men, he has a rare zest for and relish of life and the things of life. The smell of the footlights in London and the smell of the salt in Brightlingsea, the rhythm of Shakespeare and the rhythm of a pretty girl's legs, the latest star actor at the Adelphi and the newest monkey at the zoo in Regent's Park, the Duchesse de Langeais and the impresario of tipples at the Garrick Club, Marcel Proust's *A l'ombre des jeunes filles en fleurs* and the shade of a Chaumontel pear tree in a quiet English orchard—fact and fancy, fancy and fact, reality and illusion, illusion and reality, these are all equally close to him—and all one. And infinitely diverting. And of utterly no importance.

Some Theatrical Personalities

Like Huneker in the matter of certain other of the arts, however tired Walkley may periodically be of the theatre and drama, he never gives the faintest sign of being tired of criticism of the theatre and drama. He may fall asleep at a play, but his criticism of the play will be thoroughly wide awake and lively. He has the gift of making the uninteresting interesting, and—what is obviously a deal more important—of making the worth while and interesting doubly worth while and interesting. He writes with the mind of a full-flowered man and the heart and spirit of a kid. His method is to maintain an elaborate and amused pretense of playing tag with a subject and having great difficulty in catching up with it and shouting "You're *it!*" when all the time he could do it very simply and readily merely by reaching out his hand. It is his favorite diversion to run after a subject with slow-motion paces and to pass the subject, which seems simultaneously to be moving at top speed, before it goes half a block. He is privy to Huneker's trick of making the reader believe at the outset that a very simple problem is an extremely difficult one and then convincing the reader shortly thereafter that he is a master hand at cracking the toughest nut. This, as in Huneker's case, is the playboy side of the fellow. He likes nothing so much as to tie a tin can to the tail of a theory that his brother critics are disposed to pet and fondle. He is, in short, like all plausible critics, a showman. On the way into the main tent, first and foremost there are some fetching sideshows.

If the requisites of a first-rate critic are a sound admiration for fine things, a hearty contempt for spurious things, and a rich gusto in conveying his discrimination, the one way or the other, to his readers, Walkley, Arthur Bingham, is such a one. He lacks the blacksmith directness and originality of a *Saturday Review* Shaw; he lacks the enormous cultural background of a Huneker; but one can't have everything. Shaw has left the field, and Huneker has left the earth. There remains, in control of the English-American scene, this wise and engaging, this superbly perceptive and very infinitely charming little gentleman of London.

The House of Satan, 1926

Ziegfeld

A YEAR or two back I bade you conjure up the picture of the rotund, rosy, amiable little apple dumpling, begauded with a facetious derby and an end man's overcoat, possessed of a brobdingnagian horse-laugh and of the general aspect of Fatty Arbuckle reflected in a trick mirror, who represented then, as he represents still, the finest ideals, the bravest ambitions, and the most vigorous analytical and critical virtues to be found in the American dramatic theatre. The portrait was that of Arthur Hopkins. Today I give you a companion portrait.

If the picture of Hopkins suggests Hi Holler festooned for a pie-eating contest, this companion picture suggests the actor customarily engaged for the role of Joe Galvanuzzi, pal of Hop Sing, the villainous Chinaman, in *Followed by Fate*. The lavender shirt and collar of the same hue, the purple tie, the socks to match, the sassafras-color overcoat belt, the green felt hat, the Italian complexion, the drooping cigarette, the black hair thickly streaked with gray, the general aspect of yon Cassius just after dinner—

all are relevantly in it. Passing the subject on the street, one is disappointed not to see him suddenly stop short in his tracks, take three stealthy paces to the left, and hiss. His expression is constantly noncommittal; his features are ever as immobile as if he had just dealt four aces; and his taciturnity as gloomy as if someone else had been dealt a straight flush. He gives one the impression of being habitually seized with a rather wistful stomach ache; one that, while not painful, is yet sufficiently uncomfortable to make its trustee sad. I probably have not spoken twenty words to him in my life, and his fifteen or sixteen in reply have been quite as dull and uninteresting as my own. He prefers Dave Stamper to Beethoven, George V. Hobart to W. S. Gilbert, and Art Hickman to Karl Muck. And he—"Ziggy" to his help, Florenz Ziegfeld, Jr., to the public—is perhaps the greatest music-show producer that the world theatre has thus far known.

The brace of portraits, then, is the pride of the American professional theatre: the one of a man who, more than any other, has brought beauty to its dramatic stage; the other of a man who, more than the rest combined, has brought beauty to its musical. Yet the common notion that Ziegfeld is a creator in music-show production in the sense that Reinhardt, say, is a creator in dramatic production is not true. He is, like Hopkins, an editor. But, like Hopkins, an editor whose stage editorial skill has lifted the contributions of others to a plane of tripled symmetry, triply smooth rhythm, and tripled loveliness.

Both men stem professionally from the Continent: Hopkins from Germany and the German manner of production, Ziegfeld from France and the French manner. Study the settings and lightings of Reinhardt and the stage direction of Victor Barnowsky, and you find whence the art of Hopkins derives. Study the trick and manner of the

Marigny of 1909 and 1910 and 1911, and you have a view of the Ziegfeld preparatory school. But no man ever improved upon his model more than this Ziegfeld: his *Follies* and his *Frolics* are as superior to the Marigny in its heyday as the Marigny was superior to any other music hall in Europe. In every department of music-show production, save one, his stage reaches its highest level. In one department, it reaches the lowest. For Ziegfeld's blind spot is the kind of wit and humorous commentary that have periodically made the French revue famous. It would seem that this exceptional professor of the tune stage knows no sounder use for two hundred thousand dollars' worth of magnificent scenes, costumes, lights, and girls than to place them in their positions upon the stage, crack the whip, and bid them in combination work themselves up in a smashing two-hour crescendo to a joke about Henry Ford. His lighting, his scenery, his costumes, and his women are generally exemplary; his dialogue is usually as witty as a conversation between two bootleggers. Even when there comes to him ready-made something like Rip's immensely funny satirical burlesque of two youngsters from the 1920 spring *Folies-Bergère* show, he finds himself unable to appreciate it, and presents in its stead a garbled and empty paraphrase wherein for the wit of Rip he substitutes the notion of dressing Miss Ray Dooley in swaddling clothes and then causing her to crack Mr. Charles Winninger over the head with a milk bottle. But aside from this utter banality of dialogue and antic, his stage is a stage on which the light pleasure theatre triumphs as it has never triumphed before.

Until Ziegfeld came upon the scene, the American music-show stage (as well as the European) was in the main merely the conventional dramatic stage with a half-dozen extra bunchlights set up in the wings and a trapdoor cut in the floor large enough to permit DeWolf Hopper to come up through it. It was intrinsically a hybrid stage, a cold stage. Its rhythm was confined to the orchestra pit, its movement to the legs and the diaphragms of the chorus, its charm to the charm of this or that pretty girl. It remained for Ziegfeld to orchestrate it, to take its separate ingredients and fashion them into a warm composition, to put the violins in the girls' legs and the girls' legs in the bull fiddles, to make the girls melt into the scenes and the scenes melt into girls. With Ziegfeld, the music-show stage became, for the first time in America at least, a clearly individualized stage. Today it is the stammbühne of its kind the world over.

The Ziegfeld shows are a triumph of overtones. The girls are sometimes inferior to the brand that George Edwardes used to display in the London Gaiety; the dancing is sometimes inferior to that in the average Dillingham show; the tunes and lyrics are sometimes inferior to those, say, of the Kern-Wodehouse exhibits; the scenery and lighting are on occasion not better than the scenery and lighting of such a production as Anderson's *What's in a Name?* But the show as a whole is always twice as inveigling and twice as beautiful as any of these. Where the other producers present, Ziegfeld suggests. And in this suggestion, this skimming-over-the-water quality, this technique of implication, there is ever a much greater effectiveness than in italics and emphasis. George Edwardes brought out his pretty girls and turned up the lights. Ziegfeld brings out his and turns down the lights. Dillingham brings out Adele Astaire and lets her dance for fifteen minutes. She dances extremely well. Ziegfeld brings out Mary Eaton and lets her dance one minute. She dances only fairly well. But a minute of moderately good dancing always leaves a better uncritical impression than fifteen minutes of very good dancing. Anderson brings out an elaborately handsome

Japanese screen scene and lets the audience look at it for almost half an hour. Ziegfeld brings out a comparatively simple embroidered curtain that no sooner tickles the eye than it is drawn aside to make place for another.

The Ziegfeld technique is the caviar technique, as opposed to the planked-steak technique of his competitors. The latter set out to gorge their audiences, to give them a meal; the former gives them just enough to make them thirsty. The *Ziegfeld Follies* arouses curiosity; the *Greenwich Village Follies* satisfies it. From the moment one puts foot in the lobby of the theatre where a Ziegfeld show is playing and lays an eye upon the frieze of chorus girls photographically virginized by Alfred Cheney Johnston, the Ziegfeld hocus-pocus is observable. From the moment one again puts foot in the lobby on the way out to the accompaniment of a boozy, half-asleep melody, the hocus-pocus is memorialized. Ziegfeld, in a word, has adapted the Belasco abracadabra and electrobiology to the more relevant and appropriate field of the music-show stage. He has borrowed Little Bright Eyes from the spiritual world, dressed her in thin black silk stockings and pink garters, and put her on the job in the physical.

But—what's it all about, after all? ask the professors. For all the undoubted proficiency of the fellow, what's the end: what's the use; what's the good? The answer is peculiarly simple. If drama is art in so far as it teaches us to understand life, such a music show is art in so far as it teaches us to enjoy life. I, for one, have never been able to reconcile myself to the notion that a shot like this which gratifies primarily the aesthetic sense, and gratifies it soundly, isn't to be taken as seriously as a drama which gratifies primarily the intellectual. You, perhaps, may get out of Maeterlinck's *The Betrothal*, Augustus Thomas's *As a Man Thinks*, or Percy MacKaye's *George Washington* a greater aesthetic, emotional, and intellectual lift than you get out of the *Follies*, but I don't. If, on the other hand, I get something out of a drama like *Lonely Lives* that I don't get out of a *Follies,* I also get something out of the latter that I don't get out of the former. The theory that there may not be as much cultivated beauty in a music show as in a drama has always seemed to me much like a theory that would maintain that the objective beauty of Michelangelo is inevitably and necessarily less beauty than, and inferior to, the subjective and spiritual beauty of Dante.

The art of gaiety is an art no less than the art of gloom. Cabell and Ziegfeld are in their separate ways no less artists than Dostoevsky and Stanislavsky. Anything that can make the Yankee concern himself with beauty is salubrious, even if the beauty is less that of Chopin, Velásquez, and Pater than that of Chopin paraphrased, Urban, and trim ankles. Even Chopin jazzed is better than Hubbell straight. The persuasion of the American even to beautiful colors, beautiful costumes, beautiful women, and beautiful legs is something. It is the first step. It is the sprinkling-can upon a dry and dusty soul. The greenhorn who has been taught to admire a smash of color, a swish of silks and satins, a lovely face, and a smooth ankle is ready for better, and higher, things. The fibrils of beauty are beginning to sprout in him. And slowly, painfully, over the rocky road whereon his successive cultural mileposts are Urban, Rosa Bonheur, Landseer, and Millet, and the Swiss bell ringers, John Philip Sousa, Tosti, and Massenet, he will mayhap finally and in perspiring triumph arrive at the *Mona Lisa* and the *William Tell* overture. If Ziegfeld does not inculcate the love of beauty in the yokel, he at least inculcates the seed of that love. Even a stockbroker, leaving a Ziegfeld show, cannot remain wholly insensible to its callaesthetic pull. Let him have six or eight years of Ziegfeld training and he will perhaps even arrive at the point where he is enthusiastic over Leonard Merrick.

Several years ago the late Paul Potter was visiting Thomas Hardy. The latter had not been in a theatre for thirty years. "Let us go tonight," suggested Potter. "What shall we see?" "A musical show," replied Hardy. After the show—it was a revue at the Alhambra largely modeled after and cabbaged from Ziegfeld—Hardy was all excitement. "Fine, fine!" he exclaimed. "Fine and beautiful!" Contrast with this view of the sensitive artist the view of the amiable dolts who see in a show of this kind not life and color, perfect design and fluid grace, but only Dolores's thighs and Gilda Gray's umbilicus. It would seem that the female figure that indirectly made a peculiar public regard Bouguereau as an artist has rather cryptically made the same peculiar public regard Ziegfeld only as a foghorn.

I have mentioned George Edwardes. It was the trick of this Edwardes to make the girl show ladylike. It is the trick of Ziegfeld to make it glamorous. Before the inauguration of Edwardes, the average music-show girl, for all her prettiness, had a sophisticated, hard-enameled look. Edwardes dressed and conjured the girl so that she looked as if butter wouldn't melt in her mouth. He removed passion from the music-show stage and sagaciously substituted for it the thrice-sensuous innocence. Ziegfeld, as I have once before pointed out, steers the doubly shrewd middle course in bringing sophistication and innocence into sudden, violent, and hence effective collision.

To appreciate Ziegfeld, all that one has to do is to view the efforts of his American and European imitators. Even when the latter buy from him his scenes, his costume plates, his tunes, his dance numbers, and some of his girls, even when they come over here and personally study his methods of composition, even when they contract with his producing help to sail over the sea and assist them closely to duplicate his shows, even then they always find that something important is lacking. Which very important something is the M. Ziggy.

The World in Falseface, 1923

The Censor

IT HAS BECOME a platitude that when a moralist mind presently scans the drama, its attention becomes fixed almost exclusively upon sex. With the death of Anthony Comstock there passed out of moral snooping, in all its departments and ramifications, the consideration of all other offenses against the established hand-me-downs of Moses. Sex and sex alone became the turpentine that made the smut smellers squirm and heave. To the late lamented Anthony, sex was but one evil calling for the intervention of the Lord God Almighty and Police Captain Mulcahy. There was, too, a comprehensive catalogue of other instruments of Satan. There were, as we discover after a study of the eminent Anthony's tome, *Traps for the Young,* candy stores that retarded the footsteps of youngsters on their way to school and church, stories of romantic love, newspapers that printed accounts of crimes, dime novels recounting the exploits of train robbers, safe crackers, detectives, and other such crooks, novels con-

taining oaths, tales of gambling, poolrooms, raffles, lot-
teries, plays dealing with criminals, alcoholic drinks,
patent medicines, dubious professors of the spirochaeta
pallida, booklets setting forth the ways and means of
dropped-handkerchief and like flirtations, atheistic and
infidel literature, and a score of similar corruptions.

Sex, indeed, was one of the least of the nefarious nui-
sances against which the august crusader pitched his indignations. In literature and in the drama, Comstock found
many more things to deplore and prosecute than the mere
overactive libido. Among the infamies that aroused his
wrath and sent him hotfoot to the telephone to summon to
his and Jehovah's aid the minions of the law were—I quote
from his book—"coarse, slangy stories in the dialect of the
bar-room, the blood and thunder romance of border life,
and the exaggerated details of crimes, real and imaginary;
crimes which are gilded and lawlessness which is painted to
resemble valor, making a bid for bandits, brigands, mur-
derers, thieves and criminals in general; leading characters
who possess extraordinary beauty of countenance, most superb clothing, abundant wealth, the strength of a giant,
the agility of a squirrel, the cunning of a fox . . . and who
are the high favorites of some rich person who by his pa-
tronage and endorsement lifts the young villains into lofty
positions in society and provides liberally of his wealth to
secure them immunity for their crimes"; plays and stories
in which "one young girl is hired to personate a rich girl
and marry the villain in her stead," in which "a beautiful
girl, by lying and deceit, seeks to captivate one whom she
loves," in which "a man is murdered by being blown up by
explosives," in which "assaults are made upon an officer
while resisting arrests," in which there is a "conspiracy
against an officer to prevent the arrest of a criminal," in
which there is a "burglary or a woman murdered by

masked thieves," in which "an attempt is made to force a beautiful girl to marry a scoundral to save her benefactor," in which "attempts are made to coerce a girl to marry against her wishes," in which there are attempted assassinations, in which confidence games are shown or described, in which highwaymen figure, in which there is a massacre by Indians, in which "one babe is stolen to substitute for another," in which there is a clandestine correspondence between two sweethearts, in which a man deserts his first wife and marries another woman, in which there is "a disparagement of honest toil," in which such things are shown as "in what part of the body to plant pistol bullets to the best advantage and how to handle poison skillfully," and in which "there are defalcations and embezzlements." Fifteen or twenty additional items of like character are listed. Under the terms of them, Comstock advocated suppression, and not on sex grounds, of all such theatrical exhibits as *Is Zat So?*, the melodramas of Lincoln J. Carter, *Within the Law, Raffles, Robin Hood, The Bohemian Girl, Pinafore, The Prisoner of Zenda, Night Refuge, The Weavers, The Fatal Card, Sherlock Holmes, Get Rich Quick Wallingford, Turn to the Right, Strife*, and a hundred others currently regarded by his descendants in morality as innocent and harmless.

The moral order has turned something of a cartwheel since Comstock became a subject of interest for the worms. Where the moralist of the eighties saw harm in the depiction of countless human frailties and diversions, his offspring today sees danger pur et simple in sex. The drama may safely violate all the Commandments but the Seventh. Even the second clause of the Tenth is perfectly safe in any number of dramatic directions, as we know, for example, from plays, their placid courses left undisturbed, like *Pelléas and Mélisande, Candida, The Fugitive, The Joy of*

The Censor

Living, *Lady Windermere's Fan*, *The Liars*, *The Duel*, *The Galilean's Victory*, and *The Case of Rebellious Susan*. But with the Seventh it is different. And not only with that one literally, but with any and all approaches to it. One may speculate as to the reason. That reason, I believe, may be discovered in the fact, well appreciated by the blue-noses, that sex is the easiest foundation on which to erect the structure of a moral show to which the public will respond. The blue-noses seek self-advertisement above everything else; when Sumner in an unguarded moment foolishly agreed with the District Attorney's office to make his raids without publicity, he spelled not only his own doom but the doom of financial contribution to his anti-vice society, as one of his latest pamphlets calling desperately for funds demonstrates. Moral campaigns need money, and even the most sympathetic Methodist wants his neighbor to hear the click of his dollar in the collection plate. It is a well-known fact, incidentally, that those Methodist churches whose collection plates have pieces of velvet at the bottom of them are the poorest, a circumstance duly noted and rectified at the last congress of the denomination's bishops. The necessary public reaction, obviously, cannot be got from raids on plays encouraging gambling, swindling, and even murder, but only from raids on those which involve sensational sex of one sort or another. The reason for this is the same as the reason which makes one murder in actual life more engrossingly interesting to the general public than another and intrinsically just as interesting murder. Since the Leutgert affair in Chicago many years ago, there has not been a single murder case in America that has lacked a sensational sex motif and that has made the general public wait avidly at the streetcorners for the newspaper extras. Without exception, the murder cases that have most greatly made the mob lick its chops have been those in which sex played a suggestive part, and the Leopold-Loeb case was no exception. An attempt on the part of the moralists, therefore, to suppress such a play as *Crime*, for instance, on the contendable ground that it was subversive of law and order, would doubtless only cause the public to hoot. What the public wants is a good, hot show on the part of the moralists whom it regards in the light of so many paid melodrama actors, and the moralists can only give it with the actual dirt that proceeds from the prosecution of theoretical dirt. The moralists are no fools; they know which side their bread is buttered on; they know what makes the front pages of the newspapers and what does not; they know that a yokel who has been told where there is a warm belly-dance will presently want to be told where there is an even warmer one, and that he will gladly hand over his money for the tip; and they hence very sensibly and intelligently, according to their corrupt and hypocritical standards, go about their dirty business. To blame them for not going about it differently, and honestly, is to blame a shell-game operator for not using three peas.

Art of the Night, 1928

Eugene O'Neill as a Character in Fiction

THE FOLLOWING SECTION is taken from Nathan's Monks Are Monks, *a book that is neither biography, nor criticism, nor fiction, but a combination of the three.*

Eugene O'Neill as a Character in Fiction

It tells the story of Lorinda Hope, a lovely young lady, wealthy and well read, who longs to have a love affair with a celebrated writer and who in her quest learns "what is wrong with American literature."

In the literary bohemia she meets a distinguished novelist, a charming poet, a dramatist of genius, a team of critics —Morton and Norton—and a battle-scarred veteran of the first crusade to make the world safe for democracy who has put his bitter experiences into hair-raising fiction. For reasons of his own, each of these famous men refuses to comply with Lorinda's wish, and in despair she gives up literature and enters a nunnery.

Eustace O'Hara, of course, is a good-natured caricature of O'Neill, though at times he seems to be talking like George Jean Nathan. Of the sextet of authors burlesqued in the book (one is a caricature of Nathan by Nathan), he fares best and his dialogue is the most entertaining.

*   *   *

EUSTACE O'HARA, in the phraseology of modern American dramatic criticism, was the only American playwright worth a God-damn. The son of a stevedore, he had worked his way through two years at Harvard, being then expelled for making an indecent noise with his mouth during an open lecture by the eminent professor George Pierce Baker, and subsequently serving the world and his own belly as a freight-car conductor, banana peddler, on a Staten Island ferry, bathroom steward on the Albany night boat, Nantucket life-saver, Greenwich Village speakeasy waiter, and shillaber with the Sells-Floto circus. It was accordingly and promptly maintained, as is customary in such cases, that he must have inherited his talent from his mother.

O'Hara had been writing plays for only a relatively few years, but in that brief span had made his name a playhouse word not only in America but all over Europe. True enough, his dramas were somewhat too rich in hells, lousys, guts, and cheez-uses to be regarded as anything but ephemeral and rather disgusting novelties by the more scleroskeletal members of the American Academy of Arts and Letters, but to the critical gentlemen of the *Nation, New Republic, American Mercury, New Masses,* and other such organs of the devil he was the Saviour, Buddha, Mohammed, and Mary Baker Eddy of the American drama all rolled into one. "Until Eustace O'Hara appeared upon the scene," they contended, "American drama offered little for the mature European interest. The records, previous to his time, showed a number of writers and a number of plays of transient quality, some of them amusing and some of them genuinely gifted in detail, but it brought to light none that bulked with body. The roll included some good melodramas that, while they departed from knavish Chinamen, heroic ensigns, and Kentucky racehorses, were hardly worth more than a three hours' audience consideration; some workmanlike but negligible farces with drolly observed national idiosyncrasies; some comedies, patterned largely after British models, that sought to be American by eliminating the butler and pronouncing such words as secretary and cemetery in four syllables instead of three; some close caricatures of American phenomena that, while they were worthy in their way—Ade's, for example—were, after all, like most dramatic caricature, evanescent; and some heavily straight-faced dramas, elaborately conscious of their own pseudo-profundity, that momentarily managed to betrick the pseudo-profound reviewers of the day into imagining them to be something important. But the roll included nothing, or at best very little, to persuade Europeans that our drama was anything but periodically diverting nursery play. With O'Hara, however, the native drama has begun to take on at least a measure of the significance that it previously lacked."

O'Hara, in short, had come to be to the American drama what General Sheridan had been to Cedar Creek. Nor was he himself, out of any mock modesty, oblivious of the fact. "The trouble with American drama before I heaved into it," he observed, "was that it was written for the most part by fairies trying to chew tobacco."

He never minced opinions. Where his fellow playwrights, such as they were, conducted themselves politely after the manner of fashionable doctors and adhered to the principles of professional etiquette, praising and greasing one another like so many suburban neighbors, O'Hara looked matters straight in the eye and said his blunt say—and not only about other playwrights, but about actors, critics, producers, and everyone else connected with the theatre.

"There is too much blah and bushwah going the rounds of the theatre and of everyone in it," he would proclaim. "It gives me a lovely pain in the bottom. The critics, who ought to know better—though God knows why, considering the kind we've got here—peddle it until you have to get yourself orey-eyed in order to recapture your senses. Take this hoopdedoodle about important playwrights that they're forever spilling. Contrary to the layman's opinion, it's the impulse and yearning of criticism, even the most hard-boiled and long-faced, to fish up out of the shallow waters at its feet an occasional whale, so that it may lay unction to its ability at angling and perhaps subsequently have its picture taken, for the impression of everyone, alongside the catch. The average critic each night before going to sleep prays that he may someday, by his superior nose for discernment, smell out a genius either still undetected or unappreciated by his fellow critics and so have something to strut and brag about. A commendable yen, surely. But it is the misfortune of most critics that this meritorious yen, like too much equally meritorious grog, often goes to their heads and induces a considerable unsteadiness in them. The wish to discover geniuses becomes a fixation; the fixation gradually becomes a mania; the mania in turn dilutes the globus oculi; and there follows a promiscuous mistaking of sardines for monsters of the deep.

"In many critics, this passion to pull up big fish has a patriotic touch about it, indistinguishable, on another plane, from carrying along a little American flag to visit Napoleon's tomb, or ordering a Bronx cocktail at the Pschorrbräu. A national pride, perhaps even an unconscious racial perkiness over some such dazzling chapter in the Republic's history as dying for democracy in Nicaragua, insinuates itself into the critic's aesthetic armamentarium and causes him to dream of the day when Melpomene, Calliope, and the other muses may resemble just so many girls on Riverside Drive or Chestnut Street. The phenomenon isn't peculiar to American critics, however. Whereever you find critics, you'll observe it. In England, we have been entertained by the spectacle of certain critics telling St. John Ervine and a few other bunkum-busters that they don't know what they're talking about and trying to elevate Britannia into a first-rate position by hymning second-rate performances in the arts. In Germany, Von Unruhs and Neumanns are being cheered indiscriminately along with the Hauptmanns and Thomas Manns; in France, a whole herd of Vildracs and neo-Apollinaires are heralded as so many Second Comings; and in Italy, if we were to put any faith in the critical evaluations, a new D'Annunzio, with a luxurious crop of hair to boot, is born monthly.

Eugene O'Neill as a Character in Fiction

"In our own beloved land, however, there is no cause for grousing. Great geniuses are being discovered overnight today with the same assiduity that they were discovered twenty-five and thirty years ago and that they have been discovered in the intervening space of time. There are so many whales in the sea, apparently, that there is hardly enough room left for Willard Mack and Sammie Shipman to go in wading. Reading the daily newspapers and a number of the magazines, one is dumfounded by the ostensible richness of staggering talents. Greece in its heyday becomes in comparison something like Paw Paw, Missouri. We hear of poets that make Shelley and Swinburne look like Greenwich Village debutants, novelists beside whom our Dreisers and Cabells and Lewises are jokes, and dramatists compared to whom I—who the critics evidently believe have been boosted enough—seem not all that I at one time seemed. It is, as I've said, no original antic. Confining my remarks to the drama, we readily remember the first strains of the Sousa March criticism that greeted Bronson Howard and James A. Herne as rivals of the Europeans and that, gathering volume, went on to toot the glory and eminence of a rabble of third- and fourth-raters including Fitch, Klein, Thomas, Belasco, Broadhurst, Sheldon, and even the pious Kennedy. With years of practice, the brass-band boys have gained a lung-power that presently begins to outpuff even the wind of their critical forebears. Any American playwright who exhibits faint symptoms of what is known in the theatre as intelligence, which is to say a sum of wisdom and sagacity amounting in the world outside the theatre to the cerebral quotient of a bright lad of eighteen, is serenaded as a prodigy and very soon thereafter as an international genius. Any local playmaker who can write even half as well as the second level of native novelists is praised

unreservedly as a great artist, and anyone of enough sophistication to let his Magdas and Paula Tanquerays smile at
least once during the evening as a super-Continental and
a slick dramatic philosopher."

In the present European drama O'Hara found little to
interest him. "England offers next to nothing," he insisted.
"Its bigwigs in the business of playwriting have either
abandoned the theatre for the time being or are devoting
themselves to such other diversions as works recounting
in half a dozen hefty volumes the saga of some pater-
familias Britannicus, and scarcely less copious treatises in-
forming women presumably quivering with impatience
about Socialism and Capitalism, or having their kidneys
irrigated at Continental mineral springs. The English
theatre at present is given over almost in its entirety to
composers of trivial sex comedies, trivial mystery plays,
song-and-dance shows, and American box-office drivel.
France is in somewhat better state, but only relatively.
There's a measure of originality in its drama, but no
imagination and skill to convert it into anything of any
merit.

"As for Germany, the stage appears to have superseded
the drama. Following in the line of Reinhardt and Jessner,
though hardly blessed with their talent, a bird named Pis-
cator is using the drama simply as a medium for the
promulgation of his directorial and producing freakish-
ness. He gives monkey shows at the expense of plays, em-
bellishing the latter unnecessarily with moving platforms,
moving backgrounds, moving screens, and moving what-
nots that take all the moving quality out of the plays themselves. He's an expert at moving everything but his audiences. In Germany generally, this effort to dramatize the
stage itself as distinct from the script is increasingly evident. It's the fad of the moment, stemming from the

antecedent and often equally idiotic drehbühnen, treppenbühnen, and kindred bühnen with the Constructivist, Impressionist, and Expressionist settings more appropriately suited to pleasure-park roller-coasters and love-tunnels than to the authentic dramatic stage."

As to reviewers, he expressed himself so:

"The generally maintained theory that play reviewers who have to rush their review into type immediately after the play is over haven't the necessary time in which to arrive at a sound estimate of the play is flimflam. The reviewer who can't make up his mind accurately as to a play's worth immediately it's finished hasn't any mind to make up. As well say that the reader of a book must moon around for days afterward and refer back to it periodically during that time before he can tell whether it's really good or bad. A play reviewer is supposed—often unwarrantedly, true enough—to have some taste, experience, and judgment, and if he doesn't know the value or lack of value of a play after being in its company for three hours his boss should reassign him to cover fires. It's my belief that the notion in question has been set in motion by the reviewers themselves, by way of craftily letting themselves down easily and apologizing for their critical impotence. If they were given a week longer to meditate a play and arrive at a sounder point of view regarding it, it'd avail them little and it'd find them harboring their initial deductions, a fact sufficiently proven by their Sunday recapitulations, which are merely expansions and substantiations of their morning-after opinions.

"The trouble with reviewing against time doesn't lie in this direction at all. Where it lies is in the direction of a smooth, effectively written, and lifting promulgation of expressed opinion, whether sound or unsound. Some men can write quickly and clearly under pressure for a spell, but even such blessed bozos can't manage it for long. Writing takes thought, and quiet, and time. Some of the finest examples of critical writing that have come down to us from the past are as full of nonsense as some of the worst examples of the critical writing that we're getting hereabouts today. But they're nonetheless literature, and at least superficially admirable. They've got, for all their intrinsic dubiousness, a fine bounce and kick. They weren't written between eleven o'clock and twelve at night; they were written leisurely. Criticism is, after all, or at least it should be, something more than a magistrate's court or a slot weighing-machine. It should be something of an art on its own. Who cares what a poem says, so long as it's beautiful? Who gives a damn about the meaning of *Hamlet*, so long as one can delight in the soft thunder of its language? Facts and logic alone have never made criticism a full-bodied thing. They are, God knows, valuable and all too rare to it, but even a cannon, in order best to discharge its projectile, has to be carefully—very carefully and scrupulously—oiled and polished."

And as to actors, in this wise:

"The bane of the local stage today, almost any American playwright will tell you, is the pigment of effeminacy which afflicts a large portion of its performers of the theoretically male species, and which makes the casting of plays extraordinarily difficult. It isn't that the actors are biologically queer—often, it may be assumed, they aren't; it's that they possess or have acquired an air of effeminacy that, however hard or adroitly they try to conceal it, shows itself sooner or later during the course of a dramatic performance to its devastation. All of us have been witnesses of the thing. It isn't meet for one imbued with the principles of politesse to venture names and dates, but a recollection of any number of plays that have been vitiated of their force by effeminate actors in the roles of forthright males is easy enough. Time and again an important scene, and with it the play as a whole, has gone to pieces because of an intrusive nance note. Often the actor shows no signs of the note early in the play, but gradually, as in the case of an actor with a game leg strainfully made to seem normal for a while, the truth comes out.

"Just what has brought about this pervading lizzie cast among our actors isn't easy to determine. It seems to be a development of the last ten or fifteen years; certainly it wasn't in great evidence before that time. The thing resolves itself into a guessing business, and, taking it as such, I venture a few conjectures. The average American actor in more recent years, particularly the younger American actor, has apparently as his ambition a desire to emulate the English actor, who represents to him, for all his patriotic denial, the vintage mark. He thus apes the English actor's speech, dress, and comportment, and, since these quite obviously don't fit him, what results is a hybrid. The chief characteristic of this hybrid is the aspect of effeminacy always the price of English imitation. An Englishman, thoroughly male, is so physically built that a tight-waisted jacket swings naturally on his frame; an American, racially of a quite different physique, looks womanish when he adorns himself with a jacket of similar cut. An Englishmen's manner of speech, articulation, and deportment are as naturally a part of him as his bad teeth, but adopted by an American they immediately take on a pixie hue. They are, on their native soil, as virile as the English themselves, but transplanted they take on a wholly different color. The entirely male man is never an imitator of other men; the moment a man patterns his speech and conduct, however slightly, after those of other men something seems a bit queer about him and that queerness invariably

105

carries under its obvious top layer of affectation a pistillate suggestion.

"In late years, an increasing number of our young American histrios have played in England and have come back denaturalized in mien and manner. They have returned like so many cuckoos and mockingbirds, their old naturalness, simplicity, short a's, horn specs, and box-back coats laid aside and in their places an assortment of absurdly copied nonchalances, drawls, monocles, spats, and waistlines. They have pansied themselves out of their Americanism and have, by their foolishness, made themselves mongrels. The hardest job a producer has these days is finding juveniles who are distinguishable from ingenues. What we need are more actors like Jack Dempsey, who tried the stage a little while ago. Jack may not be much of an actor, but his worst enemy certainly cannot accuse him of belonging to the court of Titania. He thus is something of a relief to look at and to listen to on this fairy stage of ours. He isn't the only male actor hereabouts, to be sure; there are others; but there are so many of the other kind that every one like him is certainly a help.

"I tell you," he would say confidentially, after the tenth drink, "it's often a big wonder to me why I go on wasting my valuable time on such a doghouse of a showshop and on the rotten incompetents that are its parasites. Consider what I, certainly the only playwright worth a hang in this god-forsaken country, have had to put up with! When I worked out the scheme of soliloquies and asides to suggest my characters' unspoken thoughts, what did the jackass criticasters puke? They puked that the soliloquies and asides were unnecessary, interruptive of the action, superfluous, repetitive, and posturing. The play, already extremely long, would, they asserted, be the more compact and better without them. Exactly the same criticism, obviously, might be made—indeed, frequently has been made by the same kind of dolts—of Schubert's C major symphony, a perfect thing, as every musician knows, despite its similar musical asides, repetitions, interruptions, and alleged superfluities. As a piece of musical writing it's relatively as long as my play, and the same arguments may be used by fools against it, but it remains nonetheless—to pop a platitude—a consummately beautiful work. And if it's seldom, if ever, played in its entirety, let the critics who imagine that in that fact they've found a good argument be made aware of the equally pertinent fact that my play as it was played was also not played in its entirety, but was very liberally cut down.

"What is argued against my asides and soliloquies may just as logically be argued against Shakespeare's. If mine might be cut out as largely superfluous and interruptive of my play's action, so might Shakespeare's. Most of the soliloquies written by Shakespeare were simply put into his plays to please actors, and the plays would move much more dramatically without them. If you doubt it, read almost any one of them, even *Hamlet*, with the soliloquies and asides deleted. To contend that Shakespeare's soliloquies constitute great poetry and that mine do not is to sidestep the direct issue. That issue is simply whether my soliloquies and asides are dramaturgically valid. Poetry or lack of poetry has nothing to do with the case. In any event, the argument is based by the critical clowns, as so often happens, merely upon labels. The truth about soliloquies and asides as I employ them is that, while they are cunningly announced by me to represent my characters' unspoken thoughts—I'm a shrewd hand at concealing the obvious and artfully masking it in a way to make the impressionables gabble—they are actually nothing more than straight dramatic speeches, as anyone can readily determine by referring, for example, to the dramatic scene, say, at the conclusion of my sixth act. I've simply written my characters' thoughts in terms of straight dramatic speeches and have passed the device off on the idiotic novelty lovers by craftily insisting that they are only mute meditations.

"As to the yawps over my play's considerable length—it runs for something like five hours—we behold criticism based on the sensitiveness of the yawpers' sterns rather than on the work of art itself. A certain critic finds that his tail becomes weary after sitting out the play and hence confounds his tail with his cerebrum, which in his case is largely indistinguishable from it. Art is thus estimated not in terms of mental pleasure but of physical discomfort; the old Babbitt plaint that the Louvre is altogether too large for enjoyment and that the lulus at Bayreuth are awful. While it's not to be denied that a five-hour play imposes more of a strain on one than a two-and-one-half-hour play, the strain is no reflection on the play's quality. A Chinese drama that runs for three nights is not ipso facto worse than a play by William Hodge that runs for a couple of hours. The Oberammergau Passion Play, that runs on and on, may still conceivably be better than one of the Rev. Dr. Charles Rann Kennedy's shorter Biblical exhibits. Shaw's two-night *Back to Methuselah* doesn't impress me as being great shakes, but the fact remains that when it was cut down to one night's playing time it was made twice as senseless and twice as dull as it would otherwise have been.

"Honest to God," O'Hara would yawn, "sometimes I think I made a big mistake in the way of self-respect not to stick to that old job on the Albany night boat!"

Lorinda, after the sentimental shufflings and evasions of her poetic friend, found O'Hara a joy. His forthright manner and directness exhilarated her. Here at last, she thought, was no preposterous dodger of issues, no player of ring-around-a-rosie with himself, no altiloquent truant to life. What was more, he was very good-looking—not handsome in the lyric way that Varick was handsome, but striking in the way that certain traffic policemen and young Catholic priests are.

"I can tell by one look at you," he had said not more than fifteen minutes after their first meeting, "that you are interested in certain physical aspects of life—and, God bless you, why shouldn't you be? You are young; you are beautiful—God be praised; and"—this as if to clinch his viewpoint in the matter—"you've got good common sense."

Lorinda had contented herself with a revival of the Corot look.

"Therefore," he had continued, "we'll come to all that, with your permission, in due time. Meanwhile, I hope you don't mind my bluntness." (Lorinda's face at this moment would have delighted a satirist like Max Beerbohm.) "I am not much on manners, either in or out of the theatre. As a matter of fact, life and the theatre are one and the same thing to me; I look on life as the theatre. Any man who doesn't isn't worth a hoot as a dramatist, whatever the fool critics say to the contrary. The whole question of manners, in life as on the stage, is colored by nonsense. Take the stage and what is called polite comedy. Along comes such a play written by an American that has viewpoint, wit, sophistication, and periodically a writing skill that can match those of the best English plays of the same species, and yet it has also that apparently inevitable something that always seems to make even the most proficient American polite comedy inferior to the English. It's customary to observe in such cases that the difference lies in the direction of manners and suavity, that the American doesn't come naturally by the Englishman's grace of manner and ease and hence is on alien ground when he tries to invade the field of drawing-room comedy. This, of course, is the purest bosh, for, as everyone knows, some of the very best modern English polite-comedy writing has been achieved by Englishmen whose acquisition of urbanity and the social graces is of a distinctly recent vintage. The difference lies in another direction. Polite comedy is intrinsically not an American form, any more than journalistic melodrama is an English form or sex farce a German, and as a consequence the American, whatever his talents, is never entirely at home in it. There are certain types of plays that are peculiar to a nation and certain others that are strange to it, and the playwright of a particular country who tries to handle one of the strange types generally, because of national and racial idiosyncrasies, finds himself with his shirt tail hanging out. There are exceptions, true enough, but they're negligible. As a usual thing, the American who sets himself to write a polite comedy fails, just as the Englishman does who tries to write such a play as *Broadway* or *The Front Page*. These are as native to purely American writing as polite comedies like *The Constant Wife* and *Aren't We All?* are to purely English, and, whatever the skill of the Englishman, evade his grasp. It's as difficult to imagine an Englishman writing something as good in its way as *The Racket* as it is to imagine an American writing something as good in turn in its way as *Our Betters*. It's as difficult to imagine, indeed, as it is to picture an American completely at home in an English suit of clothes or an Englishman completely comfortable in an American.

"This seems to be true even where the American writer of polite comedy may personally have all the smooth cosmopolitanism and manners of the English writer. If this has the sound of paradox, then there's also the sound of paradox to the equally authentic circumstance that, as between an American and an English song-writer of relative national identity, pulse, and mood, the American will almost invariably be found to be the more efficient in the composing of melodies that affect the popular heartstrings, not only of his own people, but of the English as well. The essence of drawing-room comedy, to return to what I was saying, is not manners as much as it is a species of diplomacy, of subtle evasion and equivoque, of groping for truth in terms of falsehood, and to this form of playwriting the Englishman brings all the talent of his race for that other and more important diplomacy of the world beyond the stage drawing-room. The best polite comedy is a kind of masquerade attended by an assortment of plenipotentiaries and intrigants. The characters' true selves are always faintly concealed behind the masks of humor and wit. One knows who they are, but isn't in a position to swear to it. In the polite comedies written by Americans the disguises are too immediately easy and transparent; the air of masquerade and frolic is seldom even momentarily glamorous or convincing. The English playwright puts metaphorical dominoes on his characters over their evening clothes; the American puts evening clothes on his over their dominoes.

"The best polite comedy is in essence a mere concealment of insults in a veneer of the punctilio. Yet where an American writer has difficulty in giving such insults a charming grace, the English playwright manages the trick handily by writing them always as if the person delivering them didn't entirely mean them or as if the person receiving them insouciantly didn't believe them to be in the least fitted to himself. It's the mark of American drawing-room comedy that when a character is politely insulted by another character he either enters into a more or less prolonged harangue with the other character, which shifts the mood of comedy into one approaching drama, or attempts to dismay him with an assertive mot. It's the mark of English drawing-room comedy that when one character is smoothly insulted by another he sustains the mood of polite comedy either by manufacturing an epigram that has hardly anything to do with the case or, after stretching himself boredly, by announcing that he thinks he'll go out and play a little tennis."

O'Hara smiled. "I know what you're thinking; you're thinking that I talk an awful lot at a stretch without taking time out to light a cigarette or to relieve the strain and make things more gracious by saying 'Don't you think so?' or 'What is your idea?' every once in a while. But that's only a trick of bad playwrights and bad novelists who haven't got anything to say and who try to cover up their short wind and distract their audiences or readers with the shenanigan. Anyone who has anything to say, says it. You won't find such men as Shakespeare or Rostand or Shaw interrupting their fine long Hamlet soliloquies or Chantecler hymns to the sun or Caesar addresses to the Sphinx with any such childish dodges. But cheap plays and cheap novels of cheap men are so chock-a-block with idiotic 'If you don't mind my going on, Lord Whangdoddles' and 'I trust I am not boring you, Lady Balderdashes' on the one hand, and 'He interrupteds' and 'She started to demurs' on the other, that you feel like letting out a loud yell."

"I fear many critics consider you a radical," ventured Lorinda.

"Radical hell!" O'Hara shouted. "I hate the damn word. It is disreputable, and for a good reason. The disrepute that envelops the radical movement in America is, contrary to our professional and volunteer observers, traceable not to the doctrines espoused and expounded by the radicals but almost wholly and entirely to the character of the radicals themselves. The objection and hostility of intelligent Americans to their radical fellow citizens are grounded not upon the principles the radicalistos preach but upon the preachers. These, almost without exception, fail of sympathy at the hands of the intelligent American not, as is sometimes also foolishly argued, because they're loud-mouthed, ill-natured, and unkempt fellows, but, very simply, because they haven't got any sense. More, they are inarticulate in the matter of what borrowed, secondhand sense they may occasionally and conceivably posture. No man cares much what another man may look like or even smell like if he has something of interest and importance to say and knows how to say it. The American radical, however, offers to his critics only the comical look and the smell.

"The English, German, French, Russian, or Italian radical commands respect even in quarters where his doctrines prove distasteful. The radical movement in those countries has as its mouthpieces men of forceful, original, and logical mind. Some of them may look like old ragbags, but no one can deny that they have sense—or at least wit—and a lot of it. Consider England alone, and men like Wallas, the Webbs, Shaw, Macdonald, and others, together with many of the minor prophets. Or think of the character of the leaders of the radical movement in France, Germany, Russia, and Italy. These men are scholars. What have we got in their boots in America? A pack of fired and disgruntled schoolmasters, back-alley rhetoricians, Greenwich Village boys, and corn-belt indignantos, all cuckooing feebly and garbling nonsensically the precepts of first-rate intelligences overseas. Consider even the two big latter-day pièces de résistance of the movement, Gompers and Debs. Neither had a mind; both had simply a gift for soapbox spieling. The European radicals laughed loudly and impolitely at Gompers when he went abroad and did his stuff. He was the Levine of his day over there. The profoundest thing that the rank and file of American radical masterminds have been able with concentrated effort to think up to say against the American capital in the whole last thirty years is that the late J. Pierpont Morgan had a red nose and a mash on an actress."

Lorinda marveled at O'Hara's vitality, and the marveling, needless to say, gave her an infinite esoteric connotative satisfaction.

"How old are you?" she asked him.

"Forty-five," he replied.

"But you don't look a bit over thirty-one or two," she said.

"I know it," he answered. "There's only one thing that keeps a man young, and that's the thrill of large cities. I aged more in the six years I spent out in the god-forsaken little dumps than I've aged in all the years I've hung around the big towns. The oldest man this side of the grave is the American farmer of forty-five. Where his city compatriot of like age is still a fellow of considerable juice and bounce, he's already, even in those relatively tender years, in the sere and yellow. The farmer of forty-five looks like a city man of sixty or more. The reason isn't hard to get at. In the agricultural belts of the land, life is more monotonous and routine more humdrum than anywhere else in Christendom. Day in and day out, they grind along without variation, without stimulation, without a single thing to give them color or excitement. And it's under this deadly grind that the rube is reduced to an old man long before his time. The spirit of youth is kept in a man by the little galvanisms and intoxications of his environment, and in the rural districts these are practically non est. The yokel never hears music, even jazz, except on a cheap phonograph; his eye is never popped by a pretty girl; he has to do his drinking out of a dirty jug; his vista is one of weather-beaten barns, barbed-wire fences, and manure; the house he lives in is aesthetic homicide; he reads nothing but patent-medicine almanacs and the four-sheet newspaper printed in the nearest village; his cooking has no variety; there is no reason for him to shave, or ever to take a bath; there is, in a word, no challenge, no inspiration, no conflict. And, like an animal, he turns to dust long before other and more fortunate human beings. Look at the farmer of middle years and you see a man whose face looks like a dried prune and whose eyes are wholly without curiosity and sparkle and whose body is as sapless as Grandpa's. One good barbershop and one *Follies* girl in the rural countries would effect the cure for the farmers' ails that all the Peruna in the Hoover empire has so far failed to.

"And the theatre," he went on. "That keeps one young, too. To live artificially but beautifully—that's the trick! And the theatre provides the means. It keeps its people young, whether they're seventy-odd-year-old Shaws or fifty-year-old Ethel Barrymores or fifty-year-old Sacha Guitrys or seventy-odd-year-old Mrs. Whiffens. Where else will you find the youth that remains in the men and women who work about the theatre either as playwrights or actors? To believe in make-believe with all your heart—that's what Ponce de Leon might have stayed at home and learned in time—so says this Mr. Eustace Swedenborg!"

And O'Hara put his arms around her, drew her to him, and gave her a big smack.

Some Theatrical Personalities

"Forgive the hero of the melodrama!" he laughed, as he duplicated it with an even bigger one. "And speaking of melodrama—by the way, how about a little drink?—a glance at the present-day playwriting in America seems to disclose an unmistakable fact, and this is it; that where once farce was the medium most satisfactorily employed by native playwrights to reflect gamy phases and characteristics of the American scene, melodrama has superseded it. Melodrama is undoubtedly the form of drama most patly suited to the salty depiction of life in America at the present time. The country may offer excellent material for farcical and sardonic comment to the literary and critical fraternity, but to playwrights it offers especially the materials of melodrama. The America of today is, beneath its comical aspects, essentially a 10–20–30 meller, with all a 10–20–30 meller's theatrical bounce. The gunmen of Chicago, the prison-breakers of Folsom, the Administration crooks at Washington, the bootleggers, the husband-killers of New Jersey, the hullabaloos of Herrin, the evangelical scandals, the blackmailing revenuers, the automobile bandits, the night-club and police grafters, the speakeasy and gambling murders, the hold-up men, the mail-train robbers, the Oklahoma gubernatorial insurrections, the Canadian border smugglers, the Atlantic rum-runners—these are ready-made for the melodrama stage. They need only a border of footlights and a couple of smelly female ushers to convert them into vivid three-dollar theatre shows.

"The critical disrepute into which melodrama has fallen is as absurd as it's unjustified. It's simply the result of the usual professorial posturing on the part of label-licking critics with a passion for pigeonholes and bogus definitions, critics who may be identified as the kind who get a fake dignity into their critical writings by calling everybody in sight Mr. or Miss. If some gimcrack like *The Noose* or *Interference* is melodrama, so is *Macbeth*, but they conveniently choose to overlook the fact and to assuage their whiskers with the old definition, largely made up of holes, to the effect that melodrama is inevitably an inferior form of drama because in it character is determined by action rather than, as in drama, action by character. Say *melodrama* to the half-wits and their minds promptly fix with robot-like precision upon Maryland Calvert swinging on a bell, Sherlock Holmes escaping from the gashouse by fooling Moriarity with a cigar butt, or the United States Marines arriving in the nick of time, the while they remain cockily oblivious of a number of the great Greek classics, Shakespeare's chronicle plays, and other such generic melodramas."

He negotiated the sizable highball that Lorinda handed to him in one magnificent swallow. "Fine stuff," he allowed, looking around to appraise the amount of fineness still left in the decanter.

"I am often amused by what the critics who don't like you say about you," ventured Lorinda.

"I am often more amused by what the critics who do like me say about me," returned O'Hara. "But what had you specifically in mind?"

"Well, they say that you can't bring yourself to write even a simple love scene without having an ominous thunderstorm going on outside, and that you can't let a character even eat an apple without playing, by way of Freudian symbolism, the *William Tell* overture."

"Asses! Even when they do vaguely hit on the truth, they don't know how to express it. They tell the truth as women do—in terms of falsehood. Do they ever tell the exact truth about anything connected with the theatre? Indeed, do they know the truth at all? They do not. Forget me and my own plays for the moment and look at their attitude toward comedy, for instance. They deliver themselves of a lot of walla-walla on the subject and what are the real facts? Given a good enough idea and even an indifferent skill at playwriting, and an entertaining comedy will come damn near automatically writing itself. The result mayn't be all that the professor-critics might wish for, but it'll pretty generally manufacture enough laughs to atone in considerable measure for their professional depression. A poorly written comedy with a fresh and popping idea is often actually very much more amusing than a well-written one with an idea somewhat less jouncy, at least to everybody but those who still insist that laughter must be literature. It would be hard to think of a comedy with an idea as good as *The Illusionist* failing to get its effect, even though its writing were much less than admirable, which the writing of *The Illusionist* certainly is. Or of one with a thematic scheme good as *The Bachelor Father*, or *The Command to Love*, or *A Single Man* or *Seven Keys to Baldpate*, or De Caillavet's and De Flers's *The King*. It isn't Sacha Guitry's dramaturgic skill that makes his comedies the howls they are; it's the ideas on which he builds them. And, conversely, all the playwriting skill of an Augustus Thomas or an Owen Davis hasn't contrived to make amusing the comedies which they have built on banal ideas.

"A good drama may result from excellent craftsmanship visited upon a mediocre theme, but a play that aims to get laughter depends a hell of a lot more on its foundational scheme than on mere writing ability. The successes of the better modern comedy writers attest to this fact. Their most entertaining pieces are seldom their best in the way of craftsmanship and in purely critical adjudication. Shaw's *Fanny's First Play* is one of the old boy's negligible jobs, but it's surely as comical a play as he ever concocted. Lons-

dale's *Spring Cleaning* is certainly not to be compared in
any sober critical sense with even Maugham's *The Camel's
Back*, yet the idea of it provides infinitely more diversion
than all the expert technique with which Maugham tried
to hide the lackluster of his play. Pinero's *The Wife without a Smile* depends largely upon its droll idea for laughter; his better-written comedy, *Preserving Mr. Panmure*,
doesn't get half as many intelligent laughs for the simple
reason that its basic mountain-out-of-a-molehill idea is stale.

"As I say, the subject matter is all-important. There may
be some critics who maintain that good writing should still
make me laugh heartily over the comedy ideas that consist
in a widow passing off her twenty-five-year-old daughter as
a child of ten, in an unmarried couple pretending they are
married in order to inherit an uncle's money, and in a venerable bachelor's discovery that his ward has only pretended to love the juvenile in order to conceal her passionate yen for him, but I fear I don't possess the talent that
they expect of me. The object of any theatrical comedy I
hie myself to is, I take it, to amuse me, and I can't be
amused by even the most proficient literary gent telling me
an old joke. If I want to amuse myself in that way, there is
always the library.

"Or take, for example, the nonsense that these same critical donkeys write about censorship. Censorship, since the
beginning of time, has amounted to little more in the final
summing up of things than an irritating mosquito bite on
the amplitudinous body of art. It's been annoying while it
lasted, true enough, but it's never lasted very long in any
one place or in any one important direction, and no one
has suffered from it except for a relatively short and negligible period. At the moment, indeed, I can think of no
modern work of art, high or low, that official censorship
has contrived to keep from the eye and ear of any one gen-

eration; sooner or later during the life of that generation the censorship has collapsed sufficiently to release the work in point. If it's been a play that's been suppressed, the printed version of the play has become available. If it's been a book, translators have come to the rescue with editions in other languages. But even these subterfuges and evasions have seldom been necessary.

"The opponents of censorship, that is, those who make the loudest noise against it, are generally found to be professional firecrackers who have never calmly studied the question and who consequently imagine that because some official jackass claps the lid on a single book or play the entire art of literature and of drama is threatened forevermore. In the last fifty years, censorship in France, Germany, Austria, Italy, England, and America hasn't retarded literature or drama one iota. Not a single reputable book or play has been successfully and completely lodged under the ban for more than a short time and, even if it had been, common sense persuades us that it wouldn't have mattered so awfully goddam much at that.

"The chief howlers against censorship are usually of the same fraternity that gets itself magnificently worked up over theoretical atrocities in the other channels of life. You'll find them, when there is no artistic censorship to inflame them, yelling against the anti-birth-controllers, as if birth control weren't already in sufficiently practicable operation, against the Ku Klux, as if half-wits were transformed into Machiavellis by the simple process of concealing their flat-heads in diapers, against the philosophy of Tennessee yokels, as if what Tennessee hillbillies believed this way or that mattered a hoot, against a hundred and one such hypothetical catastrophes and dangers. The phrase 'the principle of the thing,' is one of the emptiest in the language. The principle of a thing may occasionally be wrong, but the thing itself, after the hullabaloo is over, is usually discovered to take care of itself pretty well. Look back over the indignations of the last century and you'll find that time has shown them to be more or less foolish. For a while they may have seemed justifiable and sound, but a few ticks of the big Ingersoll and all has become automatically daisy again. I'm against censorship of any kind in any direction at any time, but if it comes now and then I don't permit myself to get steamed up over the fact any more than I do over any other human blunder. It'll all come out in the wash, experience proves, in no time.

"The trouble with the great majority of critics is that they take almost everything for granted, provided it's been told to them long and often enough. Just because they, like everyone else, have never known or heard of a woman who married a barber, they doubtless conclude that no one ever marries a barber, yet I've never known a barber who wasn't married. But I can see that your mind isn't altogether on what I've been saying. And I have a pretty good idea as to what it is that it is on." He smiled whimsically. "Am I right?"

"Yes," Lorinda answered him, "I think you are." She paused a moment. "How about another one of those things?"

O'Hara glanced at the decanter.

"Oh, I didn't mean that!" she exclaimed.

"Those things?" O'Hara lifted an eyebrow. "Then— what did you mean?"

"This," she said. And, courageously putting her arms around him, she lifted herself up and showed him.

Lorinda, she smiled to herself, was getting on.

"Well, anyway," observed O'Hara, "I'll say you're attractive."

"Anyway?" Lorinda echoed, drawing back, aghast. "What in the world do you mean?"

"What I mean is just this," was his reply. "I think you're a swell girl and all that, but—and I'll be characteristically blunt about it, if you don't mind—I am so fed up on sex that I'm dead sick of it."

Lorinda collapsed into the nearest chair like a meatless sausage. Dismayed, she managed to blurt out: "But you kissed me first! If—why—if—"

"Damned if I know," O'Hara calmly answered. "I must have forgotten myself for a minute. I wasn't thinking. It's when I get even a moment to think about it that sex—from kissing to everything else—palls on me. Oh, I sure haven't been that way always—not by a whole big jugful—but I have been that way for this last year, and how! I'm like a bartender who has passed through the D.T.'s and doesn't want to touch the stuff any more. I've seen, heard, read, written, staged, thought, analyzed, and criticized sex until the word gives me a headache. I've seen, in the course of my more or less constant theatre-going to find out what the other fellows were writing, no less than three thousand plays on sex in the last eight years. I've heard sex, sex, sex on a hundred stages. I've read so many books on sex and so many sex novels that they've acted like a Keeley Cure on me. I've written a dozen plays on sex myself; my last one, dealing with science and religion, is the only one I've written in seven long years that hasn't dealt with sex, and I find I've been so poisoned by the contact with literary and dramatic sex that I couldn't entirely keep it out of even that one! I've directed whole herds of actors and actresses in sex scenes, and I've talked on the lecture platform about sex as I've regarded it in my plays until the icewater has given out. I've listened to thousands of people discuss sex as I've treated it and I've read hundreds of critics on the same sub-

Eugene O'Neill as a Character in Fiction

ject. I've talked and listened to my publishers on the sex element in my work and I've had many run-ins and legal scraps with the censors about it. And you wonder why I'm sick of it!"

"But you're a man and human," wailed Lorinda.

"Yes, but I am also a man and human who happens to have an awful case of sex indigestion. Consider what I've gone through! Incidentally, may I have another drink to give me a little strength and help me forget my misery? I have seen, up to date, two hundred and sixteen plays in which Lily Hollownoodle, the trusting, pie-faced ingenue, has been deflowered by the loose and cajoleful Reginald Woofus, embellished with spats. I've seen three hundred and nine in which Evangeline Mushbanks has run away from her husband, the estimable but somewhat stodgy Herman Mushbanks, and given herself to young Lord Pantscrease in the private supper-room of the Big Boar Inn at Twitchtwitch. I've seen one hundred and eighty-eight in which governesses were ruined by sophomores home from school, and one hundred and seventy-two in which financiers respectably married to brunettes have been fetched and ruined by girls with yellow hair, and four hundred and thirty-seven in which the authors confused beds with the Polo Grounds. I've seen dozens of plays in which the sum of human enterprise and endeavor has been represented as consisting in either the epigrammatic or physical violation of a woman's chastity and dozens of others in which pornographic playwrights talked sex for two and a half hours in haylofts, peepshows, and call houses. I've listened to bad Freud and Jung in terms of worse actors and actresses until my ears gave out. The theatre and everything concerned with it—and that is the life I lead—has had the same effect on me that a visit to a bordello has on the average man: when he comes out of it he is, for the time being at least, the most surfeited and moral fellow in Christendom. Can you expect a man to feel like chasing a girl around the room with any enthusiasm after he has gone through my dreadful vicarious experiences? He'd laugh himself to death and collapse before he got halfway around the table! After years of Wedekind, Strindberg, Lenormand, Brieux, and Mae West, I am just about as excited over sex as a guinea pig would be over *Fanny Hill*. When I crave a good, exciting, novel evening I go over to Newark and spend it with my old aunt. I've seen plays dealing with Lesbians, fairies, nigger-lovers, and nymphomaniacs until, I assure you, Art Young's nice cool sewer looks like Du Barry's boudoir to me. I've written plays and made a reputation and fortune for myself as a dramatist of sex until the prospect of indulging in sex thrills me about as much as the prospect of indulging in a motor ride would thrill Henry Ford!"

"But sex is life," sobbed Lorinda.

"Sex was life once upon a time, but now it would seem to be literature, or one of the other arts. At least that's the way it appears to the artist. He expends so much sex on and, more exactly, in his work that he has none left for life. He exhausts his inclinations and imagination in pen and ink, in oils, marble, and music, until the very thought of sex outside his work is like the thought of eating mustard to a man with a mustard plaster on his chest. Sex is no longer even a transient pleasure to him. A pleasure is something casual and charming; consequently, sex to a man like me who works professionally with it is approximately as casual and charming a potentiality as a fire to a fireman."

He took out a cigar and lighted it. Lorinda accordingly knew that now all was lost.

"I'll return to the subject shortly," he said, holding the cigar before him, rolling it fondly in his fingers and appraising it with admiration. "Meanwhile, why is it that my own plays on sex have been received with critical acclaim? Because, if I say it myself, I am as honest about sex and character when I write about them as I am when I speak about them to you. I don't, like most of the other joeys, arbitrarily give my villain better manners than my hero and imagine that by doing so I have achieved an equitable characterization of the villain. Nor do I, like the others, place the more unpopular opinions and philosophies in the mouths of my heroes and heroines and imagine that I have thus achieved rational and original character delineation. I don't dress up my Jack Trevors as Desperate Desmonds and my Desperate Desmonds as Jack Trevors and believe that both of them thereby achieve a closer approximation to real, living human beings. I don't go in for such buncombe. I am the Ziegfeld of the emotions and of biology. I undress them realistically and adorn them, for propriety's sake, with simply a loincloth of poetical chiffon. I refuse to affix labels to my characters or to their actions, and my refusal to do so is sometimes mistaken by the lard-heads for a posturing immorality. They think I'm an ethical bootlegger, the ninnies! Loving above everything else to pretend a momentary sophistication and emotional atheism that—when they get home to baby—they are thoroughly ashamed of, they gulp down tripe that ladyfingers sex or that shrewdly dresses up sin by Boué Soeurs and morality by Gimbel, but they gag at the perhaps deplorable facts of life as I present them, with no wisecracks to laugh them off, no incidental piano-playing of Chopin by the loose fish to prove to everyone that his heart's in the right place after all, no cute, pretty virgin cast to soften a strumpet role, and no concession on the part of any character toward any other, except anatomical.

"Sex as we find it customarily treated in the drama gets

nowhere nearer the truth of things than dirt does to an airplane. It's above the intelligence and experience of the average playwright. Hence when it doesn't bore one it stupefies one with its juvenile imbecility. A man can be fed up on and disgusted with a subject when it has long been made nonsensical as readily as he can be when it has long been made too intelligent—so my mood cuts both ways. One wouldn't relish listening to Einstein talking sense for a solid year without a let-up any more than one would looking at Charlie Chaplin dropping his pants for the same length of time. Sex, any way you take it, has become to me like those restaurants where you pay so much and eat all you want of everything in sight; you find that you don't eat half as much as you would in some other restaurant; your appetite is spoiled by bad technique. There's too much soup, meat, and pie all around you; your plate is constantly replenished. The country today is like such a restaurant. The theatre, books, movies, church sermons, lecture platforms, newspapers, and conversations are sex, sex, sex. The moment you come back home on a steamer and get near the Statue of Liberty a flock of newspaper photographers descend on the ship and begin snapping pictures of girls with their skirts up to their navels; the sex-haunted customs men dig down among your undershirts and socks for copies of dirty books; the moment you get to where you live again the elevator boy wants to know if you brought back any French postcards; and the first things you find in your accumulated mail are a joint subscription offer of *True Confessions*, the *Cosmopolitan Magazine*, and *Art Studies*, a touch in behalf of some home for wayward girls, an advertising calendar with Greta Garbo's picture on it, and a dozen catalogues from 'curiosa' book dealers."

"If the theatre and its surplus of sex bothers you so much, why don't you stay away from it?" Lorinda wanted to know.

Eugene O'Neill as a Character in Fiction

"It's too late; the damage is already done!" O'Hara sighed.

"But you even go to the theatre when you're not working, when you're abroad on a holiday. What is the sense of that?"

"The sense is obvious," he vouchsafed, facetiously blowing his nose. "There are important matters to be studied and important things to be learned. For example—and how about another little drink, incidentally, sister?—a studious survey of European theatrical conditions has convinced me of one thing, and that is that there is a lot of pretty bum champagne being produced in France these days and that the beer in Germany, while certainly nothing to make faces at, still isn't up to the standard of Hauptmann's and Sudermann's heyday. True enough, there are certain theatres in Germany where the brands on sale in the lobby are in the best tradition of classic entertainment, but there are others where what you get is a sad decline from the palmy days. I am speaking, mind you, of theatrical conditions alone. The state of affairs in other quarters is more prosperous. For example, there is a place just around the corner from one of Reinhardt's Berlin theatres where the beer is so tasty that, after, say, eighteen or twenty seidel of it, one is moved to drop into the café several blocks away, near the Kleinestheater, where the same brand is on tap but where the seidel are somewhat larger.

"While theatrical conditions are not all that one might wish for in Berlin—the beer at no less than three important theatres is slightly too warm and at not less than two others a bit too cold—the situation in Munich, Stuttgart, and Dresden, particularly in Munich, is much more encouraging. In these cities the lager itself, as well as its keeping and service, is genuinely artistic. While not detracting from the dramatic manuscripts that are put on as adjuncts to it, it offers its own raison d'être (as the Alsatians put it) in its detraction of the critical attention from the actors. I don't say that there aren't some German actors who are very talented; what I imply is that there are a whole lot more that several quarts of Löwenbräu help a great deal. But while, as I have indicated, the beer generally is all and even much more than any American deserves, something seems to be lacking. Maybe it is that the imports of Pilsner from Bohemia are not as large as they used to be. For when all is said and done, and with a due and most profound obeisance to Spatenbräu, Hofbräu, Pschorrbräu, Culm-bacher, Würzburger, Mathäserbräu, Löwenbräu, Augu-stinerbräu, Hackerbräu, Kochelbräu, and all the other es-timable German malt tonics, it was and is Pilsner, an alien brew, that made and make Germany what it is. No man who has ever drunk Pilsner, that topaz nonesuch, can ever be enchanted by anything else, however hypnotic. So I sup-pose theatrical conditions in Czechoslovakia must be better than anywhere else in Europe.

"In France, as I have hinted, much of the champagne is of the Impressionistic school. The labels are the same as in the great days of Rostand, Bataille, Hervieu, and Porto-Riche, but the product is amateurish. Here and there, if one is sufficiently experienced in the matter of Paris thea-tres and their environs, one may capture a bottle of authen-tic vintage, but what is dispensed generally to visiting crit-ics tastes as if it came from Ile de Staten. To enjoy the most dramatic French champagnes one must review the Eng-lish theatre, for London is where the best is sent. The English drama may be in the doldrums, but certainly the English theatre isn't. The bar in it is still producing some very elegant stuff. Even my nurse informed me it wasn't the fault of the liquor I drank there.

Eugene O'Neill as a Character in Fiction

"As for the Italian theatre, I don't like chianti.

"But to return to the French. Say what you will about the French theatre, it shows better sense when it comes to revues and music shows than any other theatre. As I have been observing now for a long time, no sane man can enjoy a revue or a musical show unless he has something more under his belt than his undershirt. The French see to it that he has and are duly rewarded by his going back home and proclaiming that never anywhere has he seen such shows as the French put on. As a result, the sagacious French revue producers clean up big every year by selling Ziegfeld, George White, and Archie Selwyn wonders that these gentleman only imagined they saw and that, when they look at them later on in the cold Broadway light, usually turn out to be things they themselves put on ten years before and had forgotten all about in the meantime. As I have said, however, the Frenchman knows his business, and that is part of it. Give me enough good champagne, maybe four or five bottles, and even a French chorus girl without any clothes on looks like Marilyn Miller with all her clothes on to me. And give me half a dozen ponies of cognac afterward, readily obtainable in any Paris revue house, and I am ready to enjoy immoderately all the vaudeville acts that I saw and was bored to death by on the Pantages Circuit fifteen years ago.

"Theatrical conditions in Hungary, as far as I investigated them, showed a lamentable decline in the quality of the Tokay. The drama has suffered seriously as a consequence. The Tokay of pre-war days is apparently no more; the species currently available seems to have no more body than a Lajos Biro comedy. It doesn't taste bad, but neither, for that matter, do certain brands of toothpaste. It even has some of its former mellowness. But something is wrong with it. Perhaps those twenty or thirty glasses of Prunelle de l'Isère I had before sampling it may have had something to do with it."

"I suppose now you've worked yourself up to such a pitch of homesickness that you want another highball," Lorinda remarked dryly.

"I shall overlook the irony," O'Hara observed, not without magnanimity, "and do you the honor of accepting. While your gracious hands are occupied with the decanter, I shall return to seriousness and ask you to reflect on the plays of a recent New York season and the effect they have had on me. It won't be necessary for me to name them by name; you'll recognize most of them at once. I'll state the nature of them exactly, literally, and accurately and bid you to meditate their influence upon my current mood, regarding which you seem to be peculiarly full of wonder.

"This, then, is the dose I've swallowed: a play in which an act of adultery was implied to be in exciting progress in a room adjoining the one before the audience's eyes; a play in which an apparently willing and eager young married woman went to a hotel with a man not her husband for purposes of adultery; another in which a man openly tried to seduce a young girl; a play in which a married man brought his mistress into his home that he might have her handy; one in which a young girl realistically showed symptoms of being with illegitimate child; a play in which a flapper was seduced by her own father; a play in which three married women took on three young boys as gigolos; another in which a rape was realistically attempted before the audience; another in which there was a scene between an old pervert and his young quarry; a play in which a male went after a female breathing like a lecherous bull; one in which a young woman who defended her excessive sexual promiscuity was offered as a sympathetic heroine; one in which a boy's lascivious and degenerate mother carried on under his and her husband's nose with her paramour; a play in which a married woman with a grown son enjoyed an affair with a man younger than her husband; a play in which a young woman, itching for a sexual experience, took on a tramp who casually happened by her house; a play in which a young girl married to an old man deliberately had a child by a younger man; one in which a white woman had an affair with a Chinaman; a play in which a respected lawyer entered into a liaison with his most personable client and another in which a man invaded a house and immediately seduced one of the willing lady guests; a play in which the heroine very agreeably had an impromptu baby; one in which the hero defended himself as a pimp and lived openly with his women; a play in which a sex-starved young woman deliberately went out and got what she hankered for; another in which a young wife committed adultery in order to get a job in the movies; another in which a man carried on sexually with the madam of a bawdy house, to the delight of the half-dozen fancy-women residents; still another in which a middle-aged woman tried to seduce a young boy, and another still in which a girl child urged a middle-aged man to deflower her; a play in which a scene of seduction was elaborately acted out in full view of the customers; one in which an old woman had a protracted affair with a young man; a play in which a young woman had an affair with her old suitor's young valet; one in which a married woman grabbed her chauffeur and insisted he get familiar with her person; one in which young boys openly discussed their peccadilloes with women; one in which a woman and a man were in a locked room for purposes of illicit intercourse; a play in which a married woman deliberately hied herself to a bachelor's apartment for sex purposes; four plays in which a man realistically attempted the virtue of a girl; a play in which a boy seduced the house-maid; another in which several old men carried on with the girls in a fast house; another in which a young boy and girl indulged in sexual intercourse and in which the girl be-came with child and was defended by her parents; a play in which a woman waxed eloquent over the virtues of promis-cuity; a play in which a woman lasciviously teased a man and drove him crazy with passion in order to subjugate him; one in which the heroine had innumerable affairs and was openly coveted by an octogenarian lecher; one in which a man pawed a young woman with rabbity intent; a play in which a young women had sexual intercourse with a goat; a play in which a young Englishman coveted the mis-tress of a Chinaman; another in which a woman insisted upon a man's taking her immediately; another yet in which a young woman ran away from home, had an affair that ended with child, and came back home and boasted about it; another still in which a nymphomaniac went to a brothel and took on a Chinaman; a play in which a married man seduced his chauffeur's wife; a play in which a lustful man tortured a sentimental man with accounts of his sexual success with the woman the latter loved; a play in which a young woman proposed to a man that he seduce her with-out further ado in her own home; a play in which a white man stole a colored mistress from her black lover; one in which a young girl married to a cripple and needing sexual relief took on a lusty sailor; one in which a married woman forced her way into a man's bedroom in a nightdress with a view to sacrificing her virtue; another in which a married man defended his mistress against his wife; still another in which a lumberjack tore the chemise off a young girl and tried forcibly to gazump her; a play in which an old woman, a guest in the house of a man and his mistress, prayed that a young man would soon ravish her; a play in which a young man enjoyed illicit relations with a married woman, and in which an old Lesbian made a play for young girls; one in which a young girl was debauched by a young man and had a baby by him; another in which a man exhibited violent symptoms of his unquenchable lust for a young woman; a play in which an old woman with a concupiscent mind led on a doddering old man; a play in which a naked yellow girl employed all her physical resources to get a white man in her grip; one in which a young white girl took on a number of South Africans; a play in which a young married woman went sex-crazy and seduced a clergyman; a play in which a girl told the man who coveted her body that she would gladly surrender at once to his importunities; a play in which a girl insisted that what a man could do a girl could also do, and just as often; one in which a slatternly boarding-house keeper took on a series of boarders; one in which a drunken sea captain invaded the bedroom of a sixteen-year-old girl; one in which a woman refused to leave a bachelor's rooms unless he gave himself to her; a play in which a woman frothed at the mouth with excitement upon seeing a man in the bathtub; one in which a big nigger chased and raped a little negress; one in which a young girl was hunted down by several old roués; one in which a half-naked woman was grabbed by a half-naked man and dragged off into the woods; one in which two young girls boasted of their carnalities; a play in which one man went to bed with another's girl; a play in which two married women competed with each other for the physical favors of a Frenchman; one in which a woman of fifty tried to trick a young boy into sex relations with her; one laid entirely in a bagnio, with appropriate physical exercise; one in which a woman entertained her lover in her husband's house; another in which a Chinaman locked a white flapper in a room and tried to seduce her; another in which a married woman took on a house-guest under her husband's eyes; one in which a young girl was forcibly carried upstairs by a man with obvious intent; another in which a bachelor entertained his illegitimate children by three different women; a play in which a young girl had two lovers simultaneously; one dealing with the love affair of a nance; another with those of a female invert; another—but I'm running out of breath; there's no need to go on.

"Morals or merit have nothing to do with the case. It's simply a case of sex, sex, sex without let-up! One apparently can't get away from it. Leave the drama and go to a musical show or revue and all you see are a lot of naked women who look like powdered Hamburg steaks and sketches built around either the one about the traveling salesman and the chambermaid or the one about the sailor and the deaf blonde. Leave the musical show and the revue and go to a burlesque show and all you get are a troupe of undressed women displaying their flesh to you from a runway and the act in which a frankfurter is employed as a phallic symbol. Leave the burlesque show and go to the movies and all you see is gum-sucking attempted seduction, so-called bathing girls showing all they've got, and a mess of Clara Bows shaking their thighs at you. Sex, sex, and more sex. And you still wonder why I feel as I do! No, sister, sex holds no charms for this baby!"

"Well," thought Lorinda, bitterly biting her lip and handing O'Hara his hat, "that's that."

Monks Are Monks, 1929

IV

PLAYERS

Duse · John Barrymore · Cecile Sorel
Mrs. Patrick Campbell · Clowns

Duse:

THIRTY THOUSAND dollars' worth of New York theatregoers filled the Metropolitan Opera House to the ceiling to welcome the late lamented and incomparable Eleonora Duse in Ibsen's *The Lady from the Sea*. Thirty thousand dollars' worth of New York theatregoers, with a couple of hundred dollars' worth of critics thrown in for nothing, thunderously clapped out their tribute to the woman who was incontestably the greatest actress of her time. Thirty thousand dollars' worth of New York theatregoers sat enchanted before the soft and insinuating genius of the rare woman of Italy. And then, the next morning, about thirty-five dollars' worth of the critics who had been thrown in for nothing deplored the fact, while admitting the matchless talent of Duse, that she had, for all that undisputed talent, been, alas, unable to move them.

The final appearance of Duse in America was the occasion for some very excellent critical nonsense, of which the above is a succulent *schnitz'l*. Just how this thirty-five dollars' worth of critics expected to be moved by an actress performing in a play that could not possibly move anybody without the aid of the whole Charles H. Fletcher factory passeth the understanding. If anyone has ever been moved by *The Lady from the Sea*, which is beyond doubt one of the most supine and deadliest plays that Ibsen ever con-

137

fected, that person is yet to be heard from. The play may interest one as a student of dramatic literature, but it certainly cannot move one in the theatrical sense of the word. And to have asked Duse to move one in it was to ask for the moon.

It was to be expected, of course, that the great actress would be subjected to all sorts of idiotic fancy writing, all sorts of hysterical hallelujahs, and all varieties of soniferous pugh, at the expense of calm and dignified criticism. One was not disappointed. Instead of considering her as the acting genius which she was, and discussing that genius appositely, sanely, and intelligently, the majority of her critics treated her for all the world like so many college boys with a mash on Marilyn Miller. Everything about her came in for an explosion of coconut grease—everything, that is, save her impressive acting. If the reviewers had only mentioned her legs, one might have substituted Miss Miller's name in the copy and the reviews would have done as well, so far as any sound criticism of Duse went, for *Sally*. Her interpretation of Ellida was dismissed in a sentence in favor of a dozen paragraphs of juvenile raving to the effect that at sixty-three she looked every bit as young as Marion Davies. Duse was the most wonderful actress of her day, but she was sixty-three years old, and looked it. Her technique was dismissed in a line or two, and a dozen paragraphs given over instead to her "soul." Her tremendous competence was denied analysis, and columns were given to her "aloof mystery," her "lonely, brooding nature," and her "immortal spirit." Thus was a great artiste, the greatest artiste of the theatre of her time, sacrificed to sentimental bosh. Her hands, as was to be anticipated, came in for all the familiar slobber. Whenever a critic attends a play in a foreign language with a conspicuous actor or actress heading the cast, doesn't understand so much as a single word of it, hasn't

Duse

the faintest accurate notion of what it is all about, and doesn't know what to say but has to say something to protect his job, he raves about the star's wonderful hands. Her voice, a truly beautiful voice, came in for the slobber no less, as, for example, this escallope from the esteemed *Times*: "It is the voice of a silver twilight, peopling an atmosphere Corot might have imagined with multitudinous accents of the human spirit. It is crepuscular in its plaintive repinings, as for a day that is dead—as also in its accents of a soul that struggles forward toward a glory of light beyond the far horizon. No voice has been heard even faintly resembling hers—nor is such a voice ever likely to be heard again!" This is criticism à la mode. Instead of cool appraisal, we have billets doux. Instead of dignified praise, blandishment and dalliance.

Duse was the superstar of the theatre not because she did not look her age, not because her fingers happened to be long and tapering, not because her voice was what it was, not because newspaper interviewers bored the life out of her and she had the good sense to keep away from them, not because of anything to do with her soul, not because she built up around her a romantic legend, not because she preferred to stay at home and keep to herself (this the "mystery" which they speak of) instead of hanging around the Algonquin Hotel at lunch and taking part in Equity Ball pageants—but, very simply, because she worked at her art as no other actress save Bernhardt worked in her time, because she was gifted with the great sense always to play under a role and lift it up to the heights instead of playing down upon it from above—as most of her colleagues in histrionism are accustomed to do, because her mind was naturally sensitive to every turn of dramatic writing, and, finally, because, unlike the overwhelming majority of actresses, she made her body the tool of that mind instead of

139

making the mind the tool of her body. She acted from the head down, not from the feet up. Her body was eloquent because her legs had less to do with manipulating it and guiding it than her brain. She was the magnificent, the peerless creature of the theatre—even if she didn't look younger than Baby Peggy, even if her hands were, after all, just hands, and even if her voice, as a voice, didn't move one any more electrically than the voice of Ethel Barrymore.

Where Bernhardt gained every one of her greatest acting effects by a maximum of means, Duse achieved hers with a minimum. Hers was an economy not seen in the theatre of her period. She acted the way Joseph Conrad writes, with the brilliance born of an imaginative, coherent, and exact parsimony. Nothing was wasted. But as the years sapped from her some of her earlier vigor, she came to resort to a series of admirable tricks—but mere tricks withal—to further her performances and get the effects that in the years before she was wont to achieve by sounder and subtler means. These tricks, such as the nervous, staccato cutting in on speeches, the holding up of a speech by way of gathering breath and the then sudden propulsion of the lines, the preparation for a speech by weaving its pattern in the air with the hands—these and the like were tokens of an aging actress, an actress still radiant but moving on swiftly toward the sunset whose light already fell upon her, an actress who felt the need of props for a great but age-ridden mastery of her craft.

(Duse, parenthetically, had that one thing that every great actress has had, has, and must have—something that may idiotically be described as a sad arm: that line of the arm that, when extended from the shoulder, has about it something of melancholy. The extended right arm of Eleonora Duse had in it all the tears of *Tristan and Isolde*.)

Duse

It is a peculiarity of the critical estimate of Duse that she is generally agreed to have been the greatest actress of her day by two sets of critics who oddly arrive at this estimate with arguments and reasons that are diametrically opposed. I privilege myself the suspicion that this is why Duse is called the "mystery woman." She is a mystery because she is the only actress of our time who has been eulogized by half of the critics for one thing and by the other half for the exact opposite of that same thing. I have in mind specifically her performances of the mother in Gallarati-Scotti's pious claptrap, *Così Sia*. In London, when she last performed the role at the New Oxford, she played it in the spirit of a tigress who, suddenly wakened from sleep, snaps out a flaming snarl of defiance. This mood of defiance gave way in turn to an impassioned, nay, almost a frenzied, faith, a sullen stubbornness, a burst of heart-rending appeal, and, finally, a despairful agony of self-immolation. The London critics hailed the performance as the acme of intelligent and acute interpretation and Duse as the peerless actress of the stage. In New York, when she performed the same role at the Century, she played it in the spirit of an imperturbable sexagenarian who accepts her mission coolly, calmly. This mood of resignation gave way in turn to a resigned, nay, almost a melancholy, faith, a complacent sweetness, a passive acceptance of abuse, and, finally, a welcome and highly comfortable surrender to fate. The New York critics hailed the performance as the acme of intelligent and acute interpretation and Duse as the peerless actress of the stage.

Now, surely, since *Così Sia* and the role no less are admitted, without dissenting voice, to be the veriest theatrical flapdoodle, and since, as in the instance of finer drama and finer roles, two interpretations so violently, even absurdly, antagonistic are hardly to be reconciled—surely something must, to put it mildly, be a trifle askew. The truth is perhaps not far to seek. It is not that the eminence of the Italian actress is critically arrived at from two different and each in themselves possibly valid points of view; it is that her eminence—an eminence rightly won over a long period of years and with an incontrovertible talent—has been taken for granted even when her immediate performances were such as to give the more judicious prolonged pause. I believe, with my colleagues, that Duse was the greatest of the actresses of her period; I believe, further, that the performance of *Così Sia* which this greatest of actresses gave in London was a superlatively fine performance; but I also believe that the performance of the same play which this greatest of actresses gave in New York would have disgraced the rankest amateur. It was grotesquely out of key with the play—as grotesquely out of key as her London performance was in key; it was slipshod, careless; it was downright lazy and cheating. In a word, Duse loafed on the job. For in the audience at the Century Theatre there was no Maurice Baring to catch her napping, no Chaliapin or Walkley or Archer or any other fully experienced and understanding soul to catch on to her and give her away. And she seemed to know it. Just a lot of American boobs. Just a lot of poor, affected suckers. The night she opened at the Metropolitan, she took no chances. Her Ellida Wangel was tremendous, as it was tremendous in London. Nor did she take any chances with her second audience, the audience, that is, at the second play in her repertoire. And here once again her Mrs. Alving had all the old greatness. But then—what was the use of spreading one's self for these Americans?—then came the bald let-down. The money was in; why bother? The greatest actress in the world—and she was greatest—deserved her little joke on these Americans and their—what do you call them?—critics. And the greatest actress in the world had it.

Materia Critica, 1924

John Barrymore

I TAKE IT that there is no longer much question that the proficient modern actor of Hamlet is he who acts the role not with his own intelligence but with the intelligence of his audience. In plainer words, that Hamlet is, figuratively speaking, no longer so much an actor's role as an audience's role, and that the best actor of that role is he who creates the role less than he mirrors the modern audience's creation of it. Forbes-Robertson is a master in this; and Leiber, though conceding vastly more to himself as actor, is similarly a captain of the stratagem. Barrymore comes to us with the same trick, and manages it admirably. His Hamlet is a calm, cool dramatic critic in the robes of the role; it is an analytical and synthetic shadowgraph of its audience's reactions; it is—and this is where it properly excels—a mere scenario of its emotional implications. Yet it is not, for all its undeniably sound plan and sagacious preparation, entirely successful. I am not persuaded that Barrymore's critically exact approach to the role, with its obvious wealth of study, scrupulously meticulous voice cultivation, and intensive training in gesture, movement, and facial play, has not deadened to a degree the human warmth that might have been projected from a less strain-fully perfect preliminary self-instruction and artistic casti-gation. Barrymore's Hamlet is critically so precise that it is at times histrionically defective. It gets across perfectly to all the professional dramatic critics in the audience, but I doubt that it gets across quite so effectively to those whom acting must more speciously and fully inflame if they are to be brought to an understanding and appreciation of the role with which that acting is concerned. I thus join in the praise of Barrymore, but with certain misgivings. His Hamlet, like a diamond, is glittering, varicolored, brilliant —but cold, intensely cold. We get from it the reflected rays of intelligence, but never—or at best rarely—the rays of heat. It is, this Hamlet, a dazzling and intricate piece of machinery, put together with a fine proficiency and revolv-ing with a perfect rhythm, yet condemned by its very na-ture to serve as a cooling electric fan. There is in it breath —vigorous, consistent, sweeping—but it is not the breath of life. It is all that it was mathematically and validly de-signed to be: that is at once its tribute and its detraction.

Shaw said of Forbes-Robertson's Hamlet: "He plays as Shakespeare should be played, on the line and to the line, with the utterance and acting simultaneous, inseparable and in fact identical. Not for a moment is he solemnly con-scious of Shakespeare's reputation or of Hamlet's momen-tousness in literary history: on the contrary, he delivers us from all these boredoms. . . ." Barrymore's utterance and acting are not always identical: one detects a self-conscious-ness of the importance of great occasion, of the austerity and traditions of the role. He goes at the role as a brave and gallant soldier goes into battle: with flags flying in his Sem Benelli heart and with Richard's shining sword raised courageously aloft—but with just a trace of very human timidity and fear holding him in. He is glamorous; he is percipient; he is sound in apprehension; he is eminently praiseworthy—but he is not the complete Hamlet.

Materia Critica, 1924

Cecile Sorel

THE REASON for the eminence in the French theatre of Mme Cecile Sorel is perhaps to be found in the woman rather than in the actress. Much as with the English, though to a lesser degree, are the French given to a devotion to actresses not so much for their public talent as for their private attractiveness as women. It is thus that favorites are conceived and bred, and once such a favorite is lodged in her niche nothing can remove her from it. The modern history of the English stage and that of the French is replete with the names of ladies who have been admired and eulogized over a long period of time for purely sentimental reasons. These, gifted with the power of adorning a stage without vitalizing it, have managed to confound their critics into believing that what is charming is also necessarily histrionic, and out of the confusion of values has flowered gradually the artificial bloom of their reputations.

Mme Sorel, I allow myself to believe, has profited magnificently by this critical delusion. Ask the average Frenchman what he thinks of her and you will find him admiringly replying, with unconscious significance: "Hélas! What a woman!" Not "What an actress!", note, but "What a woman!" And if there was ever an average Frenchman, I nominate as a type any one of the dramatic critics currently practicing their art in France, with perhaps the single exception of the clear-sighted Henri Béraud. The Frenchman, in the case of Mme Sorel, as in the instance of a half-dozen of her less well-known contemporaries, sees the actress in terms of what she is, or impresses him as being, off the stage. He sees the actress primarily not in her costume and greasepaint and not in her stage roles, but in her salon, her motor car, her worldly life. If that life massages his fancy with agreeable unguents, if about her there linger a tale and a tradition that gratify his imagination, he takes with him into his orchestra chair an already established idea and appraisal of her, and, whatever the quality of her art, that idea and that appraisal remain uppermost and dominant. The woman who thus strikes his fancy may be any one of a dozen kinds. She may be a creature of the gala world or she may be a homebody with two or three flaxen-haired children, the latter, particularly, if she be on the English stage. She may be the darling of princes, or the rage of Deauville and Monte Carlo, or the wife of a playwright-critic who is a member of a reciprocal back-patting fraternity. She may be a gracious and handsome woman with a gift for sweetening her five-o'clock tea with sugary glances, or she may be one who with her own hands bandaged soldiers' wounds during the war and supported twenty or thirty war orphans. She may be any one of these, or something else, and a mediocre actress. But when she sweeps through the stage door, she carries with her the external impression of her, and whether she be a Camille or a Phèdre or a Paula Tanqueray to make the very ushers gnash their teeth, she still remains in the public estimation an admired and much loved creature.

While the precise ground whence has sprung the French admiration of Mme Sorel is unknown to me, it is certain that that admiration must be founded upon other things than her histrionic virtuosity. That she knows the rudiments of her trade, that she is mistress of the many tricks of acting, and that she has even now and again, as in *Sans Gêne*, given more than a merely creditable account of herself, are not to be denied. But that she comes anywhere near being the first-rate actress that her countrymen have persuaded themselves to imagine she is is a matter for very considerable doubt. I have seen Sorel, I believe, in almost every role of her repertoire in the last fifteen years and more, and I have yet to see a single dramatic performance of hers that could be fairly put down as anything better than second-rate. In comedy, she presents a more likely talent, as I have noted, than in drama. But in neither does she present a talent that glows and glistens and that reaches out over the footlights with an entire conviction. At her best, she is artificial; one can detect clearly the turning of the histrionic wheels; one can feel always the heavily conscious performer. The heat of fine acting may conceivably be in her mind, but she is unable to coax it down into her heart.

If I have seemed to imply that only in France and England are favorites established in the manner I have intimated, I wish to correct the impression. For here in America we have occasionally engaged the same phenomenon. Maude Adams was an example. But the American goes in for that sort of thing very, very much less than the European, and, what is more, he shows signs of abandoning it altogether. I know of no actress in the American theatre today who can give a series of second-rate performances and yet by the love of the public for her bring long lines to the box-office window. In France and in England, on the other hand, one would have small difficulty in naming names.

Art of the Night, 1928

147

Mrs. Patrick Campbell

ABOUT A YEAR AGO Mrs. Patrick Campbell, after an absence of some fourteen years, made her reappearance on the New York stage at the Mansfield Theatre in a comedy called *The Adventurous Age*. In the third act of the piece the action called for Mrs. Campbell to crawl down a short ladder from the window of a house. Upon her negotiation of the feat, not without considerable visible effort and audible puffing, a great wave of applause broke over the auditorium. Though plainly unintentional, that applause was so ironically insulting that it would not have surprised me in the least had Mrs. Campbell, were she not the well-bred woman that she is, thereupon stepped to the footlights and in very polite terms bidden her audience to go to hell.

The pathos and the significance of the incident should not be lost upon us. Here was an actress who in her heyday was a celebrated beauty; here was a woman who, aside from what acting talent she possessed, was once a slim and sightly creature to stimulate men's fancy, to turn the heads of countless cavaliers, to make tom-toms of innumerable masculine hearts, aye, even to cause the dogs in Hyde Park to chase their tails with an unwonted pruritus. And what had time wrought of her? A Brünnhilde creased with the years, an old woman plainly strapped in to the point of discomfort, whose mere climbing down a few rungs of a little ladder without collapsing created a gaping astonishment in her audience. That way lay the pathos. And this way lies the significance: that no woman such as Mrs. Patrick Campbell was should, when the decades have stolen her physical splendors, risk longer the kindly derisions of an ever essentially cruel theatre.

There is nothing more sad and nothing more ridiculous than the spectacle of an ex-beauty fighting it out on the old line. The greatest actress in the English-speaking theatre of today is the memory of Mary Anderson; the most pitiable, the quondam proud beauty, whatever her name, who valiently and idiotically and very tragically tries to make the memory of yesterday still walk alive in skirts and greasepaint. With certain actresses, of course, the case is different. For there are actresses far gone in years who never capitalized on youth or beauty as their chief theatrical assets, who were made to seem relatively venerable in youth by the classics, who have devoted their careers to capturing the esteem of men who have drunk out of Shakespeare rather than out of silken slippers. These are the ageless actresses, for they never made a weapon of mere years, and they are thought of principally as actresses and not as women. The history of the theatre is not without many such names. But there are others of whom the public has been made to think first as women and secondly as actresses, and by the women themselves. These have been those who have enveloped themselves in their younger years with a surface romance of one kind or another, and with plays that emphasized the romantic aspect of them. These are the women who have made capital of their physical charms and who have presented themselves to audiences over a long period as sirens of Lake Como week ends, vampires of the Nile, and the despair of young clergymen on their way to the Holy Land. It is these upon whom time has played its foulest tricks. It is these who, grown chunky and rubber-girdled, dare the mordant appraisal of audiences when vanity sacrifices them to the sharp steel teeth of its inevitable and merciless bear-trap. Mrs. Patrick Campbell is still a skillful comedienne, but what chance does mere skill at trivial comedy stand against the recollection of a once lovely woman become sere and fat and yellow?

Art of the Night, 1928

Clowns

W**HATEVER** the poverty of the American theatre in other directions, it finds its cornucopia sufficiently full of talented clowns. I doubt that the theatre of any other country at the present time can boast so many genuinely droll fellows, or that when it comes to low comedy there is a factory so productive of salubrious guffaws. On what country's stage will you discover another Bobby Clark with his stogie butt, elegant walking stick, and illuminated diamond; Harpo Marx dragging a long rope after him, disappearing in the wings and presently reappearing holding its still trailing end; and Tom Healy trying vainly and with much grave head-scratching to figure out how his partner guesses what number he has been thinking of, when the former asks him and he tells him and his partner says "That's correct"? Or George Bickel with such a German dialect as hasn't been heard in the American air since Jim Huneker used loudly and with much banging on the table to order biscuit Tortoni at Lüchow's; Phil Baker ironically inquiring of Sid

150

Clowns

Silvers if he knows what pinochle is and Silvers replying: "Sure! Pinochle and sauerkraut"; and W. C. Fields and his majestic cuff-shooting mien, modish dickey, and very tony cigar end? Or Al Jolson swapping confidential matters with a horse; Eddie Cantor bounding back and forth across the stage, the while he with a consuming enthusiasm relates the astounding wonders of being bitten lovingly on the ear by a red-haired girl; and Bert Wheeler singing a tearful ballad the while he eats a large cheese sandwich and dill pickle? Or Poodles Hanneford with his rubber suspenders that, when he would adjust them to his pantaloons, elude his grasp, shoot back, and clap him a jolly one in the eye; Sam Mann and his lemon lozenge sucked tormentingly near the orchestra brasses; and Will Mahoney and his derby? Or Moran and Mack; Eddie Conrad and his piano act; and Frank McIntyre with his two-ton lizzie walk? Or Tom Patricola's clown clogging; Will Rogers's animadversions on politics; Julius Tannen's monologues; and Walter Catlett's priapic love-making? Or Joe Cook's reading of a bedtime story; the unmatched paint-smearing act of the Ardath Brothers; Andrew Toombes's fairy tale; McIntyre and Heath's travelogue on ham trees, pretzel vines, and pork-chop bushes; and Raymond Hitchcock's chronic case of laryngitis? Or Victor Moore's baby voice; Fred Stone with his serio-comic athletic monkeyshines; Lew Fields with his shoulder-shrugging, philosophical "Easy come, easy go," upon being swindled out of the one hundred dollars that represent his life's savings; and Don Barclay and Al Herman? Or Bozo Snyder and Sliding Billy Watson of the burlesque houses; Tom Howard and his dopey "spy" act; and Frank Tinney, on such occasions as he is out of the hospital, with his orchestra-leader conversazione? Or Joe Smith, of the Avon Comedy Four, and Ted Lewis, and, surely, Johnny Hudgins and his hoofing pantomime, and

Players

Joe Jackson and his bicycle, and the excellent Ed Wynn, and Harry Watson and his prize-fighter act, and Gallagher and Shean, and Jack Donahue, and Herb Williams and his piano act, and Gus Shy, and Chic Sale? These occur to my pencil as it travels quickly across paper. There are others, I am certain, that I have overlooked—others who rank with many of these as professors of the belly-laugh. In combination, they comprise a company the like of which only the American House of Representatives can equal.

Art of the Night, 1928

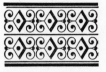

V

PLAYWRIGHTS AND
PERFORMANCE

Shaw · Rostand · O'Casey · Pirandello
Jim Tully · Galsworthy · San Secondo
Evreinoff · Marinetti · Noel Coward
Saroyan · O'Neill · Tennessee Williams
Arthur Miller · South Pacific *and Its*
Criticism · The Burlesque Show

Shaw: I

IT IS the ingratitude of criticism that it can never forgive
established genius for being anything less than complete
genius. Like a sharpshooter, it hides behind a rock on the
upward trail waiting, and not without an occasional smirk,
for genius to slip on a stray pebble and descend never so
slightly from the heights. Genius is the one thing in the
world that can never afford to be even itself; it must ever
progressively be more than itself. The artist who has
painted a great picture or chiseled out a great statue or
composed a great symphony or written a great play must
next paint a greater picture or chisel out a greater statue or
compose a greater symphony or write a greater play. If he
does not, criticism will wag its head in doubt, and speculate
on its earlier high estimate of him, and even now and again
—base ingrate!—laugh derisively. This modicum of de-
risive laughter is now heard once more in certain quarters
in the instance of George Bernard Shaw and his latest work,
Saint Joan, and in these certain quarters and among these
deplorable and ignominious scoffers I regret to report that
I find myself. For though the genius who has given us the
greatest modern English ironic historical drama and one
of the greatest of modern English comedies and the best of
all modern English satirical farces and the most intelligent
of modern English dialectic fantasies has been gradually
slipping down, down the golden trail in the last decade and
with his comparatively feeble one-act plays like *The Inca*

of Perusalem and ten-act plays like *Heartbreak House* and two-hundred-and-seventy-five-act plays like *Back to Methuselah* has gathered behind the mountainside rock an increasing number of skeptical francs-tireurs, there have been, and are still, those of us who look to him stubbornly and steadfastly to duplicate and even augment the dramatic gifts that these years ago were so dazzlingly his. But each new year with its new manuscript brings a new disappointment, and the treasures that the man of genius has given us in the past are with an ignoble thanklessness forgotten in the light of his more recent failures. I say failures, although of course such a man never fails as meaner men fail. There are streaks of diamond dust in even his shoddy. Yet one expects—has the right of expectation that the man himself has given us—that these streaks shall be not mere streaks. The cobra eyes of criticism ever fasten their deadly glare upon the artist who has already realized himself.

Thus, Shaw's *Saint Joan*, though it is a work far above the general, fails to satisfy us. From a lesser genius, it might pass muster—at least to a degree. From the hand of Shaw, it comes as an affaire flambée. We have had the Drinkwater chronicle play, and now we have a Vegetarian one. It is relatively undernourished; it cries for Old Tawny and red meat. It is as literal as the inscription on an envelope; the incidents of history with which it concerns itself are sieved through an indubitable imagination whose holes in this instance are so large that the incidents remain much as they were before. One looks for brilliant illumination and one finds but pretty, unsatisfying candlelight.

This *Saint Joan* seems to me to be for the major portion an affectation on Shaw's part to prove late in his career to a doubting world that he has, after all, a heart. Why Shaw should want to convince the world that he has a sympa-

156

thetic heart baffles me quite as much as if Darwin or Huxley or Einstein had wished or would wish similarly to convince the world of the fact in his own case. But age ever grows sentimental, and Shaw, whose genius lay in tonic cynicism and disillusion, has grown comfortably sweet. Relatively so, true enough, but the genius of incredulity and dissent cannot compromise with the angels and survive. Yet one cannot convince one's self that this late compromise on Shaw's part is not very largely another instance of his sagacious showmanship, or, in other words, conscious hokum. Shaw is undoubtedly just selling his soulfulness to the box-office devil. The sentiment of his rare Cleopatra was wise, and not without its leaven of irony, and very truly beautiful. The sentiment of his Joan of Arc is the bald sentiment of a wartime soapbox plea for money to buy milk for French babies. It is effective in an open-and-shut way, but its artistic integrity is suspect. Now and again in the course of his play Shaw, with the ghost of the Shaw of fifteen years ago mocking him, becomes for a moment himself again, and we get a flash of the old-time quick mind playing its smiling skepticism in counterpoint to the Rubinstein "Melody in F" dramatic motif. But, splendid though these isolated moments are—the speeches of the Archbishop of Rheims in the second episode and of the bench on the Inquisition in the episode before the last are Shaw at his best —they yet paradoxically, because of the confusion of the sentimental and rational keys, weaken considerably the texture of the drama as a whole. The greatest love scene in all the drama of all the world, a scene of tenderness and passion and glory all compact, would fall promptly to pieces were the heroine to hiccup or the hero, embarrassingly finding an alien particle in his mouth, to spit. Shaw's hiccuping is amusing and his expectorations are corrective and prophylactic, but they do not jibe with the story of Joan as he has set out to tell it and as actually he has told it. The story of Joan is perhaps not a story for the theatre of Shaw, after all. It is a fairy tale pure and simple, or it is nothing—an inspiring and lovely fairy tale for the drunken old philosophers who are the children of the world. It vanishes before the clear and searching light of the mind as a fairy vanishes before the clear and searching light of dawn and day. It is a tale for the night of the imagination, and such a tale is not for the pen of a Shaw. It is a tale for a Rostand, or a Barrie at his best, or maybe for some Molnar. If irony creeps into it, that irony should be an irony that springs not from the mind but from the heart.

Speaking of Shaw's *Joan* from the purely theatrical rather than from the library point of view, I cannot persuade myself that such an essentially inferior—very, very inferior—play as Moreau's on the same subject does not constitute a much more persuasive and convincing spectacle. It takes all for granted, and it accordingly sweeps the necessary theatrical emotions up into its arms. It may be a very poor play, but it never falters in its grim, artistically pitiable passion. Shaw, to the contrary, has sung his dramatic "Marseillaise" with a trace of British accent. The melody is there, still vibrant and still thrilling, but with too many disturbing suggestions of Piccadilly. *It* moves, yet *we* do not move. It thinks when we would feel; it is literal when we would soar into the clouds of fancy; it is humorous, with a Krausmeyer's Alley species of humor—as in the handling of the episode of the eggs in the first act—when we do not wish to be humorous. The old Shaw jokes on the dunderheadedness and insularity of the English somehow do not seem to belong here; the George V. Hobart dream allegory of the epilogue is the old derisory Shaw making an obviously desperate last jump for the step of the rearmost car as the train is quickly pulling out and away from him; the episode of

Joan kneeling, sword aloft, head bathed by the spotlight man, before proceeding on her way to lift the siege of Or- léans is the stained-glass stuff of the old Stair and Havlin circuit. When Shaw is literal, his literality lacks vital sim- plicity; when he is fanciful, as in the epilogue, his fancy is more literal still.

Materia Critica, 1924

Shaw: II

OBSERVES H. G. WELLS in *The Way the World is Going*: "He [George Bernard Shaw] has made free use of the phrase, the Life Force, but what meaning he attaches to these magic words is unknown. . . . He has an aversion from sex . . . which may be either Butler or temperamen- tal, and he seems to want mankind to try laying partheno- genetic eggs, and coming out of them fully whiskered."

The notion thus somewhat facetiously expressed by the acute Wells re-stimulates a similar notion that for some time has been impertinently agitating my encephalon. That Shaw, as Wells says, appears not only to have an aver- sion to sex but also what amounts almost to a fear of it has not been lost upon those who have carefully pondered his writings. The reason for the peculiar aversion and for what seems to be even fear is difficult to make out, but the an- tipathy and distrust nevertheless remain clearly visible and often emphatic. Shaw's canon plainly betrays his dislike of sex and his evasion of it. In all his work from beginning to end I know of no instance where he has not deftly avoided self-commitment on the subject or has not indulged in equivoque of one sort or another in his treatment of it.

It is impossible, within the limits of the present chapter, to go fully into Shaw's writings and draw from them a comprehensive catalogue of illustrations. But one may suggest the color of his intrinsic and general attitude by skimming through them and extracting a few sufficiently pointed and revelatory examples. That, when he laid hold of the incalescent Cleopatra, he chose to contemplate her at the age of sixteen and, in spite of the fact that sixteen was maturity in that gala era, insisted upon comfortably regarding her as a species of pre-Mary Pickford flapper, that he presented the Caesar who had a baby by her as an historical Crocker Harrington, and that he once achieved the remarkable feat of writing sexlessly about the madam of a bordello, are phenomena familiar to everyone. That, also, in the series of interviews gathered by Archibald Henderson into *Table Talk of G.B.S.*, he orally betrayed an indifference, even antipathy, to sex is as readily recalled. I quote a few passages: (*a*) "It is admitted the alleged rejuvenations (*vide* Steinach) do not prolong life. And it is longevity which interests me and not the ghastly prospect of seeing all the moribund people bustling about and pretending to be gay young dogs"; (*b*) "There is never any real sex in romance. What is more, there is very little, and that of a very crude kind, in ninety-nine hundredths of our married life"; (*c*) "One man's poetry is another man's pruriency"; (*d*) "The novel which says no more about sex than may be said in a lecture on the facts to a class of school-girls of fifteen can be enormously more entertaining than a novel wholly preoccupied with sexual symptoms"; (*e*) "I could not write the words Mr. Joyce uses: my prudish hand would refuse to form the letters"; and (*f*) "Is any treatment of sex in the interest of public morals?" And where the interviewer shot embarrassingly direct questions on sex to the interviewed, the latter is remembered as having cleverly avoided direct answers in such circumlocutions as "A playwright has no patience with novels," or in disquisitions on economics, capitalism, and what not.

Let us glance haphazardly through Shaw's work. Having presented us with a virginal Cleopatra and a Caesar whose amatory exercises are confined to lifting her upon his knee and playing horsie, he presents us with the inflammable Great Catherine as one of the Four Marx Brothers, and not Harpo either. He gives us a Pygmalion who will have none of his perfected Galatea and who, to use Shaw's own words, excuses his indifference to young women on the ground that they have an irresistible rival in his mother. "If an imaginative boy has a . . . mother who has intelligence, personal grace, dignity of character without harshness, and a cultivated sense of the best art, . . . she sets a standard for him against which very few women can struggle, besides effecting for him a disengagement of his affections, his sense of beauty and his idealism from his specifically sexual impulses. This makes him a standing puzzle to the huge number of uncultivated people . . . to whom literature, painting, sculpture, music and affectionate personal relations come as modes of sex if they come at all." He gives us even a Don Juan who moralistically announces: "I tell you that as long as I can conceive something better than myself, I cannot be easy unless I am striving to bring it into existence or clearing the way for it. That is the law of my life!" His Larry, in *John Bull's Other Island*, prefers his friend Tom to the woman who implores his love. "I wish I could find a country to live in where the facts were not brutal and the dreams not unreal," is the character's oblique anatomical lament. His Dick Dudgeon, in *The Devil's Disciple*, pro-

nounces the word *love* "with true Puritan scorn." His
Lady Britomart, in *Major Barbara*, "really cannot bear an
immoral man." And his Eugene, in *Candida*, romanticizes
his emotions out of sex.

"Moral passion is the only real passion," announces Tan-
ner, in *Man and Superman.* "All the other passions were in
me before; but they were idle and aimless—mere childish
greediness and cruelties, curiosities and fancies, habits and
superstitions, grotesque and ridiculous to the mature intelligence. When they suddenly began to shine like newly lit
flames it was by no light of their own, but by the radiance
of the dawning moral passion. That passion dignified them,
gave them conscience and meaning, found them a mob of
appetites and organized them into an army of purposes and
principles." "Virtue," Shaw notes in *The Revolutionist's
Handbook*, "consists not in abstaining from vice but in not
desiring it." Charteris, in *The Philanderer*, accused of phi-
landering, states that he is not guilty of any such low thing.
"I hate it; it bores me to distraction!" Praed observes to
Crofts of Mrs. Warren, apropos of a hint of sexual inti-
macy: "Your delicacy will tell you that a handsome woman
needs some friends who are not—well, not on that footing
with her." And Mrs. Warren repentantly thus: "Do you
think I was brought up like you—able to pick and choose
my own way of life? Do you think I did what I did because
I liked it, or *thought it right,* or *wouldn't rather have gone
to college* and been a lady if I'd had the chance?"

Speaking of the marriage contract in one of his prefaces,
Shaw alludes to sex stimulation as "the most violent, most
insane, most delusive and most transient of passions," expresses his disbelief that married people as a rule really live
together, and says that "a man as intimate with his own
wife as a magistrate is with his clerk . . . is a man in ten
thousand." In response to the General's timid "But there

are calls of nature—" in *Getting Married,* Shaw makes Lesbia reply: "Don't be ridiculous." And when the General is so much as allowed to venture on another occasion the word *assignation,* the Shavian get-out is accomplished thus: "Oh yes: she began the correspondence by making a very curious but very natural assignation. She wants me to meet her in Heaven"—the while Mrs. Bridgenorth comments on the "everyday vulgarities of earthly love." "I sinned in intention," says Juno in *Overruled.* "I'm as guilty as if I had actually sinned." Lina, in *Misalliance,* takes out her surplus energy on a flying trapeze and recommends the same diet to her adoring Tarleton. And in *Arms and the Man* we find the Shavian protagonist not too proud for sexual dalliance, but too tired.

The point is not that Shaw's imaginative writing is sexless—that is a fact too well known to call for repetition; the point is that the body of his work as a whole reveals a man to whom sex, in the sense that the word is commonly used, is at once unpleasant, deplorable, and disgusting. There are times, true enough, when he seems to advance the opposite point of view, but it will be found that, when he does so, he does so only subsequently to refute and demolish it. Nor is his argument of the other point of view even momentarily persuasive; it hasn't the ring of sincerity; it is a dummy set up merely for tackling purposes. Among conspicuous modern English men of letters and English critics of life, he alone is indefatigable in waving the white banner of biological asceticism. One of the cleverest dialecticians of our time, he is sometimes successful in concealing his true attitude for a moment, in masking his ferocious personal convictions, and in giving a bland performance in the role of a hell of a fellow, but it fools no one. Chesterton once observed that it is the weak man who always, when taking a walk, most vigorously thwacks the bushes along the roadside with his cane. A mistrust of his own philosophical attitude toward sex may similarly account for Shaw's disputatious thwacking of it.

After reading *Cashel Byron's Profession*, Stevenson wrote to William Archer: "If Mr. Shaw is below five-and-twenty, let him go his path; if he is thirty, he had best be told that he is a romantic, and pursue romance with his eyes open. Perhaps he knows it." Shaw is still the romantic that he was when a boy. And his romanticism is no more clearly to be detected than in his animadversions on sex. He declines to see it for what it is; he cannot bring himself to regard it save in terms of sentiment, love, the Indian policy, Marxian socialism, or the League of Nations. And all the fine irony and rich humor which he occasionally has visited upon the subject cannot conceal the romanticist hiding behind them and seeking to protect himself through them from the charge of romanticism. Shaw has always set up smoke screens or avoidances of the issue to protect himself from himself. The hero of his early novel, *The Irrational Knot*, in answer to the query as to what he is going to do about his wife's elopement with a former lover, says: "Eat my supper. I am as hungry as a bear." His charming Szcymplica, in *Love among the Artists*, is in her potentially most romantic moments restrained by the "soul commercial" that Shaw, with a cannily masked apprehensiveness, injects into her. Lydia Carew, whose "body is frail and brain morbidly active," is made to think coldly of the splendid Cashel Byron in terms of eugenical science. In *An Unsocial Socialist* Shaw smears his inborn convictions with greasepaint and tries to make us believe that he believes the seven deadly sins, as Professor Henderson notes them, are respectability, conventional virtue, filial affection, modesty, sentiment, devotion to women, and romance.

We have Shaw speaking of the wickedness and abandonedness of Offenbach's music and of the morals of Handel's. We find him waxing impatient with "the female figure free from the defect known to photographers as underexposure" that he encounters on the statues and fountains in Paris. He writes: "What Hofmannsthal and Strauss have done is to take Clytemnestra and Aegistheus and by identifying them with everything that is evil . . . with the murderous rage in which the lust for a lifetime of orgiastic pleasure turns on its slaves in the torture of its disappointment and the sleepless horror and misery of its neurasthenia, to so rouse in us an overwhelming flood of wrath against it . . . that Elektra's vengeance becomes holy to us. . . ." "In our sexual natures," he states in the preface to *Androcles and the Lion*, "we are torn by an irresistible attraction and an overwhelming repugnance and disgust." Again: "Marriage turns vagabonds into steady citizens; men and women will . . . practice virtues that unattached individuals are incapable of." In the preface to *Overruled*, thus: "That jealousy is independent of sex is shown by its intensity in children." Again: "Adultery is the dullest of themes on the stage, and from Francesca and Paolo down to the latest guilty couple . . . the romantic adulterers have been bores." Yet again: "It is ridiculous to say . . . that art has nothing to do with morality."

"If a young woman, in a mood of strong reaction . . . were to tell Mr. Herbert Spencer that she was determined not to murder her own instincts and throw away her life in obedience to a mouthful of empty phrases," he once said, "I suspect he would recommend the 'Data of Ethics' to her as a trustworthy and conclusive guide to conduct. Under similar circumstances I should unhesitatingly say to the young woman: 'By all means do as you propose. Try how wicked you can be. . . . At worst, you will only find out the sort of person you really are. At best, you will find that your passions, if you really and honestly let them all loose impartially, will discipline you with a severity your conventional friends . . . could not stand for a day.' " In the preface to *Getting Married* we come upon this: "The assumption that the specific relation which marriage authorizes between the parties is the most intimate and personal of human relations . . . is violently untrue." In *The Apple Cart* we engage the anatomically paradoxical spectacle of a King's platonic mistress. And, by way of a climax, we have a Garden of Eden in *Back to Methuselah* in which, when Shaw's Eve learns the secret of sex, "an expression of overwhelming repugnance" crosses her features and she "buries her face in her hands!"

Testament of a Critic, 1931

Shaw: III

I SURELY ADVANCE no stunning morsel of news when I intimate to you that it has for some time now been the generous conviction of his many admirers that something ought to be done—by way of preserving the reputation he has antecedently established for himself—to make Mr. George Bernard Shaw shut up. To those of us who have been so greatly and so often soundly entertained by him for many years, the immediate institution and subsidy of an aesthetic Ku Klux with his muffling as its sole purpose would be a fond and gratifying thing. For, crossing the line of seventy some five or six years ago, the erstwhile

Grand Old Boy of English drama and letters has, to the grief of the loving and yet judicious, made pretty much of a damned fool of himself. As *damned fool* is the exact phrase, I see no need for a more literary and genteel circumlocution. And not only has he made this damned fool of himself, but, in addition, he has turned out to be a very lamentable bore.

Any man, whether in his later or earlier years, is privileged to make something of a fool of himself if only he accompanies the act with a palliative dose of consoling humor or wit or with a persuasive and even slightly substantiating mocking philosophy. Any man is not only privileged to make a fool of himself, indeed, but, as human nature goes, is apparently pretty well by the Fates bound. Yet when a man of Shaw's previous humor, wit, intelligence, and very considerable dialectical skill makes a monkey of himself and no longer displays the humor, wit, intelligence, and dialectical skill to make his public not only swallow the fact but like it, it is high time that some kind friend took him gently by the ear, led him back home to mama, and begged her, in his best interests, to keep a close eye on him and not let him out at night any more. The trouble with Shaw is that, metaphorically, he has been going out at night when his venerable years and enfeebled powers have made it more or less obvious that he should have had his glass of hot milk by nine o'clock and been put safely to bed in his long woolen underwear. Yet what has he done? What he has done, careless of his literary, dramatic, critical, and disputatious health, has been to persist in frisking anciently about under the young stars and the inhospitable winds of the new springtime, with forced antic gaiety croaking a song of the early nineteen-hundreds and with strained jocularity mimicking the noises of yon treetop cuckoo. Where certain other quondam distinguished valetudinarians have, like the M. Maeterlinck, run off with a young girl, Shaw, being a vegetarian, has run off with an old joke.

Consider some of our erstwhile hero's septuagenarian monkeyshines. He has had his photograph taken in a state approximating the altogether. He has descended to a talking picture of himself wherein he has clownishly turned himself this way and that, instructing the onlookers to observe the rich beauty of his profile. He has made radio speeches in the language of Mr. Rube Goldberg's comic-strip "balloons." He has entered into Shakespearean discussion with prize fighters, has played tag for the cameras on the Riviera with movie pantaloons, and has clambered laboriously atop a cannon in Moscow and cracked cheap vaudeville wheezes. He has engaged in sober philosophical discourse with one of the Four Marx Brothers and has given out interviews so silly that American newspaper editors, disbelieving that anything so juvenile could emanate from a mouth once so intelligent, have cabled to England for verification. He has taken up with the British haut monde and proudly posed for photographs with his bedizened hostesses. He has anticked for reporters at Malvern, performing circus-ring stunts with an umbrella. He has vainly insisted upon his youthfulness by going out in the rain barehead and by being ostentatiously disgusted with persons who have sense enough to go in when it rains. He has made speeches on German railway platforms, on his return from a trip to Russia, so obviously manufactured for their publicity value that everyone has snickered at his performances. He has, in short, done just about everything that a dignified and still partly intelligent man could not think of doing. And, what is worse and what is our more immediate and relevant business, he has grown quite as dull and quite as stupid and quite as tiresome in his literary and dramatic enterprises as in his extra-literary and extra-dramatic.

In *The Apple Cart* we had a premonitory indication that a multiple, or brain, sclerosis had begun to attack Shaw. And now, in *Too True to Be Good*, his latest substitute for playwriting, the doctor has told us the worst. I believe that I do not exaggerate when I say that, were any other name in the whole world of drama or literature attached to the play as author, no theatrical producer, white or black, would hesitate for a moment in throwing it forthwith into the trash basket. Aside from one or two moderately fresh and faintly amusing flashes of paradox, it amounts in sum not only to a weary reiteration of all the antique Shavian opinions but to a restatement of various other opinions on the post-war degringolade, the post-war spiritual uncertainty, the futility of carnage, etc., as stale and obvious as an old gin breath. It is dull, dull, dull, perhaps the dullest play, indeed, that a playwright of sometime high position has ever contributed to the theatre. And, being that dull, it carries with it a shade of sadness that its author, long so close to the admiring humor of most of us, has not at length the sagacity and wisdom to call it a day and, in some quiet corner of England, does not for the rest of his years sun himself peacefully and satisfiedly in the warm afterglow of his earlier career.

The Intimate Notebooks of George Jean Nathan, 1932

Shaw: IV

R E-EMERGING for a single appearance after three years of inactivity, the little group of Washington Square Players brought their resources to the trio of minor Shaw efforts noted [*The Dark Lady of the Sonnets, Overruled,* and *How He Lied to Her Husband*] and, while the performance was of an inconsiderable nature, the coincident re-emergence of Shaw after the local theatre's later-day neglect of him provided, despite the inferiority of the selections, a touch of that brio which John Bull's other islander even in his lesser dramatic self has seldom failed to impart to a stage so often in need of it.

May God in His infinite wisdom spare the grand old boy to us for many another year, but, since mathematics seem to be inexorable in the scheme of Divine Providence and since he is now ninety, the Great Bookkeeper may have other ideas. It is this unhappy thought that prompts, while he is still alive, an all too brief reckoning of what he has meant, among so many other things, to the world of drama.

When in his earlier day as a critic Shaw looked upon the English stage, what he found, in the plays of Pinero, was simply a romantic servant girl's view of sex made palatable to her even more romantic employers by identifying it with persons of a somewhat fancier social class. What he found further, in the plays of Henry Arthur Jones, though he deemed him Pinero's superior, was a relation-

ship of men and women predicated solely upon its avail-
ability for ready theatrical effect, and a philosophy of that
relationship facilely concocted by placing a sliver of banana
peel under Pinero's moral rectitude. What he found yet
further, despite the strong wind beginning to blow down
from Norway, was a drama still artificialized out of all
reality by French influences. What he found in sum and
in short was an English stage which interpreted life largely
in terms of the powdered mentalities and evening-dressed
emotions of high-life puppets or in the even more laugh-
able terms of paper-knife melodrama.

Since critic and crusader are generally one and the same,
for all the critic's customary lofty disdain of the impeach-
ment, the disgusted Shaw didn't wait long before exchang-
ing his critical robes for playwriting armor and, his red
whiskers breezing behind him, riding forth to battle. With
the earlier help of his fellow critic Archer he drew first
blood, if but a dribble, from the heathen by heaving onto
the stage of the Independent Theatre Company of London *Widowers' Houses*, which, though paradoxically imi-
tative of the very drama he was tilting against, dared to
introduce sociology and economics into the hitherto sac-
rosanct drawing-room. This was the start, modest enough,
but the start nonetheless of the putsch that was to revolu-
tionize not only the modern drama of England but to a
considerable degree the drama of the rest of the civilized
world.

It was not, however, too easy going. The English were
still happily swooning over the pretty parlor woes of Mrs.
Tanqueray and her sisters when Shaw had at them with
the ironic whimsicalities of *Arms and the Man*, which they
appreciated only as a stage Russian pretends to relish
licorice-pellet caviar, and, unforgivably, with *Mrs. Warren's Profession*, which, while essentially not altogether

dissimilar to Mrs. Tanqueray's, nevertheless so outraged the British morality that its production was forbidden.

Chuckling in his beard, Shaw thereupon said to himself: Very well, if the numskulls prefer sentimentality, I shall give it to them, but in such clever and witty wise that they will not recognize the deletion of the *ality*. *Candida*, that most adroit of sentimental comedies, was the result. And slowly, like a tortoise making for a lily pond, the English public began to respond. And slowly its esteem for Pinero's innocent young women whose reputations had been knavishly stained (*The Benefit of the Doubt*) and less innocent older ones who melodramatically burned Bibles by way of justifying their illicit relations with politicians (*The Notorious Mrs. Ebbsmith*) began faintly to fade. Nor did Jones's Michaels and their lost angels or Wilde's ideal husbands bring the color wholly back to its cheeks. For Shaw, not dismounting from his charger for a moment, kept prodding sardonically with lances like *The Devil's Disciple*, which invited audiences to bring with them into the theatre fewer glands and more brains and which pleasantly surprised them by being not at all as painful as they had anticipated but, on the contrary, surprisingly amusing.

From this point on, Shaw's crusade was, as the vulgar Yankee expression has it, pretty well in the bag. It was not that the English, who steadfastly worship anything old, whether a philosophy, an actress, or a bathroom, deserted en masse the dramatic order of yesterday. Very far from it. The Episcopalian indiscretions of lords and manicurists (*The Gay Lord Quex*), the Lake Como moonlit adventurings of elegant strumpets (*Iris*), the spectacle of cross-examined "good" women battling to preserve their honor (*Mrs. Dane's Defense*), the necklaces of Mrs. Gorringe, the amatory maneuvers of Jane, and the various princesses and butterflies still exercised their perfumed influence. But that influence was not exactly the puissant thing it once was. And gradually and surely it was to become less and less so under the Shavian pressure. And where in several other and more progressive countries it had not been earlier recognized, it was now not long before St. George was hailed as the voice in the dramatic wilderness, and the prophet of the new dramatic order.

Having already produced the beautifully witty *Caesar and Cleopatra* on a stage chronologically identified with the sweetly cologned *The Gay Lord Quex*, Shaw forthwith pitched in in earnest. *Captain Brassbound's Conversion*, after a lapse in *The Admirable Bashville*, was followed by *John Bull's Other Island* and that by *Major Barbara, The Philanderer*, and *Man and Superman*, the three last produced in a single year. Scarcely had audiences recaptured their wind when *The Doctor's Dilemma* was heaved at them, and then in quick succession *Getting Married* (*The Shewing-Up of Blanco Posnet* suffered a deferred production), *Misalliance*, and *Fanny's First Play*. And, not so very long afterward, *You Never Can Tell* and *Pygmalion* and, to the bewilderment of any possible remaining doubters, that most remarkable of modern historical fancies, *Saint Joan*.

Shaw's position as the greatest dramatist in the English-speaking theatre of his time was now secure. Nor could that security be minimized by his later and enfeebled work. Though his *The Apple Cart, The Simpleton of the Unexpected Isles, Too True to be Good, Back to Methuselah, Geneva, In Good King Charles' Golden Days*, etc., marked a clearly visible and here and there sorry decline, there were still traces of the real Shaw detectable in them. And at their worst, save in the case of *Geneva*, they were better than the overwhelming majority of plays that emanated from the English theatre in the same period.

Playwrights and Performance

It was not, throughout his theatrical career, that Shaw was the revolutionary dramatic thinker he was esteemed to be by critics and audiences given to a confounding of impudent intelligence with a quietly reasoned and profound philosophy. Much of what was accepted as daring had already long been tried and tested when Shaw offered it. It was rather that he had the great ability to restate platitudes in such a manner that their weariness left them and that they took on again the color of youth. He brought with him many of the old stage toys, but he painted them up in such brilliant and dashing colors that they seemed new. He laughed at the old conventions of the drama, nevertheless kept them and, by playing his wit over them, gaily deceived his willing customers that they were right out of the bandbox. And, above all, he had the enormous theatrical skill to make cynicism a merry thing.

Gratuitously to analyze his plays too closely is to look the gift horse in the mouth, for they have given their recipients some of the happiest hours the stage has afforded them since their earliest birthdays. *Caesar and Cleopatra* overdoes the business of deriding the British? Perhaps so, but it nonetheless remains the best play of its kind written in Shaw's time. The epilogue of *Saint Joan* is greasepaint humbug? True, but the play remains the best play of *its* kind in that same time. *Fanny's First Play* is on the trivial side? Again true, but where a better and more hilarious trivial one? The Life Force business of *Man and Superman* and the pursuit of man by woman is out of Schopenhauer, with a bow to Nietzsche for the Superman business? So what? Maybe the play as a whole isn't plentifully superior to it?

I am not offering definitive criticism; I am offering definitive appreciation of dramatic and theatrical favors. I may deplore with the more definitively critical and worthy P. P. Howe Shaw's admiration for confusing such a character's name as Mr. Redbrook with Mr. Kidbrook or Ftatateeta with Teetatota and, with Howe, condemn it equally with Wilde's having named a character Kelvil in order to be able later on to call him Kettle (or even equally with Shakespeare's bequeathal of the name Elbow to subsequent punning ends), but since it occupies only eight seconds out of two otherwise amusing hours, I shall not complain too loudly. I may also make a wry critical face over the old vaudeville funny business of a woman getting drunk, but *Candida* is *Candida* just the same. I may professionally yelp a little when the great Catherine rolls around on the floor like a pair of 1890 German and Irish comedians, but the short play is pretty entertaining in spite of it. I may groan a bit over such undergraduate pleasantries, so Howe terms them, as "No man is a match for a woman except with a poker and a pair of hobnailed boots," but there are a hundred such compensating lines as "Captain Bluntschli, I am very glad to see you; but you must leave this house at once" or as "Life does not cease to be funny when people die any more than it ceases to be serious when people laugh." And I may, as a critic who gets paid for it, frown gravely over any number of other obvious shortcomings in the great old boy's plays, but, as a man who doesn't get paid for it, I smile and laugh and moisten at so much that is otherwise in them that I nevertheless kiss him on both cheeks.

There is that word *moisten*. It would take a pretty tough character, or a Viola tricolor, to resist Shaw at his sentimental best, for in that best there is a world of tender wisdom distilled into some of the most beautiful prose that the modern stage has known. Caesar's speech to Cleopatra . . . Candida's gentle philosophy . . . Dubedat's bequest to Jennifer—these and a dozen, two dozen, others confound the criticism that once, and then seemingly not with merit, held Shaw to have a heart compounded half of secondhand Butler and half, in Wells's phrase, of parthenogenetic eggs.

And so when it comes to sex. The Shaw who once said: "There is never any real sex in romance; what is more, there is very little, and that of a very crude kind, in ninety-nine hundredths of our married life"; the Shaw who observed: "One man's poetry is another man's pruriency"; the Shaw who asked: "Is any treatment of sex in the interest of public morals?"; the Shaw who remarked: "The novel which says no more about sex than may be said in a lecture on the facts to a class of schoolgirls of fifteen can be enormously more entertaining than a novel wholly preoccupied with sexual symptoms"—the Shaw who has uttered such beliefs has trouble explaining himself to the Shaw who, albeit perhaps unwittingly, has created some of the most desirable heroines that the modern stage has shown. It is his paradox that his own passivity has created warmth in other men. Though he often hopes to write brilliantly of women as if they were so many lamps without shades, the softening shades are nonetheless born of his prose. And of his own irrepressible sentiment no less.

Dick Dudgeon in *The Devil's Disciple* pronounces the word *love* "with true Puritan scorn," Mrs. Bridgenorth in *Getting Married* comments on the "everyday vulgarities of earthly love," and so with many another of his mouthpieces. But, as Stevenson hinted long ago to William Archer, Shaw was nevertheless born a romantic and continues to be one to this day. And, as I myself observed years ago, his romanticism is no more clearly to be detected than through such of his animadversions on love and sex. He pretends not to see the latter for what they are and for what, deep inside him, he knows them to be. But all the fine irony and humor which he has visited upon

176

them cannot conceal the romanticist hiding behind that irony and humor and slyly through them seeking to protect himself from the charge. If the author of the rare and beautiful letters to Ellen Terry is not one of the most deeply romantic natures of his time and if he was not then, psychologically speaking, one who cunningly dismissed sex only and simply because he wished to safeguard his pride and disappointment in the presence of his successful rival, Irving—if Shaw was not and is not all of that, these observations are those of a two-year-old, and a backward one.

The great man is nearing the threshold of the hereafter. The theatre has not seen his like before, and will not see it soon again. He has brought to it a merry courage, a glorious wit, a musical tenderness, and a world of needed vitality. He has laughed at the old gods, and, to give them their due, the old gods have enjoyed it. And outside and beyond the theatre he has let a wholesome breeze into more assorted kinds of national, international, private, and public buncombe than has any other writer of his period. Therefore, hail, Shaw, hail and—I hope I shall wait long before saying it—farewell!

The Theatre Book of the Year, 1945–1946

Rostand

LA DERNIÈRE COMÉDIE DE DON ROSTAND—I allude, obviously enough, to *La Dernière Nuit de Don Juan,* a play profoundly born, profoundly wise, and profoundly beautiful. Three times in nine months I have read it, and three times, intoxicated by its beauty, I have found myself periodically raising my eyes from the manuscript and pausing to address to myself a glowing critical soliloquy. For here are the laughter and tears of genius woven into a great, gay ache—a super-Schnitzlerian tapestry shot through with the brilliant threads of fancy, poetry, and sardonic pathos. For here are literature and drama inextricably intertwined; a masterpiece of the modern theatre.

Like fine drama of its kind ever, there is something remote about the play. You make to touch it with your fingers, and it is not there. It is a mood on the wind, springtime melting into summer and fading into autumn in the snap of a moment. From the time its Don Juan reclimbs the steps of Hell to enjoy his respite in the world of women —repeating with each upward step the name of Ninon . . . Laura . . . Armande . . . Jeanne—to the time the devil metes out to him his ironic punishment as the reincarnation of Punchinello in a traveling marionette show —from beginning to end it is as present, and yet as elusive, as the memory of a forgotten tune. Its episodes are a succession of dramatic jewels.

Where Molière's *Le Festin de Pierre* ends, Rostand's work begins. (The prologue has been reconstructed from the author's notes, and is only an outline.) The play carries its central character through scene after scene of wit, charm, and tender derisory philosophy. Beside it, all the Don Juan plays ever written, from Zamora's to Grabbe's, and from Molière's to Tellez's and those of the modern continental comedy school of Hans Otto, Von Schmitz, and Thaddeus Rittner, take on a varying sense of imaginative pallor. Rostand's is an infinitely impudent, infinitely dreamful, infinitely delicate Don Juan. "I am of another essence than your Doctor Faust who wished nothing better than a little German girl," he boasts; "A town of love has watched my natal day; my dying day should see a town of love. Only one epitaph is fitting for Don Juan: 'He was born at Seville and died at Venice!' " he dreams; "I have traveled everywhere, like a fairy tale," and his words are fragile and far away. . . . Rostand's Don Juan is at once a wit, a philosopher, and a child. "One is burned when one has said 'I love you,' " he reminds Punch. "Then how is it done?" asks Punch. "By nudging her? By making eyes?" "That is too stupid; 'tis too carp-like," replies Don Juan. "How should I look?" then Punch. "Like a chasm," replies Don Juan.

Here is Rostand's indomitable Aiglon, grown mature, and off the field of Mars and in the court of Venus: "I am a monster with a soul, a wild-beast archangel, who has preserved, in his fall, his wing." Here is Rostand's Chantecler in doublet and hose: "I am the nostalgia of all. There is no work—despite your hissing, oh ancient adder—no virtue, no science and no faith which does not regret it is not I." "What," asks the devil, "will remain of that?" And Rostand's Cyrano with the small nose answers: "That which remains of Alexander's ashes, and knows that it was Alexander!"

For sheer poetic loveliness there are a half-dozen scenes in the play that are not surpassed in modern dramatic literature. Of these all, most noteworthy perhaps is the scene wherein the devil tears into as many small pieces the list of Don Juan's one thousand and three conquests and sends them, like snow, out upon the moonlit bosom of the Adriatic, there each suddenly to be transformed into a gondola bearing the spirit of the woman whose name was written thereon. I say most noteworthy, and promptly doubt my words. For even finer is the ensuing scene wherein the thousand shadows of silver blue mount silently the stairway to challenge and torment Don Juan's memory of them—he cannot penetrate their masks, their masks of what passed for love, and blindly, desperately, he searches face upon face—it is . . . it is . . . it is—to the curtain fall. And finer, more beautifully imagined still, are the scenes wherein the shadows slowly, derisively, yet tenderly, strip Don Juan of his amorous gasconade and wherein Don Juan, at the devil's bidding, collects in a frail chalice the frozen teardrop that each shadow wears, like a jewel, in the corner of her mask—which tears the devil, peering through an enormous lens, then ironically analyses.

The life of the theatre lies in plays like this. For one such, a thousand deadly evenings are gladly endurable. Such episodes as that of the secret tear, the only one the devil may not touch, the tear of pity for Don Juan; such profound mockery as the paint-and-canvas hell to which the still strutting Don Juan is in the end consigned; such humor as lies in Don Juan's pathetic serenity before the cavalcade of his shadow loves, and such poetry as lies in the one white fragment of the torn list—these are the stuff of a glorified and imperishable theatre.

The World in Falseface, 1923

O'Casey

SEAN O'CASEY'S *Juno and the Paycock* is noteworthy for two very good instances of character drawing, for its measure of warm and comprehending humor, for its curiously

effective handling, in a suspensive manner, of the character of the son of the Boyle household who has betrayed a
fellow patriot, and for a brief flash of moving drama, toward the end of the play, in the boy's death at the hands
of his colleagues' avengers. It is deficient in the trick of so
assembling these virtues that the whole shall produce a
play as meritorious as its component parts.

The price of O'Casey's imperfect maneuvering of his
materials is, after the evening has passed its middle mark,
tedium. Everything is on the stage to make a consistently
holding play, but the materials are like a troop of fully
armed soldiers whose commander is down with the measles
and who accordingly hang around, their rifles cocked, wait-
ing vainly for orders to move forward. Time and again the
smell of approaching drama is in the air and the nose sniffs
in eager anticipation only to be disappointed. The first act
proceeds smoothly and amusingly, centered as it is upon
the character of the lying, bragging, lovable loafer Boyle,
quondam sailor on a coal barge that never got further than
Liverpool, but in his own tireless imagination and gabble
a sea dog among sea dogs. The colloquies between Boyle
and his bootlicking neighbor, Joxer Daly, are as diverting
as anything you'll find in the playhouse at the moment.
But once the flush of this initial act is over, O'Casey's fancy
and dexterity give out, and after a half-hour more his play
drops with an audible bump.

The failure of O'Casey to master his materials is readily
discernible in the length to which he goes to conceal his
dramatic nervousness in heavy exaggeration of dramatic
and comic episode. Not only does he so overdo the burlesque song renditions of his characters in the second act
and the tragic melodrama of his last act that these portions
of his play lack all conviction, but, to boot, he so segre-
gates comedy and drama that one kills the effect of the

other. His second act is almost entirely in the low-comedy vein and his third act, cut off from the other as with a meat ax, piles tragedy upon tragedy so exaggeratedly that it would take a professional pallbearer to profess any show of sympathy over his characters' plight. The impression is of a man stopping suddenly short in the midst of a comic story to tell the plot of *Oedipus Rex*. Tragedy, to be convincing, must mount cumulatively and slowly; O'Casey directs it in the tempo of a rapid succession of unanticipated fire alarms. Within the space of a comparatively few minutes he betrays his young heroine and gives her an illegitimate baby, causes her lover to swindle the family out of a rightful inheritance and run off to England, brings the son of the household to be shot to death in a gutter, separates husband and wife, desolates the home of his protagonists to the extent of removing its last chair, gives his central character delirium tremens, induces the young man who has planned to marry the daughter to sneak away, and suggests that the cause of Irish freedom is up a tree. His traffic in tragedy reminds one, indeed, of nothing so much as the familiar smoking-car story about the sorely harassed parent whose steadily augmenting family woes are brought to a climax by his small son Abie's unhousebroken deportment and who, at his wit's end, is informed by an old gentleman seated back of him in the day coach that, unless he mend his Abie's ways at once, the old gentleman will make trouble for him.

In his later *The Plough and the Stars*, on the other hand, O'Casey has produced a piece of work not less full of defective detail than his *Juno and the Paycock* but, for all that, a drama excellent in its characterizations, rich in an irony that reaches the heights of cruelty, and paradoxically powerful in lasting impression. Three or four of the episodes have the stamp of unmistakable dramatic genius;

quietly as a cannon on rubber tires O'Casey rolls them toward the footlights and suddenly thunders them into the startled consciousness of his audience. As a surgical picture of the Irish, I know of nothing in drama or literature that comes anywhere near this play. That the Irish merely gave vent to catcalls and eggs when it was shown in Dublin is surprising; that they didn't bomb the theatre is even more surprising. O'Casey takes his people, themselves, their ambitions, their dreams, their pretenses, and their innermost philosophies, and doesn't leave a green thread in their chemises when he gets through. His clinical portrait is the most vicious thing in modern dramatic literature, but the viciousness is that of a deep understanding, a profoundly critical love, and a prophylactic hairbrush swatting a turned-up child. His play is long, too long. As in *Juno and the Paycock*, he doesn't seem to know exactly when to let go. The technique in both plays is much the same, although it is exaggerated in the one under immediate discussion. O'Casey busies himself leisurely with character for the first thirty-five minutes of each act, and then suddenly in the last five minutes recalls that, after all, a drama should have at least a little drama in it and belatedly dramatizes in a few moments the ambling antecedent business. The break is not too well dovetailed. The effect is of a Dutch concert disconcertingly interrupted by a pistol shot. Again, as in *Juno and the Paycock*, the dramatist piles on the final woe to such an extent that a measure of persuasiveness is deleted from his work. His wholesale murder, sudden death, and general desolation are Shakespearean in every way but the compensatory one of great poetry. The stage at the conclusion of his tragedy resembles nothing so much as the floor of a slaughterhouse. Those characters who haven't been shot and killed are either dead of tuberculosis, insane, in the last stages of alcoholism, or being led off the stage for no good purpose. Still again, as in the other play, *The Plough and the Stars* overdoes to the point of irritation the vaudeville trick of repeating a word or phrase for humorous ends. It was Pinero who once pointed out the limit to which this device could prosperously be used, and then topped it by one. O'Casey tries to top it by ten or fifteen, and naturally fails. He also goes in once again for the mispronunciation of words by way of getting a cheap laugh, as in the instance of *chaos* in *Juno* —and he repeats and repeats. But—when the play is over, the effect the playwright has set himself to get is as peculiarly and bafflingly there as the hair in your nose. You carry with you out of the theatre a merciless, yet sympathetic, vision of Ireland and its youngsters in grown-old bodies. You feel the utter futility of a people and a purpose, the tragic ridiculousness of a nation of eternal children playing politics with loud nursery rattles and playing soldier with popguns. You look upon this picture of the Irish by an Irishman, one of the most articulate fellows on the Emerald Isle, and you smile and wince at the same time.

There isn't a character in O'Casey's gallery that isn't well drawn. Some are superbly drawn. There is, for example, the carpenter Fluther, the alternately genial and bellicose souse who is constantly swearing off the stuff for good and who is as sharply perceived a study of an Irishman, down to the smallest detail of thought and act, as the drama has given us. There is the little old querulous Irishman Peter Flynn, proud as a peacock over marching in meaningless parades in elaborate and meaningless regalia. There is the young Irish liberal and dreamer, constantly mouthing an ill-assimilated amount of sociological information; there are, in sharp, brief little strokes, portraits of Irish women and of Irish ballyhoos and of English militiamen. Some of the episodes, as I have said, have the vital smash of kindly gunpowder: the scene at the saloon bar with Irishmen getting indignantly cockeyed while, outside the place and as counterpoint to the bibbing inside, other Irishmen, equally indignant, are haranguing their fellow countrymen to defend their immemorial rights with their eternal souls; the climax to the second act wherein, the political indignation reaching its zenith, one of the Irishmen lets off his accumulated martial steam by fighting another Irishman, both of them drunk, for an insult offered by the latter to an Irish prostitute's virtue, and then goes off with the woman for the night; the richly comical yet searching episode in the following act in which, with Dublin strewn with English bullets and Irishmen dying on every hand, the women make the practical best of the situation, news arriving of the pillaging of shops and stores, by taking a baby carriage, previously the subject of acrimonious dispute among them, and with true sisterly concurrence hustling off to load it with pink lingerie, white shoes, parlor lamps, and other treasures out of demolished show windows; and the final moment of the play wherein two English petty officers, with the results of carnage all about them, quietly observe that it is five o'clock and settle down to drink the tea that has been set out by an Irishwoman for her soldier husband dying somewhere in the gutter below the tenement.

Art of the Night, 1928

Pirandello

THE MAJOR PORTION of the drama of Pirandello consists in a kind of metaphysical masochism. The Italian lays hold of a philosophical paradox and derives an intense orgastic pleasure from belaboring himself with it. Where Shaw takes the same paradox and uses it sadistically upon his audience, his Latin contemporary bares his own flesh to it. In his ability to laugh at his self-imposed torture lies the latter's genius.

The technique of the outstanding Pirandello drama is that of a philosophical detective play, with Truth as the mysterious and evasive culprit and with all the characters of the play as sleuths. The play called *Right You Are If You Think You Are,* for example, is typical of the leading elements in the Pirandello canon. As a tour de force in mystification, it must rank as a noteworthy achievement. Composed of materials that are essentially of dubious dramatic value, it is so ingeniously contrived that time and again when it seems that the whole structure must be on the point of collapsing, the uncommon wit of the author astonishes one with its jugglery of the theme back into renewed life. When the curtain falls on the first act, that theme strikes one as having been rounded out; there seems to be little that the playwright can bring to it to sustain it further. Yet the second act no sooner gets under way than what appeared to be a complete statement and relative solution of the theme is seen to have been but dexterous preparation. The same impression persists after the fall of the second curtain only to be dissipated by the rise of the third. The fault of the play theatrically, as with the bulk of the author's work, lies in its prolonged and unrelieved argumentation. It is mentally dramatic, but, after all, the theatre calls for the use of the eye as well as the ear, and the Pirandello drama has the air of being written for intelligent blind men. I do not make a point of mere physical action, plainly enough; what I mean is that Pirandello seeks to dramatize abstraction in terms of abstraction rather than in terms of theatrical concreteness. One sees his characters move about the stage, but the movement always impresses one as having been wrought by the stage producer rather than by the dramatist himself. For all that it matters, the actors might just as well be wooden dummies and their lines spoken by a ventriloquist.

Pirandello's favorite theme is the shadowy line that separates and distinguishes truth from fantasy, what is real from what is not real, and what is believed to be fact from what may conceivably not be fact at all. His method of presenting this theme dramatically is to lift it completely clear of the drama as we generally recognize it and to play it like an old-time minstrel show, without castanets and tambourines, but with the conventional interlocutor at center interrogating in turn the performers seated to his left and right and commenting whimsically upon their replies. In *Right You Are If You Think You Are*, for instance, the interlocutor is clearly identified in the person of Lamberto Laudisi, who, throughout the main portion of the play, sits elegantly aloof from the other metaphysical minstrels, periodically inquires of each of them the philosophical equivalent of "Who was that lady I seen you on the street with?" and upon each metaphorical reply that

that was no lady, that was my wife, lifts his eyebrows quizzically and observes slyly that the minstrel addressed only thinks it was his wife as, under the laws of certain states and countries, no marriage would be recognized and hence the imagined wife was actually nothing more than the lady initially alluded to.

Where Shaw possesses the most agile mind in contemporary drama, Pirandello possesses beyond question the trickiest. In the matter of philosophical paradox there is no one like him in the field of modern dramatic writing. It is not, however, a mere superficial trickiness, but one that springs from a shrewd combination of introspective wisdom and a profound cynical humor. The virtue of Pirandello lies in the quality of his meditations and conclusions; his weakness in his failure thus far to evolve a thoroughly satisfactory species of dramaturgy to quicken them into consistently holding theatrical exhibitions. The greatest admirer of the Italian has difficulty in reconciling his considerable intellectual interest in Pirandello's stage with his relative theatrical disinterest. The theatre, after all, is a place where ideas must not merely live but must also move. The ideas of the theatre of Pirandello are alive, as healthy human beings dreaming interesting dreams in their sleep are alive, but they are not dramatized in terms of their waking hours. Critics of the printed drama may justifiably take the opposite point of view, but critics of the theatre who do not confound a merely unusual and startling novel theatrical evening with sound and lastingly effective acted drama cannot help but deplore the circumstance that allied to the engaging Pirandello mind there is not the theatrical craft of some such worker in the sociological and economical phases of the Pirandello what-is-truth motif as John Galsworthy.

Art of the Night, 1928

Jim Tully

WHILE THE DRAMA may be many miles ahead of Jim Tully, I doubt that the theatre has yet caught up to him. He is too cruel, too forthright, and too raw for an institution that, for all its progress, is yet in many of its phases, by virtue of its democratic nature, still an antechamber to the kindergarten. Tully goes down into the sewers of American life for his fiction and dramatic materials, and out of those sewers he fetches forth characters dripping somewhat too fetidly for the pleasure of the native aesthetic tenderfoot. When his *Beggars of Life*, as fine a book of its kind as has been written in our day, was lifted over onto the stage, it was found necessary, after the initial performance, to doctor up the element of incest that the weak stomachs of theatre audiences might not gag at it. The novel *Jarnegan* contains stuff that has outraged many; certain of its phrases would make Petronius himself rush for the smelling salts. This is true also of *Circus Parade*. And we find in the play called *Black Boy* still further indications that the last thing in the world that the stage can do is hold the mirror up to nature and get away with it.

This *Black Boy* is, in its technical phases, a play as crudely wrought as is *Jarnegan* a novel. Tully misses all sense of form; he has no more finish, in the accepted sense of the word, than a medicine show; he grabs all the blinding scarlets of the palette in his fist and, with one smash,

smears them flat against the wall, from which they proceed
to drip in ugly splotches. As I say, form is lacking, but if
there is a writer in America today who can lay hold of
mean people and mean lives and tear their mean hearts
out with more beautifully appalling realism, his work is
unknown to me. This Tully is the Weyler in modern
American literature. Even his casual journalistic interviews, the best interviews that you will find in the public
prints, have the flavor of the King's utterances in Scene 2
of the third act of *Richard II*. The simplest chronicle of a
movie queen's rise to eminence is not complete for Tully
save it include an account of the way her illegitimate Hun-
garian uncle bit off her mother's ear in a fit of delirium
tremens, of the attempt made by the vice presidents of the
six largest moving-picture companies to lure her into white
slavery on behalf of the presidents, of the three or four directors who were mysteriously shot by other directors for
trying to force their wicked wills upon her, of incredible
machinations on the part of Jewish purveyors of Swedish
bathing beauties to destroy her prestige by spreading in-
nuendoes concerning her and a San Francisco Chinaman,
and of the manner in which the proud beauty was cured
of an Oriental disease only after years of mixing mercury
with her gin. His stories of hoboes, yeggs, harlots, jailbirds,
niggers, of all the riffraff of humanity, crawl among the
vermin in the cellar beneath the cellar of Gorky's *Night
Refuge*. Their lusts and oaths and miserable bravery sound
in a barroom bacchanale. For when Tully approaches a
character, he approaches that character's soul only after he
has first ripped off the last shred of his undershirt, torn off
his trousers, and given him a contemptuously critical boot
in the rear. The fellow has about as much delicacy as an
iron-riveter. But, when his job is finished, no one can say
that he hasn't got the smashing effect that he has gone after.

And what is more—and this is the important point—that he hasn't got that effect legitimately. He is often cheaply melodramatic; he is sometimes so loud that he is unintelligible; but, when the roar of battle has died down, he has got his man.

Black Boy, as it comes to us in the theatre with the name of Frank Dazey, author of the gimcrack *Peter Weston*, significantly added to Tully's on the playbill, is surely not the play that Tully originally wrote. The play that Tully wrote, if I am any judge of him, estimating him from his antecedent work, certainly made no such compromises with an audience's tender feelings and prejudices. I point to a single example. The play tells the story of a humble Negro's dream of grandeur that lies in the title of heavy-weight champion of the world, in the attendant wealth and power, and in the love of a white woman. And it tells then the story in gradual diminuendo of the toll of vainglory and dissipation and of the final vanishing of the last wisps of that dream in the discovery that, like all other illusions in this world, the white woman, whose arms hold in them the fellow's unreal heaven, is only a high yaller. Or, at any rate, that was the story, unless I am in error, that Tully's play once told. But when that play came traveling into the timid theatre, things happened to it. An audience would resent the spectacle of a big Negro—and the role was to be played by an actual Negro—indulging in amorous contacts with a white woman, or one who it was persuaded to believe was white. Did not, forsooth, such resentment show itself when the theme of O'Neill's *All God's Chillun* was announced? It would be unwise to take chances. And so the script was duly altered to include two "plants" assuring the audience in the earlier portions of the play that the woman, for all her appearance, had colored blood. Obviously, the whole point of the play was thus got rid of at one swoop, and the eventual disillusionment of the central character deleted of all dramatic force. A number of other changes are as clearly evident, all contributing to a weakening of Tully's original. Yet, weakened or not, and with all its crudity, this *Black Boy* is nevertheless a living breathing thing. It has more vitality, more kinship with actuality, and more reality of character than nine tenths of the artfully tailored plays we get in a round of a theatrical year.

Art of the Night, 1928

Galsworthy

It is UNFORTUNATE that Mr. Galsworthy should elect the play *Escape* as his swan song to the theatre. A dramatic career as distinguished as his has been deserves a better ending. To wind it up with this play is much as if Shaw had trusted to *Press Cuttings* for his final blaze of glory, or Hauptmann to *Die Jungfern vom Bischofsberg*. While I do not mean, plainly enough, to place Galsworthy in the high company of the aforementioned dramatists, his position in the contemporary theatre has been sufficiently important to merit a sounder adieu than this. For *Escape* must rank with such of his works as *The Fugitive, A Bit o' Love, Windows, The Skin Game,* and the like, as one of his feeblest enterprises. One cannot help believing that its reception in certain quarters as a meritorious job must be attributed to the critical philosophy set forth by one of the critics in *Fanny's First Play*: that if the play be signed with

the name of a good author, it is a good play, and if it be
signed with the name of a bad one, it is a bad play.

Escape, though it bears the name of a good dramatist,
is none the less a bad play. Its creator has imagined an excellent theme—the reactions to the predicament of an
escaped convict on the part of a diversity of his fellow
countrymen—and has done little more with it than to permit it to be commented upon by a series of flapper intelligences. At only one point in the play, in the very last
scene, does he bring his theme face to face with a relatively
critical mind and a critical philosophic situation, and then
all he has to offer is the bewhiskered speculation, favorite
to a whole library of second-rate sentimental fiction, as to
what Christ would have done in a like juncture. The body
of the drama is taken up with the attitudes toward the
escaped convict of an undeviating procession of soft-
heads: a susceptible ingenue, a child who collects auto-
graphs, a sweet one in blue pajamas and a pink neglige, a
young woman who sentimentalizes the hunting of foxes, an
addle-pated fat wench who enjoys roadside picnicking, a
hotel chambermaid, a doddering old man, a couple of jail
wardens given to a high delight in moving pictures, a silly-
ass musical-comedy Englishman stepped straight out of the
comic weeklies, a village constable, a yokel, and a couple of
stonecutters. It is through such instruments that Galsworthy filters his theme, bringing into conflict with it upon
no single occasion anything approaching a real mind or an
experienced emotion. The one trivial exception is to be
had in the case of the clergyman in the final episode, and
there, as I have observed, Galsworthy merely continues his
complete surrender to sentimentality.

Escape belongs to the catalogue of Galsworthy's valentine drama, along with *A Bit o' Love* and similar plays.
Sentimentality is thick upon it, like steam in a candy

kitchen, and obscures any values that the drama might have possessed. I may exaggerate somewhat when I say that the impression that one gains from it is much like the one induced by the old Hanlon tinsel shows, in which the hero, a handsome fellow in purple tights in quest of the elusive blonde prima donna, passed through a dozen scene changes beset variously by acrobats dressed as devils, contraltos in the robes of witches, and contortionists with sinister eyes painted in the middle of their foreheads, but I believe that I do not exaggerate too greatly. The conflicts that Galsworthy interposes in the path of his migratory hero are largely of a piece with these old extravaganzas. Were so much as a single character from one of Shaw's plays—or even one of Brieux's—to wander into the text for a moment and deliver a few remarks on the subject in hand, the play would promptly take on a sliver of the conviction it lacks, for then at least one or two of the sensible questions that presently rattle rebelliously, insistently, and impatiently in the audience's head might be posed and so momentarily dissipate the all-enveloping sentimental fog. As the play stands, all the author does is to ask sociological questions of the kindergarten class. In addition to the dubious thematic handling, Galsworthy has never written poorer drama. Such an episode as that dealing with the two wardens waiting to capture the convict on the dark moor, with its jokes about Charlie Chaplin and Duggie Fairbanks and its slapstick finale with the cops rolling around on the ground in each other's arms, constitutes a revue skit of the cheapest sort. Nor are such jejune observations as the streetwalker's "Clean streets!—that's the cry. Clean *men*! That'd be better!", such dramatic devices as the whistling of a popular music-show tune by way of a signal, and such jocosities as concern painful corns entirely what one has a right to expect from a man of Mr. Galsworthy's eminence.

Mr. Galsworthy's eminence? To what, looking back upon his long and honorable career as a dramatist, has that eminence been due? It is the custom to answer that it is and has been due to certain qualities of mind, an intelligence at once calm and discerning, and one expert in surveying both sides of a question and meditating more or less profoundly the tilting of the scales now this way and now that. But I doubt it. The eminence of Mr. Galsworthy in the field of drama is and has been due to the dignity not of his thought, but to the dignity of his emotions. One can name a number of dramatists with minds on a level with Galsworthy's who have not achieved anything like his eminence, for they have not, like him, possessed synchronously the emotions of scholars and gentlemen. The true mark of an artist is to be found not in his head, but in his heart, or at least in what passes for the seat and capital of his emotions. Many a playwright with a clear head has had muddy emotions, and many a playwright with a soundly reasoning mind has found it corrupted, in dramatic practice, by cheap feeling. Galsworthy's emotions are those of a civilized gentleman. The emotions of so many of the younger British playwrights of the day are those of wise and sophisticated, and very clever, bounders. It is, to conclude, therefore a great pity that so worthy an exponent of the modern drama should say good-by to it with so puny and discreditable an example of the art he has dignified and adorned.

Art of the Night, 1928

San Secondo: The Question of Passions

THE CONVENTIONAL criticism of any such play as, for example, Rosso di San Secondo's *Marionette, che Passione!* is that the emotions and perturbations of its characters are too alien either to persuade or interest the Anglo-Saxon spectator. It is a criticism that we hear whenever one of the more intensely amorous dramas of the Latin countries comes our way, and it is a criticism that, for sheer sophistry, one must go a long distance to equal. That the Anglo-Saxon cardiac psychology is somewhat different from that of the Latin needs no arguing, but that this difference makes the Anglo-Saxon unresponsive to plays emphasizing it calls for a great deal. The criticism is merely a convenient cloak under which its expounders conceal their inability to get at the core of the matter.

It is not the passions of the Latin drama that seem unreal and indeed often mutinously humorous to the Anglo-Saxon audience, but the Anglo-Saxon actors who are put forth to affect them. The case is different, as everyone knows, when an Italian or Spanish or French drama of the species under discussion is played in an Anglo-Saxon community by Italians, Spanish, or French actors. One hears no snickers then, save from persons who do not understand the language and to whom the drama accordingly and as a matter of course takes on the air of a somewhat comical moving picture. But when the drama is translated

San Secondo: The Question of Passions

into English and the passions of its Pietros, Gonzalos, and Raouls are put into the mouths and antics of Piccadilly and Broadway actors, they quite naturally strike the spectator not only as alien but as extremely jocose. I am speaking, of course, of the modern drama, for once you put actors into costume and relegate their activities to a past period, an audience is ready to grant anything, bad acting in particular, and to enjoy it. But when you show an English or an American audience a painfully obvious English or American actor in a Hawes and Curtis suit and a sanitary barbershop haircut who is put down in the program as Don Basilio Ramón Gumersindo Contreras and who, after calling upon his ancestor, Solórzano y Pereira Mendoza, to bear witness to the outraged family honor, pulls out a sixteenth-century stiletto and stabs himself through the liver because his sister has married a peon—well, I ask you.

The majority of the kind of plays I am alluding to are produced in just this way. The translations are often good enough, the décor is often sufficiently apposite, and the producer generally goes so far toward verisimilitude as to hire a real Italian or Frenchman to play the part of the waiter in the private supper-room scene, but the actors who are disclosed in the important roles are uniformly by nature, temperament, and physical appearance about as aptly suited to them as a company of Italian, Spanish, or French actors would be to *Is Zat So?* or *Porgy.* The argument here, of course, is that competent English or American actors should be able so to alter their actual personalities as realistically to suggest the nature and deportment of the alien characters entrusted to them, but an argument, however convincing, is one thing and established fact is another. And the established fact, with so few exceptions that they may be dismissed, is that when English or American actors

197

try to make persuasive the passions of D'Annunzio, Guimerá, or Porto-Riche they almost always succeed only in making their audiences laugh. If there is another reason for the failure of an Anglo-Saxon audience to react satisfactorily to the stranger emotions of an alien drama, I am at a loss to account for it. Surely no one would be so foolish as to contend that Anglo-Saxons are as generally unresponsive to so-called alien passions when they are set forth in translated modern novels; the success of any number of such novels in England and America, from those of Anatole France to those of Blasco Ibáñez, is ample proof of the emotional receptivity of Anglo-Saxons when no disconcerting barriers are put in the way. Surely, too, no one would think for a moment of arguing that an Anglo-Saxon audience is unresponsive to the unusual passions of much of the classic drama. And, to go even further, we may convince ourselves that, when it comes to these theoretically alien and unfamiliar emotional disturbances, we have considerable evidence from the daily newspapers—not counting the tabloids—that Italian, Spanish, and French passions are in as full operation on the part, say, of New York and Chicago Americans as they are in their native lands. It is not the alien passions that generate the Anglo-Saxon titters. When an audience sees Mr. Frank Morgan, for example, a man as completely suggestive of Broadway as *Variety*, pretending, without make-up, in the San Secondo opus, that he is a passionate Italian, conducting himself like a libretto by Leoncavallo and drinking a glass of poisoned champagne because his fair one has gone to the Italian equivalent of Atlantic City with a rival, it is readily to be forgiven for echoing the sentiment of a certain illustrious, if deplorably vulgar, predecessor of Kriegsherr Foch.

Art of the Night, 1928

Evreinoff: The Theatre in Life

HE BELIEVES that he has discovered a new instinct, hidden from psychologists until this year of grace—the instinct of transformation, or the instinct of theatricalization." Thus, one of the literary critics in a summation of the latest philosophical crumb of the Russian Evreinoff. That our Slav friend has actually discovered something new, however, is to be believed only by those who are unaware of John Palmer's distillations from the elaboration by Wilde of Shakespeare's meditations upon the same subject. Taking the latter's familiar "All the world's a stage," Wilde pursued the truth further in his equally famous treatise on nature's invariable imitation of art. And taking Wilde's animadversions as a springboard, Palmer splashed around amusingly in the theory that so great was life's imitation of the drama that today when a man found his wife had been unfaithful to him he generally met the situation with a line out of a Pinero play. All that Evreinoff has done is to expand Palmer's idea, originally set forth brilliantly in an essay in the *Saturday Review,* into a book. And as a book, whatever its shortcomings, always makes much more impression than an essay—in the same way that a skyscraper always makes much more impression than a smaller building, however superior architecturally the latter—we find Evreinoff hailed as a profound fellow while Palmer is brushed aside.

Playwrights and Performance

The impulse toward theatricalization has long been as habitual to human beings as their impulse to lie to themselves in most other directions. It begins in childhood with boys playing the roles of Indians, firemen, and policemen, and with little girls "playing house" and mothering doll babies; it continues into adolescence with an imitation in dress and deportment of objects of their admiration; it goes on into the twenties with boys patterning their conduct after celebrated football heroes and movie actors, and girls patterning theirs, in turn, after the heroines of romance; it grows, rather than diminishes, with age's coming and finds men and women offering to the world spurious and somewhat idealized projections of themselves, that the world may be persuaded to accept them for what they actually are not. It is thus that we have the Napoleon complex in countless businessmen, the Valentino complex in innumerable fake cavaliers, the Nietzsche complex in various jitney radicals, the Tunney complex in weaklings—after they have swallowed a couple of cocktails—and the Cleopatra face powder and lip rouge of shopgirls, together with Turkish incense attempting to lend an Oriental air to Harlem flats, clerks dressing up to look like an approximation to the Prince of Wales, bowlegged and knock-kneed women trying to short-skirt themselves into the wallop of a Peggy Joyce, and thousands of Fords equipping themselves with twenty-five-dollar foghorns and hoping to convince startled pedestrians that they are Hispano-Suizas.

The tremendous jump in the trade of interior decoration, with its penchant for converting bedrooms of the Benjamin Harrison period into Du Barry boudoirs and Grand Rapids sitting-rooms into George Alexander drawing-rooms, marks simply the growing tendency to bring the stage into the American home. So, too, does the increase in the use of soft lamps, and the increase of English servants, and the increase in triangular emotional sport. In the way of individuals, it was at times impossible to distinguish William Jennings Bryan from Robert B. Mantell, just as it is at times difficult to distinguish between the Hon. Mr. Dawes and a dress rehearsal for *What Price Glory?* A Mrs. Snyder plays the role of a Paul Armstrong heroine; a governor of the State of New York acts the role of a Paul Bourget hero; a hundred thousand little stenographers droop their mouths like Dolores Costello and drive their bosses to drink making Mae Murray bedroom eyes. Small wonder that theatrical and moving-picture censorship is a grim necessity.

Art of the Night, 1928

Marinetti: Theatricalized Theatre

A FEW YEARS AGO there appeared an article in the Italian periodical *Le Futurisme,* by one Marinetti, of Milan, urging against the present-day theatre the fact that it lacks all bounce and gaiety. Not the stage of the theatre, which now and then discloses something to lift the miserable human psyche into the celestial regions of amusement, but the theatre itself, which seldom discloses anything of the kind. The theatre itself, the writer pointed out, is generally a dark, damp, forbidding house, as unsuggestive, physically, of gaiety as a Milanese scudería. What it needs is something to convert it from its present austere and chilled condition into a place that wears at least a string of bright beads and a few vine leaves in its hair. What it needs, in short, is less of a show on the stage and more of a show in the auditorium, since the theatre of today is actually only one-fourth theatre (that part of it that is the stage) and three-fourths (or the rest of it) cold, hard, uninviting chairs surrounded by bleak walls that make it indistinguishable from an undertaking parlor, minus only the latter's cheerful flowers and stimulating organ.

There are, of course, occasions when the theatre is properly of such an austere mien, say, when fine dramatic art occupies its stage. But for one such occasion there are a hundred when an austere air is no more suited to it than it would be to a hot-dog stand. In the theatre as we engage it in the world today, we find that a particular playhouse often discloses a platform that, in a single season, is held successively by tragedy, comedy, melodrama, pantomine, farce, musical comedy, and what not. There are exceptions, to be sure; there are certain theatres that resolutely dedicate their stages to a specific form of drama; but, in the main, one encounters stages that, as units, are given over indiscriminately to Shakespeare one day and Mephistophelian-looking gentlemen who make bowls of goldfish disappear the next, to problem dramas one week and the next to Hindu gentlemen who can have pins stuck into their epidermises without feeling them, and to *Iphigenia at Aulis* one month and to a colored song-and-dance show the month after. Surely a theatre that houses a farce in which a fat man hides under the bed to avoid the ingenue's irate Uncle Adolph should look and actually be a bit different from a theatre that houses a tragedy in which all the leading characters have inherited lewd spirochaetae and blow their brains out. It caters to people in an entirely different mood; but, though it caters to such people, it fails to cater to that mood. The Comédie-Française or the Deutsches-Theater or the Hampden in New York are all right as they are; their physical atmosphere is appropriate to their stage traffic. But the majority of theatres to the left and right of them in their respective cities and similar theatres in Vienna, Madrid, Rome, London, and Chicago four times out of five no more satisfactorily reflect their proper natures than so many profusely fly-specked mirrors. Thus, today, seeing *John Gabriel Borkman* in a theatre where, only the week before, one has seen a music show is much like asking one to listen to *Vom Tode* in a night club and expecting one to enjoy it.

Discussing specifically the subject of vaudeville theatres, the Italian writer pointed out the complete absurdity of playhouses resembling in every detail dramatic theatres yet offering to their audiences such violently discrepant and utterly discordant things as trained geese, red-nosed comedians in green pants, soft-shoe dancers, and virtuosi of the banjo. Such theatres most assuredly should mirror their stages and should themselves inculcate in their audiences at least a measure of the mood which the platform didos were designed and seek to inculcate. It was the writer's suggestion, for example, that the vaudeville-auditorium chairs should be of the trick variety, that at intervals the ushers should sneak up behind fat, bald-headed men in the audience and tickle their pates with feathers, that as the older and more sedate ladies of the audience entered the door they should have "Please kick me" signs stuck onto their bustles, and that the houses should be sprayed along toward the middle of the performance with some kind of powder that would make everybody sneeze. These may not be exactly our Italian friend's suggestions—my memory is not too accurate on the point—but they hint at the general contour of his recommendations. Exaggerated though they are, they indicate to a degree just what is lacking in the vaudeville dumps and what, by virtue of this lack, is gradually putting the vaudeville business in limbo. Go into any first-class American vaudeville theatre today and you will catch sight of a house full of faces that, whatever the nature of the stage performance, are in the main as long and sour as the faces at a performance of *The Cenci*. It is only along toward 10.15, if the bill is a sufficiently amusing one, that the management succeeds in making the audience melt even partly and give way to its funny bone. The theatre itself has stood in the way in the meantime; it has taken the audience the intervening hours to surmount and conquer the heavy mood which the playhouse has superimposed upon it.

The changes that certain revue and music-show producers have made in their theatres in recent years, together with the devices that have been exercised by various purveyors of other forms of light entertainment, show clearly that our impresarios are beginning to be aware of the truth of the new theatre theory. The runway, installed in revue houses, to bring gaiety from behind the footlights into the midst of the audience; the broad stage aprons whereupon dancers and clowns cavort in close proximity to the customers; the use of the aisles for chorus numbers; the monkeyshines of "plants" in the boxes; the gorillas that run up and down the aisles pursued by a dozen actors dressed as policemen; the distribution of "plants" among the audience to give the latter the feeling of sharing in the stage traffic; such things as illuminated auditorium sidewalls and cages of canaries which Reinhardt put into his Berlin Kammerspiele; such theatres as the Redoutensaal of Vienna; such tricks as smelling up the house with various kinds of perfume, a device of music-show producers to "get over" their flower songs; the use of incense in Oriental plays, the fumes of which spread over the auditorium; the chorus custom of playing ball with the members of the audience and of entering into similar intimate amusement relations with the trade in the seats—all such things are an indication that something has long been lacking in the theatres themselves and that the lack is being gradually appreciated. In due time it will be rectified completely. And the moment it is thus rectified we shall see the dawn of a newly prosperous theatrical day. The French saw the need, in part, years ago, and their music halls, at least, have been coverted into physically relevant and appropriate houses.

But there are theatres other than revue houses that call for a change. A theatre in which a loud, low farce, for instance, is being played should be a theatre that itself has something of the loud, low farce's spirit. As a usual thing, at least in America, however, it no more cultivates the farcical spirit in its sitters than a dentist's chair cultivates the spirit of romance. What is needed on such occasions is a house that imparts a sense of fun the moment one enters it. The ticket-taker should be dressed up as a "What Is It?" and should trip up each patron as he crosses the threshold, the house manager should stand in the lobby and pass out loaded cigars, the ushers should wear sleigh-bells and the programs should be on long rubber bands which would cause them to snap back out of the customers' hands, the backs of the chairs should have trick mirrors on them, the chairs themselves should every once in a while collapse and land their occupants on the floor, the gallery patrons should be supplied with confetti, there should be toy balloons for the butter-and-egg men and their sweet ones, the candy on sale in the rear aisle should be filled with red pepper, the stairs leading to the smoking-room and ladies' parlor should be collapsible, the arms of the chairs should be connected with an electric current which should be turned on at appropriate moments during the course of the evening, and everyone should, upon entering the theatre, be given a colored paper hat, a set of false whiskers, a pair of cardboard ears, a boutonniere that squirts water, a few rotten tomatoes, and a tack to place on his neighbor's seat. And what is true of the farce theatre is true of the melodrama theatre and each of the other relatively unimportant yet presently absurdly dignified and overly serious theatres. Each of these should, in its different way, be treated as treatment has been suggested for the farce lusthaus. For example, the mystery-melodram theatre should have a bizarre and spooky illumination, the ushers should be dressed as ghosts or burglars and should shoot off pistols as they show the patrons to their seats, the lavatory should be entered through a sliding panel, there should be secretly manipulated trapdoors under the seats through which the patrons' hats might periodically be made to disappear from under their chairs and then again to reappear, the box-office attendants should wear black masks, sudden terrifying screams should issue during the entr'actes from the ladies' room, and Mr. William Lyon Phelps should be mysteriously kidnapped by the house manager sometime during the first act.

As I have said, one of these days our managers will wake up to the situation and theatregoing will then become almost as much of a sport and pleasure as bullfighting or lynching. For let these managers remember, if they believe that I am given to deplorable levity, that the auditorium show, in the broadest and best sense of the word, was not above the Greeks in their heyday nor above the playwriting and managerial genius of a fellow named Shakespeare.

Art of the Night, 1928

Noel Coward

ONE IS CONSTANTLY reading and hearing of Mr. Noel Coward's wit. One has been reading and hearing of Mr. Noel Coward's wit for some years, ever since, in point of fact, his first comedy was uncovered to the British and American ear. And one has been reading of it, in the reviewing columns, and hearing of it, by word of audience mouth, threefold since his recent comedy *Design for Living* has been made manifest. This enthusiastically applauded wit, it saddens me to report, I cannot for some reason or other, despite painstaking hospitality, discover. I can discover, with no effort at all, several amusing little wheezes, but all that I am able to engage in the way of the higher jocosity called wit is a suave prestidigitation of what is really nothing more than commonplace vaudeville humor. This vaudeville humor Mr. Coward cleverly brings the less humorously penetrating to accept as wit by removing its baggy pants and red undershirt and dressing it up in drawing-room style. But it remains vaudeville humor just the same. .

I take the liberty to offer, seriatim, a number of examples from this *Design for Living*:

No. 1: GILDA: "You've called me a jaguar and an ox within the last two minutes. I wish you wouldn't be quite so zoological." (In the old small-time vaudeville halls it ran as follows: "So I'm a goat and a jackass, huh? You talk like you was in a zoo!")

No. 2: GILDA: "Don't take off your coat and hat." OTTO: "Very well, darling, I won't, I promise you. As a matter of fact, I said to myself only this morning, 'Otto,' I said, 'Otto, you must never, never be parted from your coat and hat!' " (The old vaudeville dialogue went thus: WOMAN (*sarcastically*) : "You ain't going, are you?" MAN: "No, darling, I ain't. As a matter of fact, I says to myself only this morning, 'Oswald,' I says, 'Oswald, you must never disappoint a lady. When she says "you ain't going," you ain't going!' ")

No. 3: GILDA: "They call the Mauretania 'the Greyhound of the Ocean.' I wonder why?" LEO: "Because it's too long and too thin and leaps up and down." (Chronicle of obvious vaudeville genealogy unnecessary.)

No. 4: (*The telephone rings*) LEO: "Damn!" GILDA: "Oh, Death, where is thy sting-a-ling-a-ling." (One recognizes immediately an old favorite in the Orpheum Circuit sketches.)

No. 5: GILDA: "I never said she wasn't intelligent, and I'm sure she's excellent company. She has to be. It's her job!" (Fanchon and Marco version: "That baby is good company, all right! In fact, she's so good she's incorporated!")

No. 6: LEO (*at telephone*) : ". . . Of course, I'd love to. Black tie or white tie? No tie at all? That'll be much more comfortable!" (Old Keith-Albee version: "I'd like to come, but I ain't got a thing to wear. Come anyway? Fine! That'll be much more comfortable.")

At this point the reader may conceivably imagine that—following the habit of critics who are intent upon proving a point—I have studiously combed the text of the play for a few particularly poor specimens and have deliberately overlooked and shrewdly concealed the more luscious. To dispel any such belief, let us proceed.

No. 7: BIRBECK: "Do you believe the talkies will kill the theatre?" LEO: "No, I think they'll kill the talkies." (Who doesn't recall Tony Pastor's "So the bicycle has hurt the theatre, has it?" "Well, not so much as it's hurt the bicycle rider.")

No. 8: BIRBECK: "What are your ideas on marriage?" LEO: "Garbled." (Old Poli version: "How do you stand on marriage?" "Straddled.")

No. 9: GILDA: "That was Miss Hodge. She's had two husbands." OTTO: "I once met a woman who'd had four husbands." (Too sour even for vaudeville.)

No. 10: OTTO: "Why do you say that?" GILDA: "I don't know. It came up suddenly, like a hiccup." (Vaudeville version: "What did you say?" "I didn't say nothing; that was just a belch.")

No. 11: OTTO: "What delicious-looking ham! Where *did* you get it?" GILDA: "I have it specially sent from Scotland." OTTO: "Why Scotland?" GILDA: "It lives there when it's alive." (I quote from my records of a vaudeville act at the Palace in 1918: MAN: "These are swell frankfurters! Where did you get 'em?" WOMAN: "From Madison Square Garden." MAN: "Why Madison Square Garden?" WOMAN: "That's where they lived when they were alive.")

No. 12: OTTO (*reproachfully*): "I don't paint their faces, Gilda. Fourth dimensional, that's what I am. I paint their souls." GILDA: "You'd have to be eighth dimensional and clairvoyant to find them." (Does one have to search one's vaudeville memory laboriously for "So you painted her soul, did you, you mug? Well, you musta been a detective to find it!")

Still a bit skeptical? Let's go on.

No. 13: GILDA: "I'm always gay on Sundays. There's

something intoxicating about Sunday in London." (Pantages 1899 edition: "I'm always jolly on Sundays. There's something about Philadelphia on Sunday that gets me!")

No. 14: OTTO: "Let's have some more brandy." LEO: "That would be completely idiotic." OTTO: "Let's be completely idiotic!" (Sam, Kitty, and Clara Louise Morton version: "Let's have another drink." "That'd be foolish." "But who wants to be sensible?")

No. 15: LEO (*drinking*) : "Very insipid." OTTO: "Tastes like brown paper." (From the Watson, Bickel, and Wrothe act, A.D. 1897: "This here drink tastes like butcher paper." "I neffer haf tasted butcher paper.")

No. 16: ·GRACE (*shaking hands with Otto and Leo, who are both in evening clothes*) : "Oh—how do you do." LEO: "You must forgive our clothes but we've only just come off a freight boat." (From the Billy Watson Beef Trust show, circa 1907: Low comedian in sleeveless undershirt and tattered pants: "Don't pay no attention to my clothes, lady; I just come off the train from Newport.")

Let us now turn to the inner machinery of Mr. Coward's "wit." This machinery whirrs entirely, we find, around the stalest and most routinized of humorous devices. Device No. 1, a favorite of Mr. Coward's, is a character's repetition in a later act, for comic effect, of a line spoken seriously by another character in the earlier stages of the play. Device No. 2, believe it or not, is the periodic use of the "go to hell" line. Device No. 3 is the serio-comic promulgation of specious sentimental eloquence. I quote an example: "There's something strangely and deeply moving about young love, Mr. and Mrs. Carver. . . . Youth at the helm! . . . Guiding the little fragile barque of happiness down the river of life. Unthinking, unknowing, unaware of the perils that lie in wait for you, the sudden tempests, the sharp, jagged rocks beneath the surface. Are you never afraid?" Device No. 4 is the employment of a word or name possessed of an intrinsically comical sound. For example, Chuquicamata. And Device No. 5 is—also believe it or not—the causing of a character, who in a high pitch of indignation sweeps out of the room, to fall over something. (Sample stage direction: *"He stamps out of the room, quite beside himself with fury: on his way into the hall he falls over the package of canvases."* Whereat the characters on the stage *"break down utterly and roar with laughter."*)

Now for the original and profound philosophy underlying Mr. Coward's great wit. I exhibit samples:

No. 1: GILDA: "Why don't I marry Otto?" ERNEST: "Yes. Is there a real reason, or just a lot of faintly affected theories?" GILDA: "There's a very real reason." ERNEST: "Well?" GILDA: "I love him."

No. 2: LEO: "I'm far too much of an artist to be taken in by the old cliché of shutting out the world and living for my art alone. There's just as much bunk in that as there is in a cocktail party at the Ritz."

No. 3: LEO: "I'm dreadfully suspicious of people liking things too much—things that matter, I mean. There's too much enthusiasm for Art going on nowadays. It smears out the high-lights."

No. 4: GILDA: "Do you know a lot about ships now?" OTTO: "Not a thing. The whole business still puzzles me dreadfully. I know about starboard and port, of course, and all the different bells; but no one has yet been able to explain to me satisfactorily why, the first moment a rough sea occurs, the whole thing doesn't turn upside down!"

No. 5: GILDA: "I think I want to cry again." OTTO: "There's nothing like a good cry."

No. 6: OTTO: "Have I changed so dreadfully?" GILDA: "It isn't you that's changed—it's time and experience and new circumstances!"

No. 7: Gilda and Otto have been discussing what Mr. Coward alludes to as "love among the artists." OTTO: "But we should have principles to hang on to, you know. This floating about without principles is so very dangerous." GILDA: "Life is for living!"

No. 8: LEO: "Science is our only hope, the only hope for humanity! We've wallowed in false mysticism for centuries; we've fought and suffered and died for foolish beliefs, which science has proved to be as ephemeral as smoke. Now is the moment to open our eyes fearlessly and look at the truth!"

No. 9: GILDA: "The human race is a let-down, a bad, bad let-down! I'm disgusted with it. It thinks it's progressed but it hasn't; it thinks it's risen above the primeval slime but it hasn't—it's still wallowing in it! It's still clinging to us, clinging to our hair and our eyes and our souls. We've invented a few small things that make noises, but we haven't invented one big thing that creates quiet, endless peaceful quiet . . . something to deaden the sound of our emotional yellings and screechings and suffocate our psychological confusions." (Ah there, Shaw, Priestley, and Co.!)

We now pass to a consideration of the freshness of Mr. Coward's broader humors. Herewith, specimens:

No. 1: LEO: "I remember a friend of mine called Mrs. Purdy being very upset once when her house in Dorset fell into the sea." GRACE: "How terrible!" LEO: "Fortunately, Mr. Purdy happened to be in it at the time."

No. 2: GILDA: "It's very hot today, isn't it?" ERNEST: "Why not open the window?" GILDA: "I never thought of it."

No. 3: GILDA: "We must get it straight, somehow." LEO: "Yes, we must get it straight and tie it up with ribbons with a bow on the top. Pity it isn't Valentine's Day!"

No. 4: LEO: "Doesn't the Eye of Heaven mean anything to you?" GILDA: "Only when it winks!"

No. 5: GILDA: "Think if television came in suddenly, and everyone who rang up was faced with Miss Hodge!" (*Miss Hodge enters. She is dusty and extremely untidy.*)

No. 6: OTTO (*at telephone*) : "Dinner on the seventh? Yes, I should love to. You don't mind if I come as Marie Antoinette, do you? (*Pause*) I have to go to a fancy dress ball."

Mr. Coward's "daring sophistication" is still another enchantment of his public and his critics. Let us, in turn, consider this daring sophistication in the light of its most trenchant specimen lines:

No. 1: GILDA: "After all, it [the London *Times*] is the organ of the nation." LEO: "That sounds vaguely pornographic to me." (Regards to Mae West.)

No. 2: GILDA: "The honeymoon would be thrilling, wouldn't it? Just you and me, alone, finding out about each other." LEO: "I'd be very gentle with you, very tender." GILDA: "You'd get a sock in the jaw, if you were!" (Regards to Michael Arlen.)

No. 3: GILDA: "Tell me, Mr. Mercuré, what do you think of the modern girl?" LEO: "A silly bitch." (Regards to Elmer Harris.)

No. 4: OTTO: "Are you trying to lure me to your wanton bed?" GILDA: "What would you do if I did?" OTTO: "Probably enjoy it very much." (Regards to Valeska Suratt, Paul Potter, and *The Girl with the Whooping Cough*, A.D. 1908.)

In order to deceive his audiences and critics into believing that all this vaudeville-hall humor and juvenile naugh-

tiness is excessively recherché stuff, it is Mr. Coward's practice, as I have hinted, to have it spoken by actors in evening
dress and to intersperse it liberally with worldly allusions
to the more fashionable restaurants, hotels, yachts, duch-
esses' houses, and watering places. When Mr. Coward is
not alluding condescendingly to something like the Duke
of Westminster's yacht, one may be sure that he is either
alluding affectionately to the Carlton Hotel or commenting somewhat superciliously on the marble bathrooms at
the George V. His plays are also usually rich in references
to the bigger ocean liners, modern French painters, various
opera composers, the better sherries and brandies, Clar-
idge's, fashionable London churches, valets—always "in
white coats"—butlers, footmen, upper housemaids, secre-
taries, the Ritz, smart house parties in Hampshire, back-
gammon, squash courts, terraces "with striped awnings,"
some casino or other, and the more expensive makes of
automobiles. And, naturally, to emphasize the magnificent
modishness of it all, Mr. Coward is careful to derogate at
due intervals such bourgeois institutions as world cruises,
newspapers, households that can afford but one maid, and
the music of Richard Wagner.

In order to establish beyond all audience doubt the perfect equilibrium of his sophistication and to persuade it
that he is superior even to his own highest flights of philosophical reasoning, it is Mr. Coward's habit to disgorge the
philosophical pearls reposing in his mind and then to
bring another character to offer a facetious remark about,
or to chuckle derisively over, each of the aforesaid pearls.
Either that or, by way of passing himself off for a mag-
nanimous intellect, to place his most serious convictions in
the mouth of a character who is slightly intoxicated. Thus,
let one character speak Mr. Coward's mind about some
cynical aspect of civilization, and another like clockwork

Noel Coward

is ready with some such retort as "That is definitely macabre!" Thus, let a character express a sentiment of some delicacy and another is ready with a deprecation of him as a rank sentimentalist. Thus, let the action turn to normal drama and a character is ready with the mocking exclamation: "Bravo, Deathless Drama!" Thus, let Mr. Coward venture what he considers in his heart to be a first-rate and saucy bit of humor and another character is ready with "That was a cheap gibe!" And thus, let a character express Mr. Coward's sober convictions as to Life and another is in the offing duly to jump in at the conclusion with a facetious "Laife, that's what it is, just laife." And so it goes —always the pseudo-philosopher and commentator taking what he writes with perfect gravity and surrounding himself, fearful and feeling the need of ideational protection, with a procession of minstrel end-men to hop up after each observation and minimize it with a joke.

Mr. Coward occupies the successful place in our theatre today that the late Clyde Fitch occupied twenty and thirty years ago. Both are of a playwriting piece, though Mr. Coward has not yet contrived anything nearly as good as Fitch's *The Truth*. And both have been overpraised and overestimated ridiculously. Where are the plays of Fitch now? Where will the plays of Mr. Coward be when as many years have passed? As in the case of my critical reflections on Fitch in his fashionable heyday, I leave the answer to the calendar.

As to *Design for Living* specifically—it has been greeted by the reviewers as something very remarkable—I can see in it little more than a pansy paraphrase of *Candida*, theatrically sensationalized with "daring," gay allusions to hermaphrodites, "gipsy queens," men dressed as women, etc., and with various due references to "predatory feminine carcasses" and to women as bitches. The big scene is simply a rehash of the one played by the two drunken women in the same author's *Fallen Angels* and here given, relevantly, into the hands of two men.

Passing Judgments, 1935

Saroyan

Is SAROYAN CRAZY? That is the question which for some time now has been occupying the nation. There are two opinions. The advocates of one maintain that Saroyan undoubtedly is. The advocates of the other indignantly deny any such thing and maintain that he is only half crazy. Both argue their convictions with what they believe to be equally convincing proofs. And, illogical as it may seem, both present much the same evidence.

Exhibit A is their Specimen's unremitting proclamation, usually accompanied by a loud pounding on the table and a kiss handsomely bestowed upon the nearest waiter, that he is a genius. Even some of the critics who admire his writings enormously assert that this is an unmistakable sign of the fellow's insanity. No man who is really a genius, they say, goes around telling people he is. It's not polite.

Exhibit B is their Specimen's oft-printed remark that the main difference between himself and Shakespeare is that Shakespeare wasn't an Armenian. Bernard Shaw years ago said that the main difference between himself and Shakespeare was that he knew how to write much better plays than Shakespeare. And, argue the alienists, every-body knows that Shaw is crazy.

Exhibit C is their Specimen's various published state-ments of his Credo. "The American theatre has been wait-ing for me, me Saroyan; no one else in it knows how to write plays. I am happy and proud to come to its res-cue." . . . . "I have just gotten up and have had no coffee. So I want to explain everything in six or seven words. The world is *the* theatre. The other theatre—the one which charges admission—is *not* the world. Therefore, the the-atre does not exist. Only the world exists. Therefore, there is no point in going to the theatre. There is no art in the world, therefore; or in the theatre; or in people; or in nature." . . . "I learned by the end of seven days that to enter a saloon and belong you had to be completely aloof. I got the idea from alley cats, whom I had watched carefully."

Further items under Exhibit C: "By the time I was nine and in the third grade I was well along in the art of satire, parody, subtle contempt for ignorance and pomposity, and kindly recognition of virtue and charm." . . . "I read *Lady Windemere's* [sic] *Fan* when I was fourteen and the same day wrote a very good play in imitation of that worldly and brilliant style." . . . "What I mean is, it's a cinch *something* is delighted by the delightful, saddened by the sad, and so on." . . . "I have especially liked the *bad* bad play, the unmitigated lousy play, with superbly lousy characters. I have liked this kind of play more than the finest fine play." . . . "To hell with the gag. What is truth? Everybody knows what it is." . . . "How to make a movie for $300? Frankly, I don't think it can be done."

Still further items under Exhibit C: "Mr. Medford be-came my movie agent before I had a chance to drop my hat and asked me if I had a story on the new type of locomotives and Pullman cars the Union Pacific was introducing. It so happened that I had just such a story. It was a love story." . . . "Light a match and you see beauty so amazing it is almost unbelievable, and you know there is nothing like it even in art any more: in music sometimes there used to be, but no more. Now we have jit, which is O.K., but strictly a gadget, too." . . . "The kicking and turning of Follies girls should by now be in decline as *the* American rhythm, the tempo and calculation of American life. It's all right, but it doesn't get anywhere." . . . "The writing of plays is an art. Eating a herring is, too. Let's not be dull about anything. Everything can and should be an art."

Exhibit D is their Specimen's complete disregard for plot in the plays he writes. Take *The Time of Your Life,* for example. It may be a fine play, they say, but it has no plot. Why? Take *My Heart's in the Highlands,* for another example. It may be a beautiful play, they say, but where's the plot, the meaning? Take *Love's Old Sweet Song.* Take *The Beautiful People.* Same thing!

Exhibit E is their Specimen's assertion that it takes him only a few days to write a play. And as for a musical show, why, he wrote all the sketches for a projected Minelli one in an afternoon. And as for the ballet—there is nothing he will not tackle—well, he wrote *The Great American Goof* in exactly thirty-three minutes, including the time he lit half a dozen cigarettes, ate two frankfurters, and read the sports pages in the *World-Telegram.*

Exhibit F is their Specimen's program note to the aforementioned ballet: "The dancers in a ballet ought not to be mistaken for people . . . Even so, in writing this ballet, I was not able to forget that the living inhabit the world. This happened no doubt because I don't know the first thing about ballet . . . As I see it, the living prob-

ably deserve nothing better than they get, although this
irritates me personally. It irritates me because nobody
other than myself seems to understand that the world is
not real. That in reality there is no such thing. What I
myself do is ignore the world, keeping a clear eye on it all
the time, of course. In everything I have ever written, from
psalm to saga, I have mentioned the world only because it
gets in my way. What I say is, What world? What this
ballet says is that you need six or seven thousand years to
get this place out of the idiot nightmare it's in now. By
the way, for all we know, there may be a place in which it
will be posible for the living really to live, instead of having all this Shakespearean fun they're having all the time.
In addition to this balletplay, I have written another. It
is called *The Poetic Situation in America Since Alexandre
Dumas*. It may or may not be accompanied by music and
choreography some day. Even so, it is something that can
be read for itself. I plan to continue writing for this form.
As *I* write it, it is a new American form."

So much for the evidence provided by those who think
that Saroyan is crazy and by those more charitable and
humanitarian persons who think he is only half crazy.
Now for those of somewhat broader vision who think he
is only one-third crazy.

Those who give him two thirds of the benefit of the
doubt offer in his defense the following evidence:

EXHIBIT A: If Saroyan frequently publishes philosophies that give pause to the judicious and hint that he is
a bit bughouse, consider these fulminations from other
loons:

1. "Not to go to the theatre is like making one's toilet
without a mirror." Schopenhauer is the particular hazel-
nut responsible for that one.

2. "If a second- or third-rate play is performed by sec-

ond- or third-rate actors, no one can wonder if it is utterly ineffective." Goethe is the papiya who pulled that hot one.

3. "The word tragedy is derived from the Greek word which means goat and the Greek word which means song. Tragedy is then, as it were, a goatish song—that is, foul like a goat." That one is the cerebration of the screwball Dante.

4. "The reason is perspicuous why no French plays, when translated, have succeeded or ever can succeed on the English stage." The sage in the strait jacket who negotiated that one is Dryden.

5. "Good music is a remedy against tediousness." And that one is the profound, original, and novel philosophy of the loco Napoleon Bonaparte.

EXHIBIT B: If Saroyan is entirely crazy, so, admittedly, was Strindberg, yet Strindberg is regarded as the greatest dramatist of his day. If Saroyan writes plotless and meaningless plays, so at times did Strindberg, and the critics have long esteemed them as classics. Perhaps, therefore, observing the plotty and meaningful plays so many presumably sane, if stupid, writers are producing, and further observing the plays regularly denounced by the critics, Saroyan isn't so crazy after all and is sagaciously and deliberately strindberging himself and writing the kind of plays the scholars and critics in secret honestly admire.

EXHIBIT C: The breakneck speed at which Saroyan boastingly writes his plays, etc. Lope de Vega and Goldoni among others—and they weren't especially hypped—often beat him at it.

EXHIBIT D: Is the personal proclamation that one is a genius always and inevitably proof that one is not only crazy but a negligible writer? If so, Shaw is not only crazy but a negligible writer. And what of Nietzsche? And of Swift? And of Jean-Jacques Rousseau? Of course, there are always Ezra Pound and Maxwell Bodenheim, but we'll skip them.

EXHIBIT E: If Saroyan's program notes on his ballet, because of his bumptiously confessed ignorance of the ballet, sound foolish, consider these in the same program by Alexandre Benois, who was responsible for the world-famous Diaghilev *Les Sylphides*: "High noiseless flights, full of tender, slightly devitalized grace, give a definite impression, and this in spite of the lack of any story, of a strange, phantasmal romance, a hopeless infatuation of disembodied beings, who know neither fiery embraces nor sweet kisses, and for whom all that is bacchic or passionate has been replaced by a sad tenderness, by the merest fluttering suspicion of physical contact."

Is that so very much clearer than loony Saroyan's "The world which everyone other than myself seems to have identified and accepted as the world is in reality a figment in a nightmare of an idiot. No one could possibly create anything more surrealistic and unbelievable than the world which everyone believes is real and is trying very hard to inhabit. The story of my ballet is on this theme. The figure of the attractive but unkind woman is not a symbol of beautiful women in the world. What she really is is the bright potential in all things which in the world is never visible to men. She takes on the architecture of the beautiful female body in the ballet because that is the easiest way out, and no harm to anybody. And because if there is to be a misunderstanding, it isn't likely to be the worst in the world, inasmuch as, for those who choose, she *could* be simply a magnificent wench who cannot be taken by rape, acrobatics, or gentle words."

So much, in turn, for the testimony introduced by those who believe that Saroyan is still a few steps this side of the asylum. And now, again in turn, for those who do not consider him at all cracked, among whom I number myself, which probably proves that I, too, am cracked.

Let us admit right off that Saroyan is peculiar. So am I, very. So, for that matter, in all probability, are you. If perchance you are not, you are just another human nonentity and may as well go on being an insurance salesman, bookkeeper, or society portrait-painter for the rest of your life.

Saroyan's peculiarity in insisting that he is a genius, for example, is peculiar only in that he does his insisting publicly. Most of the rest of us writers do it in private. We tell ourselves we are geniuses, and he tells us he is. That is the only difference. Well, is he, though, a genius? No. But he has a fine and original talent, and it is only natural, relative youth that he is, that he should grandly mistake it for genius. When I was very young—around ten, I think—and wrote a kid school piece that was posted by my teacher on the school bulletin board as a commendable instance of belles lettres, I was sure that I was a genius and lorded it about for a whole week. Even my parents were rather persuaded that I was on the way to becoming a second Walter Pater, which numerical status convinced me they weren't so very perceptive and still had a great deal to learn about the relative eminence of literary masterpieces. If Saroyan thinks he is a genius, let him think it. He will either get over it in time or prove to us that he is right. Meanwhile, such a belief in himself is a good thing; it will drive him into a higher resolve.

Saroyan's complete freedom from the customary inhibitions surrounding the punctilio are further mistaken for a loose screw, especially by those given to a strict adherence to the accepted social procedures. If, for example, a critic denounces one of his plays, he will not only write a voluminous letter to the critic pointing out the excellent, aye, the really remarkable, qualities in it that the critic overlooked, but will insist that the fellow view the play again in his company in order that he, Saroyan, may explain to the fog-head what the latter could not discern for himself. I can't see any particular harm in this, save that it is a waste of precious time on Saroyan's part, inasmuch as if the critic does not recognize a good play when he sees one he is a dolt not worth bothering with, and if, on the other hand, he recognizes a bad play for the bad play it is, he is not going to bother with Saroyan anyway.

Saroyan's gasconade in print may not be in the best of tact and taste, but tact and taste have nothing to do with mens sana. J. B. Priestley is often just as boastful and tactless and tasteless as Saroyan, and, while he is nowhere the latter's equal as a playwright, he is certainly otherwise very far from identity with the Cuculus canorus. If Saroyan's manifestoes are at times silly, which they are, they reflect not upon his sanity but solely upon his momentary intelligence and lack of experience. Yet even at his silliest I doubt if Saroyan has been any sillier than such nationally accepted philosophers as Dale Carnegie or such internationally accepted ones as Frank Buchman. The trouble with Saroyan is simply that when he expresses a thought, whether intelligent or unintelligent, he is firmly convinced that he is the first man to be on deck with it, like a youngster who with his first girl discovers the only true meaning of love. No harm in that either. We have all gone through that phase and we all, with increased wisdom and experience, grow out of it. Well, maybe not quite all—I can name at least two gross of writers of maturer years who still believe that their platitudes are new tablets from Jehovah.

If Saroyan, it is argued, were completely balanced he would write plays that could more readily be understood.

Playwrights and Performance

Dismissing the excessive and unnecessary point that bean-brains are still trying to understand certain of the plays of Ibsen, Pirandello, and other such crackpots, it remains that Saroyan's produced plays to date are so easy and simple of comprehension that they are veritable A B C. Their very absence of so-called plot only makes them easier of that comprehension. Plot is sometimes confounding rather than clarifying, as witness such recent instances as Elmer Rice's *American Landscape*, Dostoevsky's *The Possessed*, Lonsdale's *Foreigners*, Harold Igo's *Steel*, Paul Vincent Carroll's *Kindred*, Gustav Eckstein's *Christmas Eve*, and Syd Porcelain's memorable barbouillage, *Alternate Current*. Plays like *My Heart's in the Highlands*, *The Time of Your Life*, and *The Beautiful People* are purely dramatizations of emotion, and as such are essentially much more readily assimilated than emotion dramatized in terms of thought —or, more usually, what passes for thought. Relevantly, they are drama in terms of human music, and music doesn't have to be understood to be felt and appreciated, save by pundits, senescent critics, and intellectual posturers.

But even to the determined ratiocinator it must occur that Saroyan's plays, superficially aberrant though they are, present less difficulty to intelligent understanding than any number of presumably more clearly defined plays. Surely in none of Saroyan's plays—and that includes *Love's Old Sweet Song*, which, incidentally, has all the plot the dullest dope may cry for—surely in none of his plays is there any such thematic muddledness and obscurity as is to be found in Maxwell Anderson's *Key Largo*, with its meditative, war-tortured, cosmically agitated, and cowardly protagonist finding hearty resolution in the challenge of a petty Coney Island roulette-wheel faker transplanted to a Florida tourist dump. Or in the aforementioned exhibit by Elmer Rice wherein the ghost of Moll Flanders, of all people, comes to Connecticut and persuades an American not to sell a plot of ground to the Nazis. Or, to shorten what might be a long catalogue, in some such play as Carroll's aforementioned *Kindred*, which contends that the world should be run by artists and then offers as its representative of these heavenly creative spirits and potential world managers a cadging violinist who plays nothing but jalopyan tunes on his fiddle, who sponges on decent tradesfolk, and who is the epitome of bounderism in every respect.

Saroyan is regarded as shatterpated because he has gone in for writing a ballet without knowing anything about ballet. Well, he went in for writing a play without knowing anything about playwriting and in *My Heart's in the Highlands* wrote the best play of its year. His ballet, true enough, is pretty dreadful; it is, despite his conviction that it is tasty stuff, nothing but an old hokum modernized morality play, the kind that Henry W. Savage and Morris Gest used to sicken the critics with, with Doubt relabeled American Goof, Temptation called The Bright Potential, Ignorance dubbed Old Man in Prison, and Tradition relabeled The Dummy. Having the dancers speak a few words now and again may be a novelty—Saroyan proudly announces that it is a "new form"—but, while it may be a novelty and a new form in the sense that serving flat beer in a cupped phonograph record is a novelty in the case of the beer and a new form in the case of the phonograph record, it is at once gratuitous, irrelevant, and impracticable. A ballet should no more be spoken than a play should be danced. The mood established by choreography is dissipated by speech. In addition, as the presentation of this talk-ballet fully demonstrates, it is as quixotic to expect ballet dancers to be proficient in the reading of dramatic

lines as it would be to expect Lunt and Fontanne satisfactorily to comport themselves in Mordkin's *Voices of
Spring* or, for that matter, in even Cole Porter's "Begin
the Beguine."

It isn't that Saroyan wrote a ballet that counts against
him. It is merely that he wrote a bad one. But so also, for
that matter, did the great Marius Petipa, the founder of
the Russian ballet; he composed not one bad one, but at
least thirty-five out of a total of sixty.

And so we give over the great Saroyan case to the jury.
But before the jury leaves the room to retire to its five
minutes of reflection and six hours of portentous time-
killing pinochle at the expense of the taxpayers, I wish to
say a few words on all four sides of the question.

On behalf of those who think the defendant is crazy,
I wish to quote, with the defendant's suspiciously ready
and even eager full permission, a program note to another
play he has written and which still awaits production. The
title of the play is *Sweeney in the Trees*, and here is the
note: "This is a play, a dream, a song, a poem, a travesty,
a fable, a symphony, a parable, a comedy, a tragedy, a
farce, a vaudeville, a song and dance, a statement on
money, a report on life, an essay on art and religion, a
theatrical entertainment, a circus, anything you like, or
whatever you please." Yes, sir, that's the note! What is
more, on behalf of these same persons who think the defendant is crazy, I wish further to quote, similarly with the
defendant's suspiciously ready and even eager full permission, a program note to yet still another play he has since
written and which also awaits production. The title of the
play is *Jim Dandy*, and here is the note: "This play is for
babies, the enwombed and the long since unenwombed,
the now full-sensed and perishing who constitute the present immortality of living things. It contains no characters,

no imitations of people, and no plot. . . ." Yes, sir, that's
the note! Furthermore, the scene is described as "A portion of what we choose to call the fiction room of the
Public Library in San Francisco but is actually no such
thing." (Further still, the play suddenly concludes in
nubibus with the line: "The writer got bored, so the play
ends.") Yes, sir, that's the general idea!

On behalf of those who think the defendant is only
half crazy, I wish to point out that that happens to be exactly what the first play really is and what the second
honestly at least partly is.

On behalf of those who think the defendant is only
one-third touched, I wish to hint that there is some very
good stuff in both plays.

And on behalf of those who think he isn't crazy at all,
I wish to say that if he only will work on the scripts a little
longer and with more patience and will give them just a
little more organization and direction, he will have produced two other highly imaginative and deserving contributions to the American drama, and two which will
doubtless make the fish who now consider him crazy believe that he is crazier than ever.

In conclusion, a few words on behalf of myself. In this
William Saroyan, crazy or not crazy, the national theatre,
I believe, has discovered its most genuinely gifted new
writer. His plays singly and in combination have disclosed
and further argue a talent which, as yet undisciplined,
vainglorious, cockeyed, and pigheaded, is nevertheless the
liveliest and most bouncing that has come the way of the
local stage in some equinoxes. In that talent, which still
resembles a fountain contending against a strong head-
wind and helplessly splashing itself all over the place, we
engage a whimsical imagination, a lenitive sentiment, a
fertile humor, and a human wonder and ache uncommon

to our drama and which in sum make his plays, whatever their occasional critical subordinacies, such welcome additions to the file of American playwriting.

He is a peculiar mixture, this young Saroyan, one of the most peculiar it has been my adventure to experience among writers for the lighted platform. Although as unabashedly sentimental at heart as the inside of an old-fashioned lace valentine, he has the dramatic gift of making his emotional syrups not only palatable to the most realistically minded auditor but immensely moving. Although his dramaturgy is sometimes as sketchy as a child's drawing of Santa Claus or a moo-moo, he not only gets the effect more usually contrived by the more precise artisan but here and there achieves it with a doubled power. And although he seems superficially to sustain his characters, orchid-like, on the thinnest of thin air, they come to us at the end rounded, whole, and completely intelligible. He writes much too hurriedly and impatiently, a symptom of his brash overconfidence. And his plays, accordingly, are not fully what care and meditation might make them. But I, for one, would rather have them in all their relative crudity than any ten dozen others sedulously polished, like old pairs of cheap shoes, into a surface acceptability.

The Entertainment of a Nation, 1942

O'Neill: I

WHENEVER, as in the case of such of his plays as *Welded* and *The First Man*, Eugene O'Neill tries on the whiskers of Strindberg, the results are singularly unfortunate. Following the technique of Strindberg, O'Neill sets himself so to intensify and even hyperbolize a theme as to evoke the dramatic effect from its overtones rather than, as in the more general manner, from its undertones. His attempt, in a word, is to duplicate the technique of such a drama as *The Father*, the power of which is derived not by suggestion and implication but from the sparks that fly upward from a prodigious and deafening pounding on the anvil. The attempt, as I have said, is a failure, for all one gets in O'Neill's case is the prodigious and deafening pounding. The sparks simply will not come out. Now and again one discerns something that looks vaguely like a spark, but on closer inspection it turns out to be only an imitation lightning-bug that has been cunningly concealed in the actors' sleeves. O'Neill, in such instances, always goes aground on the rocks of exaggeration and overemphasis. His philosophical melodrama is so full of psychological revolver shots, jumps off the Brooklyn Bridge, incendiary Chinamen, galloping hose carts, forest fires, wild locomotives, sawmills, dynamite kegs, time fuses, mechanical infernal machines, battles under the sea, mine explosions, Italian blackhanders, last-minute pardons, sinking lines, and fights to the death on rafts that the effect is akin to trying to read a treatise on the theme on a bump-the-bumps. He rolls up his sleeves and piles on the agony with the assiduity of a coal-heaver. He misjudges, it seems to me completely, the Strindberg method. That method is the intensification of a theme from within. O'Neill intensifies his theme from without. He piles psychological and physical situation on situation until the structure topples over with a burlesque clatter. Strindberg magnified the psyche of his characters. O'Neill magnifies their actions.

Materia Critica, 1924

O'Neill: II

AND HAD YOU chosen Eugene O'Neill, who has done nothing much in the American drama save to transform it utterly in ten or twelve years from a false world of neat and competent trickery into a world of splendor, fear and greatness, you would have been reminded that he had done something far worse than scoffing, that he had seen life as something not to be neatly arranged in a study, but as terrifying, magnificent and often quite horrible, a thing akin to a tornado, an earthquake or a devastating fire."— *Sinclair Lewis, in his Nobel Prize address to the Swedish Academy.*

Among the items in Mr. Lewis's disquisition which

came in for waspish comment, both printed and oral, at the hands of American writers who didn't get the prize and who were consequently displeased with the intelligence of the Swedish Academy, this presented itself as perhaps the most riddled target. Facetiousness over both Mr. Lewis's rich encomium and the measure in which O'Neill had justified it, or rather not justified it, laboriously insinuated itself into at least one half the clippings patiently scissored by the indefatigable Dr. Romeike. There was derision for Mr. Lewis's "world of splendor, fear and greatness," and for O'Neill's tornadoes, earthquakes, and devastating fires. There was a mocking of Mr. Lewis's faith in the transformation of American drama, and of O'Neill's share in that transformation. There were amused hisses and boos and catcalls, and not a few senile eggs and pre-Raphaelite tomatoes. In the midst of the ironic din, a critic of the drama may have been privileged to retire for a moment to the peace of his chambers, there to determine what sense there was to the business.

After about a quarter of a minute's prolonged and studious meditation, the critic came to the conclusion that, despite the pardonable smiles induced by Mr. Lewis's conviction that the American drama had been transformed utterly in ten or twelve years from a false world of neat and competent trickery into a world of splendor, fear, and greatness, there nevertheless was a very fair relative degree of truth in his statement, and that certainly if anyone was responsible for any sort of transformation in the American drama, O'Neill was that person. The American drama may still be very far from what one might desire it to be; but that in the last decade it has got much nearer to that desideratum than ever it got before must be obvious to anyone not wholly blind or British. It would be pleasant to believe that this great change for the better had been of slow, steady, and relentless growth, that it had come as a result of gradually seeping revolution, and that O'Neill was simply the man who had grabbed the flag from the hands of the forces that step by step had paved the way for him and had then accompanied him shoulder to shoulder on the valiant march. But, pleasant though it would be, it would not be true. For the truth of the matter is just what Mr. Lewis announced it to be to the Swedes, to wit, that O'Neill alone and single-handed waded through the dismal swamplands of American drama, bleak, squashy, and oozing sticky goo, and alone and single-handed bore out of them the water lily that no American had found there before him.

I do not argue, in my somewhat dubiously poetic metaphor, that O'Neill, since first he invaded the swamp, has always come out of it bearing the gift of a water lily. There have been times, as in the case of *Welded* and *Dynamo*, when what he has brought to shore has resembled rather more closely a cauliflower. But I do argue with Mr. Lewis that to O'Neill alone must go the credit for transforming the American drama, if not quite entirely into a world of splendor, fear, and greatness, at least into a world at length wholesomely free from fear and, thus freed, possibly on the way to splendor and greatness. When O'Neill came upon the playwriting scene, the American drama—even at its least hypocritical, at its least sentimental, and at its bravest—had still the air of a female impersonator removing his wig and implying his perfect masculinity in a movement of his jaws on an imaginary hunk of chewing tobacco. Such antecedents of O'Neill as Augustus Thomas ("dean of American playwrights") with his interpretation of life in terms of osteopathy and thought transference, as Charles Klein with his stenographers outwitting actors in the roles of Rockefellers and Morgans, as George Broadhurst with his boy politicians putting an end to municipal corruption by the exercise of what are today known as wisecracks, as Eugene Walter with his Rector's restaurant tragedies, and as William Hurlbut with his studies of New York in terms of the violation of an ingenue's virtue and with his Ibsen distillations like *The Writing on the Wall*—such antecedents surely left no inspirational legacy to O'Neill. Life, as he saw and wrote of it when first he began to take pen in hand, may not always have been akin to a tornado, an earthquake, or a devastating fire, but at least it was never akin to a Belasco conservatory, a Liebler drawing-room, or a Broadway supper café.

With O'Neill's acceptance and success in the theatre, American playwrights suddenly took courage and proceeded, as best as in their fashion they could, to set themselves to a species of drama far removed from that to which they had been devoting their efforts. The newer and younger writers, led by O'Neill, threw off the shackles at once and tried to write honestly, faithfully, and truthfully; the older ones—men like Owen Davis—at least temporarily abandoned the further confection of mush dishes and tried to follow the changing taste with imitations, very pathetic, of the O'Neill drama. Even criticism, long tied to the apron strings of sentimentality, moral cowardice, and dramatic falsehood, began slowly to get onto its own legs, to wag its tail independently, and to bark loudly and defiantly in behalf of the new order. And audiences, growing steadily in receptivity and intelligence, joined in the barking.

The result is apparent. Where once—and not so long ago, as the clock ticks—the American stage, even in its then most reputable aspect, was occupied by such stuff as *The Witching Hour, Paid in Full, As a Man Thinks,* and *The Man of the Hour,* it has in the last ten years gained respectability with plays like *The Great God Brown, Strange Interlude, Craig's Wife, A Texas Nightingale, Street Scene, Chicago, Desire under the Elms, Another Language, What Price Glory?, Saturday's Children, The Hairy Ape, The First Year, Ambush, Rain, Sun-Up, The Green Pastures, Veneer, The Front Page, The Left Bank, Brief Moment, The Vinegar Tree,* and numerous others. Sinclair Lewis may have been guilty of second-degree hyperbole, but down under it he knew pretty well what he was talking about. . . .

It must not be imagined, however, that one sees O'Neill as a compendium of all the virtues, a fellow purged of all sin, his head encircled with a critical halo and his nose magnificent with a brass ring. He has his faults, as he has, more richly, his virtues. Of both, though of the latter more especially, *Mourning Becomes Electra* is an illuminating mirror. It once again discloses its author as the most imaginatively courageous, the most independently exploratory, and the most ambitious and resourceful dramatist in the present-day Anglo-American theatre. It once again gives evidence of his contempt for the theatre that surrounds him and of his conversion of that contempt into drama that makes most other contemporaneous drama look puny in comparison. It dismisses the little emotions of little people in favor of emotions as deep, as profound, and as ageless as time. It opens the windows of the stage, so habitually shut against the world of pity and comprehension and terror, to that world again. But so heroic is its intention, its sweep and its size, that its characters, like the characters in certain other plays by the same author, are themselves not always up to the sweep and size of their author's emotional equipment and emotional dynamics. In other words, it sometimes paradoxically happens that it is O'Neill, the dramatist as man, rather than his characters and quite apart from them, who agitates and moves an audience. In other words still, the characters that O'Neill creates are at times the after-images rather than the direct images and funnels of his torrential and unbounded emotional imagination. They are periodically too inconsiderable to contain him. They sometimes give one the impression that the load he has placed on their shoulders is too heavy for them to carry. They present themselves occasionally in the light of characters valiant, faithful, and obedient, yet not equal to the demands their creator has made of them. Thus, though *Mourning Becomes Electra* is indubitably one of the finest plays that the American theatre has known, its Greek emotions now and again embarrass the American characters into which the author, loosing the floodgates of his copious emotional fancy, has projected them.

In the modern drama to which we are accustomed, the emotions of the characters are often more trivial than those of the members of the audience. It is a rare play nowadays that imposes anything more than the most superficial of emotional demands upon an audience. For it must be remembered that the theatre audience of today is a different audience from that of other years. It is, in considerable part, the intelligent, experienced, and sophisticated residuum of the erstwhile heterogeneous mass of theatregoers that embraced the presently happily expatriated movie, talkie, radio, and other such elements. Its elected and most prosperous dramatic fare is no longer such stuff as *Strongheart, Classmates*, and *Brown of Harvard*, but *Strange Interlude, The Last Mile*, and *The Barretts of Wimpole Street*. The larger number of dramatic exhibits offered to this new audience by the commercial producers fail to satisfy it. It is a platitude that intellectuality has little more to do with drama than with music, poetry, or home brewing, and that, as with these other arts, it is largely a question of emotion or nothing. And the emotional content of forty-nine out of every fifty present-day plays is approximately that of a clam-juice cocktail. As a consequence, they fail to stir an audience in the slightest degree, for the audience, as has been observed, is usually just about twice as dramatic and twice as emotionally competent as the plays. The average man and woman in the selected theatre audience of today have in their own lives, and consequently in their own theatrical imaginations, emotional resources considerably superior to those of the usual play characters that they waste three dollars to watch. They are thus not even vouchsafed the pleasure of enjoying a vicarious emotional experience, for the dramatic emotions which they attend are largely those of emotional fledglings and so are not only insufficient to provide them with any reaction but are, to boot, pretty often unintentionally humorous. It is no wonder, under the circumstances, that the intelligent theatregoer often presently patronizes music shows in preference to drama and that, when anything at all possible in the way of open-and-shut farce comes along, he gallops to it for the dose of catharsis usually denied him in the serious theatre.

Into this theatre and into this audience, starved for an emotional purge. O'Neill has come with the physic that both have longed for. Into a theatre that night after night has dribbled out the meagre little emotions of ladies' maids dressed as grand ladies, of Cockney actors listed in programs as builders of empire, and of men and women generally with passions as persuasively incendiary as warmed gumdrops, he has brought, since almost first he began to write, a new full heat and fire. The little faint flickers of dramatic flame that now and then lap pathetically at the edges of the Anglo-American stage have been stirred by him into something more like a conflagration, whose incandescence has reached even beyond that stage to the stages of Scandinavia, Russia, and Germany.

In *Mourning Becomes Electra*, an independent reworking in terms of modern characters and the modern psychology of the Greek Orestes-Electra legend of Aeschylus, Sophocles, and Euripides, O'Neill has once again taken over the present-day theatre and made it his own. From five in the afternoon until close to midnight he harrows and mauls, taunts and tortures, prostrates and exalts his characters, set into the New England scene at the close of the Civil War, with the lash and the blaze of his passionate inspiration. It is this inspiration, mighty and crimson, that transcends his characters and play and that, like the glow of a steel furnace against the heavens, impresses the vision, the feeling, and the fancy even though the furnace itself be a mile away. The characters are metaphorically this furnace, sometimes remote, not always immediately actual, and not always plausibly determinable—the affinity between the psychology of the son of Agamemnon and the son of a New England Yankee soldier, for example, is not always altogether convincing; but the glow, spreading over all, luminous and radiant, is the glow that is O'Neill.

A parenthetical observation in conclusion. To superficial critics of O'Neill's writing career, the trilogy idea is associated specifically with his more recent development. A study of his canon, however, reveals the fact that from his earliest beginnings his dramatic mind, if not always his actual dramaturgy, worked with and toward that idea. The trilogy impulse is readily to be detected in three of his short plays of the sea, published under the general title of *The*

Moon of the Caribbees. Beyond the Horizon, as he himself now sees it in retrospect, was essentially a trilogy arbitrarily compressed within a single, regulation-length play. *Dynamo,* as is well known, was the first play of a trilogy the writing of which he abandoned. *Strange Interlude,* as he originally visualized it and as he outlined it to his friends years before he set himself to its execution, was a super-trilogy. There is even a hint of the trilogy sequence in the nature of the emotional philosophy and its development in the recurrent battle of the sexes and Mother Earth theme in certain of his other plays. The dramaturgical form that the volcanic emotionalism of *Mourning Becomes Electra* takes is thus simply a natural outgrowth of a seed that has been in his work since first he began to write.

The Intimate Notebooks of George Jean Nathan, 1932

Tennessee Williams

THE PLAY [*A Streetcar Named Desire*], which might well have been titled *The Glans Menagerie,* has been criticized in some quarters as an unpleasant one. The criticism is pointed. But the fact that a play is unpleasant, needless to say, is not necessarily a reflection on its quality. *Oedipus, Lear,* and *The Lower Depths,* to name only three out of many, are surely very far from pleasant, yet it is their unpleasantness which at least in part makes them what they are. There is a considerable difference between the unpleasant and the disgusting, which is the designation Mr. Williams's critics probably have in mind, and his play is not disgusting, as, for example, is scum like *Maid in the Ozarks* and *School for Brides*. The borderline between the unpleasant and the disgusting is, however, a shadowy one, as inferior playwrights have at times found out to their surprise and grief. Williams has managed to keep his play wholly in hand. But there is, too, a much more positive borderline between the unpleasant and the enlightening, and he has tripped over it, badly. While he has succeeded in making realistically dramatic such elements as sexual abnormality, harlotry, perversion, venality, rape, and lunacy, he has scarcely contrived to distil from them any elevation and purge. His play, as a consequence, remains largely a theatrical shocker which, while it may shock the emotions of its audience, does not in the slightest shock them into any spiritual education.

Eight years ago, at the beginning of his career, Williams wrote a play called *Battle of Angels*, which closed in Boston after a brief showing. It hinted at his preoccupation with sex in its more violent aspects, which continues in the present exhibit. It also, while not nearly so able a play, betrayed his apparent conviction that theatrical sensationalism and dramatic substantiality are much the same thing and that, as in the present case, one can handily pass the former off for the latter, and for something pretty artistic into the bargain, by gilding it with occasional literary flourishes accompanied by offstage vibraharps, flutes, and music boxes. The hanky-panky may work with a susceptible public, but not with the more ingressive criticism. There is a considerable difference between Wedekind and Wedekindergarten. To fashion any such festering materials into important drama it is essential that they be lifted out of life into a pattern larger than life, as, among others, Strindberg and his contemporary disciple, O'Neill, have appreciated. Williams in considerable part leaves them where he found them and deludes himself into a belief that he has made the gutter a broad sea by now and then sailing in it little papier-mâché poesy boats, propelled by doughty exhalations.

Impressionistically, the play suggests a wayward bus occupied by John Steinbeck, William Faulkner, and James Cain, all tipsy and all telling stories simultaneously, and with Williams, cocking his ear to assimilate the goings-on, as the conductor. Critically, it suggests that he is a little deaf and has not been able to disentangle what may be valid from the bedlam and assimilate it to possible meritorious ends. Theatrically and popularly, however, the result will surely impress a lot of people, even such as will pretend for appearances' sake to be offended by what they will allude to as its "strong meat" and who after seeing it will profess that they long for a breath of fresh, good, clean glue.

Like a number of his contemporaries, Williams seems to labor under the misapprehension that strong emotions are best to be expressed strongly only through what may delicately be termed strong language. I am not, you may be relieved to know, going to take up again the already overargued question as to whether such language has any literary justification. I am as tired of the discussion as undoubtably you are. But, justified or not in certain cases, it seems to me that in this specific instance he has at times used it not because it is vitally necessary but for purposes of startle and because his dramatic gifts do not yet include the ability to achieve the desired effect without easy recourse to such terminology. His writing—to fall back on a description I have used before—sometimes sounds altogether too much like a little boy proudly making a muscle.

Tennessee Williams

The play centers on a Southern schoolteacher whose youthful marriage ended in tragedy when her homosexual husband committed suicide, who has vainly sought nepenthe in miscellaneous sex, and who has become an incurable neurotic with delusions of grandeur. It develops her amatory life with her sister's husband and with the latter's crony. And it ends with her mental disintegration and deposit in an asylum. That it holds one's interest is not to be denied. But it holds it much as it is perversely held by a recognizably fixed prize fight or a circus performer projected out of what appears to be a booming cannon by a mechanical spring device. It is, in other words, highly successful showmanship, but considerably less than that as critically secure drama.

In this general view of the play, I hope that no one will suspect that I am subscribing to such definitions as Jerome's "Ugliness is but skin-deep; the business of Art is to reveal the beauty underlying all things." Such sweet sentiments, though generally accepted as true, are much too broad and sometimes faulty. The revelation of fundamental ugliness and depravity has been known to be not only the business of art but even occasionally its triumph. The form and style and manner of the revelation may be beautiful, but the revelation itself is not. A better definition might be that the business of art is to reveal whatever is basically true, whether beautiful or ugly, in terms of the highest aesthetic competence. The ugliness in Williams's play may in the definition of the Jeromes be only skin-deep, but the ability to prick deeper into it and draw from it the blood drops of common humanity, and in them a true count of dramatic art, is absent. It scarcely throws one off critical scent to quote in the program verse, by Hart Crane, about "the broken world," "the visionary company of love," and "its voice an instant in the world."

Playwrights and Performance

It is not enough to substitute the ingenious stage magic of lights and music for the equally seductive but more definitely powerful magic of poetry. For what still mutinously forces itself upon one in this tale of a prostitute who would envelop hideous reality in the anodyne of illusion and supplant the world of pursuing lust with one of pure love is, save in a few valid scenes, the impression of a Pirandello theme dramatized by a hopeful aspirant to dramatic lyricism and which periodically—and I am not being as facetious as you may think—converts its characters into rampaging approximations to Harpo Marx.

Contributing greatly to the external successful aspects of the play are admirable direction by Elia Kazan and a uniformly excellent acting company in which, supported by Marlon Brando, Karl Malden, and the rest, Jessica Tandy in the role of Forever Streetcar gives one of the finest performances observed locally in several seasons. Also helpful is Jo Mielziner's variant of his scenic design for the same author's *The Glass Menagerie*, though one may wonder how he reconciles an acutely realistic lavatory with the rest of his fancifully imagined and dreamlike interior of a dwelling in the Vieux Carré.

The Theatre Book of the Year, 1947–1948

242

Arthur Miller

Arthur Miller

W. H. AUDEN has thus differentiated between them: "Greek tragedy is the tragedy of necessity; that is, the feeling aroused in the spectator is 'what a pity it had to be this way'; Christian tragedy is the tragedy of possibility, 'what a pity it was this way when it could have been otherwise.' "

The definition again is found to be snugly appropriate to Miller's work [*Death of a Salesman*], and evidently no one appreciates its aptness more than he does. But where other playwrights often have usurped to themselves the Christian pity, he, though doubtless he experiences it himself, prefers to leave it to his audience. Therein lies one of his play's chief merits, for it does succeed in substantially evoking both an immediate and a lingering compassion not alone for the life its protagonist lived but for the life he might have lived in its stead, and with none of the more usual playwright's hard insistence.

There are other merits. The writing is simple; there is no slightest pretentiousness; and, though the play, because of its basic disorganized expressionistic form, is susceptible of strained effort, little sense of strain is felt by its auditors. There is, moreover, none of the heavy striving for lyric tone common to the plays of prosy writers who seek to conceal their prosiness in something they choose to imagine is poetry, yet something of a poetic tinge nonetheless at times issues from it. And, finally, though it misses the spiritual exaltation that is the requirement of fine tragedy and though its end effect is rather acute depression, it triumphs over itself by virtue of the uncompromising honesty of its emotion.

That the play must have a considerable internal force becomes apparent when one considers that it registers the effect it has registered in spite of several confounding production elements. Though Elia Kazan, aided greatly by Mielziner's imaginative setting, has directed admirably the physical flow of the tragedy, his direction of the vocal is often so bad that its intrinsically gentle spirit has a difficult time in establishing itself. Lines that should be read quietly are so shouted and yelled that it seems at times he is determined to make the play a melodrama in spite of itself. There are moments, indeed, when the melodramatic screaming becomes so loud that it is next to impossible to make out what the father or his two sons are talking about and not to feel that Lincoln J. Carter will pop in at any minute with a scene showing the father in his automobile racing against the tooting New York, New Haven and Hartford on one of his selling trips to Boston.

There is, too, the casting of Lee Cobb as the salesman doomed by false standards and self-deception to humiliation and failure. I can well understand the wisdom of avoiding the conventional in casting the role not with the Donald Meek type of actor but with one of strength and size, since the theatrical effect of tragic decline is thereby heightened. But Cobb is so bullish not merely in physical person but, more disastrously, in elemental grain and spirit that one feels, wrongly to be sure, that the playwright is arbitrarily pulling him into the picture and that, were the character left on its own, his life would have taken a decidedly different course. And there are, as well, several additional points in the staging which take unhappy advantage of the author. The direction resorts to such obvious stuff as indicating the now aged salesman's once younger nature by having him jovially kick up his heels in a kazatska, his love of his elder son by causing him so to overdo camaraderie in pawing embraces and hearty yawping that he seems less the potential figure in a tragedy than a onetime understudy for Sam Bernard in *The Rich Mr. Hoggenheimer,* and his pretense of bravery in the face of consciousness of defeat by such a bellowing as was never equaled by the late Melbourne MacDowell, a booming mountebank if ever there was one, as the Duke de Gonzague. Some of my colleagues, I note, have described Cobb's performance as "tremendous." It is. As a boiler explosion.

That the play is weakened not only by such things but by Kazan's favorite occasional melodramatic emphasis on the box office's behalf is clear. One periodically gets much the impression one would have got if they had brought in Paul Armstrong and Wilson Mizner to pepper up a play like *Our Town.* But the innate silent power of Miller's script, the reticence of much of his writing, and the intermittent excellent flashes of imagery—such, for one example, as the memory of road drummers "riding on a smile and a shoeshine"— combine to make one sufficiently oblivious of the disturbances and to react to the whole as the author hoped.

Henry Arthur Jones once observed that "unless drama is touched with a sense of eternity, wrapped 'round with the splendor of heroism, and imbedded in what is primary and of everlasting import, the mere reproduction on the stage of the commonplace details of everyday life must always be barren, worthless, and evanescent." There is much to be said for the definition. *Death of a Salesman,* by it, does not measure up, does not measure up by a very considerable margin, to a tragedy of real artistic stature. Its touch with a sense of eternity is but flicking; there is in it little splendor of heroism; it is imbedded but sketchily in what is primary and of everlasting import; and it reproduces merely the commonplace details of everyday life. But it remains not barren, nor worthless, nor, possibly, evanescent, because it touches these commonplace details with a sense of deep and pitiful recognition, because there is splendor of a sort not in any heroism but in its very human cowardice, and because, at least for the time one is in its presence, what may not be primary and of everlasting import is made out of one's immediate won sympathy to seem so.

Whenever a critic, reviewing a play of some pretensions of quality, employs the word *melodrama* in a derogatory sense, other critics who are extreme in their regard for the play are certain to take him acidly to task with the now familiar remark that, since melodrama is the tone of today's world, it is asinine to use the term in condemnation of it. The gentlemen seem to overlook three small points. First, the fact that melodrama seems to be the present world's chief characteristic does not necessarily justify it as a chief characteristic of dramatic or any other art. Secondly, there are various kinds of melodrama, and the melodrama that the critic has in mind in the instance of the play he is considering is the kind which in the interests of theatricalism raises its head at debatable moments. Where, in a word, completely honest characters would comport themselves with some intellectual, psychological, and emotional reserve, the characters purely for the sake of theatrical effect are arbitrarily made to dive off the Brooklyn Bridge and hold up a mail train. And, thirdly, the melodrama is resorted to in order to lend a surface excitement to what a better dramatist might make even more exciting through emotional and physical reserve.

Sometimes the melodrama, which, incidentally, is the easiest of all dramatic forms to master, is unintentional on the part of a playwright, who confuses it with inner intensity of theme and character. Sometimes, when intentional, it gets out of hand and so supervises character that the latter explodes into nothingness from spontaneous combustion. And sometimes, of course, it is well considered and completely and properly in key. But much more often in the work of various American playwrights, whether deliberately or not deliberately, it has the air of an exclamation point inserted into what is essentially a passive sentence, the aspect of red-painted fingernails on a small girl child, and the sense of pulling the lever of a street-corner fire box and bringing on the engines, hook-and-ladders, and hose carts in a false alarm. It is, in short, frequently a youngster's "boo" designed to startle other youngsters, a little boy's Indian whoop hopeful of scaring his quietly amused father. And it also, even when there is nothing intrinsically wrong with it, is sometimes so whimsically out of the immediate surroundings that it sounds something like the majordomo of Buckingham Palace elegantly answering the telephone and exclaiming: "Why, yes, of course, Mrs. Greenberg."

This was the kind of melodrama that, among other things, made Miller's widely admired previous play, *All My Sons*, strike me as an inferior performance. I have already spoken of the dubiety of his character drawing in that play, as well as of other elements in it that were open to skepticism. Since this subsequent play, *Death of a Salesman*, is clear of all such defects, it is gratifying to hear Miller confess that he himself now sees the faults of *All*

My Sons, and equally encouraging to observe that some of those critics who were most enthusiastic about it now see it also, belatedly, as having been what they admit was a "contrived job."

As will be remembered, *All My Sons* was a dramaturgically conventional play of the rococo "well-made" species. Commenting on it, Miller says: "The Conventional play form forces the writer to siphon everything into a single place at a single time, and squeezes the humanity out of a play. Why shouldn't a play have the depth, the completeness, and the diversity of a novel? I felt I had to perfect conventional technique first and *All My Sons* was an exercise."

Death of a Salesman is no such exercise; it is the result of profit from trial and error, and not merely in respect to dramaturgy. There is complete honesty in most of the characters; there is absolute honesty in contemplation of its theme as against the sense of fabrication one had in the case of *All My Sons;* and there is, unlike in that play, a minimum of theatrical compromise. Even in the few instances where one feels that perhaps Miller operates to avoid a possible monotony by including episodes of some forced, theatrical color, the episodes themselves—as, for example, the scene in which the sons entertain their father in a Sixth Avenue corner saloon fabulously equipped for champagne service—somehow do not seem altogether too removed from truth. And the point of view throughout, in its challenge of popular conceptions, is strikingly intelligent. The popular credos that nothing is more valuable to a man than being liked; that sincere, hard work is bound to reap its ultimate reward; that children, even if they conceal the fact, have an inborn love for their parents; that loyalty is always a virtue; and that only the incompetent fail in this world—such beliefs, with no show of facile cynicism, Miller punctures. His tragedy of the little man has in it also, if obliquely, a little something of the tragedy of much bigger men, whether successes or failures by the world's standards.

In a preface to the published play Mr. Miller goes to considerable lengths to justify his belief that the tragedy of the little man may be quite as exalted dramatically and artistically as that of the classic kings and emperors. He need not have gone to so much trouble. It may be, but there are two points which, seemingly in the interests of his own play, he chooses to overlook. Save the little man have something of a mind, which Mr. Miller's protagonist has not, his tragedy, while it may be moving, is in finality without universal size and is like the experience we suffer in contemplating on the highways a run-over and killed dog, undeniably affecting but without any profound significance. The tragedy, accordingly, becomes that not of a full-winged human being but merely that of a mindless clod, at once pitiful and touching but lost from the outset in the maelstrom of inevitable circumstance. And his struggle against his surroundings becomes not cumulatively holding but obviously foredoomed, since there is no share of intellect even modestly to assist him. Great tragedy is the tragedy of man's mind in strong conflict with the stronger fates; minor tragedy that of mindless men already beaten by them.

The second point is the language in which tragedy is written. The fall of kings calls for a splendor of prose or poetry, otherwise it may be quite as unimpressive as the fall of little men. But the tragedy of the little man, to be as impressive as that of a king, calls as well for such treatment. It is not the story of and the reasons for a ruler's tragic end that remain in our hearts and memories but the flights of language through which they are related. Commonplace language, though it may be exactly suited to the tragedy of the underdog, may make for first-rate theatre but scarcely for first-rate and overwhelming drama.

In defense of his point of view, Mr. Miller concludes: "It is time, I think, that we who are without kings took up this bright thread of our history and followed it to the only place it can possibly lead in our time—the heart and spirit of the average man."

We are not without kings, though they may not wear the royal purple. We have men of heart and spirit—and also mind. They are or may be the meat of important tragedy. The average man's, the common man's tragedy, save it be laid over and lifted above itself with the deceptive jewels of the English speech, can be no more in the temple of dramatic art than the pathetic picture of a lovable idiot lifting his small voice against the hurricane of the world.

The Theatre Book of the Year, 1948–1949

South Pacific *and Its Criticism*

LITTLE IS MORE DANGEROUS to the prosperity of women and musical shows than crediting them openly with too much intelligence. Some time ago Elsa Maxwell paid that doubtful compliment in her syndicated newspaper column to the charming actress Lilli Palmer and was subsequently told by the latter that it had succeeded in depriving her of a job for a full year and a half. To say of a musical show that it is intelligent is similarly to scare people away from it, since to speak of intelligence in connection with any such exhibit is like touting a drama for its stupidity. There is, moreover, often some reason in the people's fright. A musical show, as I have noted in the past, is in its very nature properly a holiday from the mind; it is, or should be, a pleasant lunacy in the midst of the world's struggle for rationalism; and the intrusion into it of too much sense spoils the party.

Do not be unduly alarmed, however, when I describe *South Pacific* as an infinitely more intelligent musical than most. Though its story line and many other things about it have been contrived with more brains than we are accustomed to in such cases, its creators have warily seen to it that its savvy does not get out of control and throw a wrench into the works, and the consequence is an unusually satisfying evening. Almost everything connected with the occasion indicates an uncommon taste, expertness, and quality of theatrical mind. The book, derived from two of the Michener stories and ingeniously combined and edited, concurrently narrates two love stories: one, that of an American wartime nurse and a French exile planter with two children by a Polynesian woman, the other of a young American marine aviator and a Tonkinese girl, and employs both for a glance at inborn or acquired prejudice against race and color. But the theme is not pointed up and stressed: the idea is allowed to develop quietly, gently, and very naturally from the acted story. The music is close to Rodgers's best; the songs dramatize character and action and are part and parcel of the play and, above all, are independent of the common musical psychology described some years ago by the late composer and producing musical director of Broadway shows, Herbert Stothart.

"Musical scoring," he observed, with both motion pictures and their Broadway stage counterparts in mind, "is, I believe, largely a matter of psychology. The composer, through experience, learns which elements generate certain moods. Anger can be generated by what I call 'red' tones, which slightly clash in orchestration and so mentally irritate. A tranquil mood can be inspired by quiet, gently flowing melody. Alarm can be created by clashing harmonies; unrest by the monotonous beat of tom-toms, and by effects strange in musical principle, hence played to unaccustomed ears. Sonorous bells and deep tones of the organ inspire reverence. These are all matters of elemental psychology. By deciding to what extent to us them, one gets the shades in between the basic classifications."

No such nursery nonsense for Rodgers. He writes a score not, as do various of his colleagues, for the table-d'hôte but, with some slight respect, for the à-la-carte ear. Most of his songs are delightful: "Dites-Moi Pourquoi," "Some Enchanted Evening" (with a hint of Lehar), "There Is Nothing Like a Dame," "I'm in Love with a Wonderful Guy," "Younger Than Springtime," "Happy Talk" (with its delicately lovely pantomime by Betta St. John as the Tonkinese girl), "I'm Gonna Wash That Man Right Outa My Hair," and "This Nearly Was Mine." Nothing, to be sure, to threaten the reputation of Franz Schubert or Arthur Sullivan, but delightful none the less. And all set to the kind of words—simple, unaffected, tender, humorous, and never strainfully sophisticated—which Hammerstein alone in our musical theatre seems to be able to write.

Logan's staging of the show is exceptional, even down to the matter of the actors' facial expressions, and the performances of most of the roles could scarcely be bettered. Ezio Pinza, recruited from the Metropolitan Opera, in voice, acting, and bearing takes chief honors; his is by far the best performance the local musical stage has seen in some time. Mary Martin, who has never been one of my passionate enthusiasms, for the most part is excellent as the Arkansas nurse; she has developed her comedy in a notable manner; but her occasional tendency to black-smith overemphasis calls for the rod. Others, like Juanita Hall as a native peddler of grass skirts, shrunken human heads, and girls of saleable virtue; Myron McCormick, William Tabbert, and Martin Wolfson as part of the United States military personnel; and the earlier mentioned prehensile Betta St. John as the secondary love interest are in every way exactly what they should be.

If these impress the reader as pretty big words and ones he has not often been accustomed to in the critical vocabulary of the present recorder, he should read for relative size those of most of that recorder's confreres. As with *Death of a Salesman*, the press reviews of the show bordered on an ecstasy that in the former case would have seemed more fitting to something like *Electra* and in this to *Lohengrin*. But, since daily journalistic criticism is conducted largely on a basis of comparative Broadway values, they were in this present instance justified, even if some of the more extreme raptures obliquely reminded us of the time-honored Broadway view of theatre criticism in general, to wit, that it too frequently is tragically deficient in such theoretically contagious warmth and excitement which sends customers rushing posthaste to the ticket window. It thus has been that in the last quarter of a century not more than four out of the many practitioners of the craft—the four given to an irradiation of heat exceeded only by a like number of Pittsburgh blast furnaces—have been esteemed as authentic, A-1, white-headed boys. These four were members, respectively of the Oh-What-A-Genius! school, the Horticulture-And-Hat-Removing school, the Dancing-In-The-Streets-And-Hat-Tossing school, and the Glauber's-Salts-or-Self-Purgative school, all closely affiliated.

The first of the tropical quartet was Acton Davies, of the Oh-What-A-Genius! school. When Davies wound up, the heat was such that one had to wrap a cold towel around one's head to read him. His especial fanaticism was the late Belasco, and herewith a sample of the pyrexia induced in and spread by him: "When we take stock of true genius, the kind associated with the names of such immortals as Michelangelo, Mozart and Dostoievski, where can we find a truer, more beautiful and complete flowering of it than in the superb art of David Belasco's magnificent production of *The Darling of the Gods?* The answer, plainly, is nowhere! It makes your pulse bounce with renewed life and your brain buzz with such visions of grandeur as are rarely the gift to us mortals. It makes you shout for supreme joy and, seeing it, it is all you can do to keep from rushing up to the nearest stranger on the street and hugging him while you cry out in happiness over such stunning mastery."

Following Davies came Clayton Hamilton, a member of the Horticulture-And-Hat-Removing school. It was sometimes impossible, reading him, to know whether you were looking at a seed catalogue, a Stetson advertisement, or a theatre review. When he got up full steam, you had to turn on the mechanical piano with the mandolin attachment for an accompaniment. Did J. M. Barrie come forth with a play in which little babies were so much as mentioned once, and Clayton wept into his beer: "Art has here sprung alive into the world with music of a million Easter-lilies leaping from the grave and laughing with a silver singing." And as to the hat motif, a typical morsel: "In this particular part [*Boys Will Be Boys*, by Irvin S. Cobb] Harry Beresford reaches greatness: and whenever greatness is achieved, all lovers of the arts should rise to their feet and stand reverently, hats off, with uncovered heads!"

Hamilton's successor in the Broadway affection was Alexander Woollcott, a member of the Dancing-In-The-Streets-And-Hat-Tossing-In-Air school. As a street dancer, Alec rivaled Carmen Amaya in her youth, and as a hat tosser he was the theatre's William Jennings Bryan. Let Mrs. Fiske or Ethel Barrymore or any one of two or three dozen older actresses appear and, whatever her vehicle, Alec's review would contain enough hoofing on the boulevards and projection of his beanie into the ether to make the Fourteenth of July in Paris look like Black Friday. The dancing in the streets and hat-tossing were also occasionally supplemented by reverential crawling, as in the instance of an actor named Jacob Ben-Ami, of whom Alec rhapsodized: "See him by all means, even if you have to crawl on your very hands and knees to get to the theatre where he is playing!" But when it came to the mimic Elsie Janis, he got really hot: "When she danced her moonlight dance . . . when she sang her moonlight song . . . when, above all, when she stood there in the uniform of a French chasseur and sang 'Madelon' . . . well, these were great moments not to be forgotten. . . . All of which is solemnly reported by one who finds it difficult to keep from growing incoherent in the process!"

There was no stopping the boy once he started to unbosom himself. "Perhaps," he would write, "it does not choke you up a little when, from some high-walled schoolyard, you hear suddenly the shrill clamor of children at recess. If it does not, the play *Five O'Clock* would have no particular call upon your sympathies." Or: "A little of the real flame is in Edward Robinson. You have only to see his performance as Satin [*Night Refuge*] to realize it and to realize, too, how all-compensating is the real fire. Here is a

young actor seeming without an atom of what is feebly
called 'personal distinction.' His speech, and Satin was supposed to be a man of education, is what dear Mrs. Sanders
used to call 'barbareous.' He takes the keynote speech of
the play, wherein Satin cries out: 'What is truth? Human
beings—that's the truth,' and devastates it by saying 'youman beans.' Yet he is still worth his weight in gold!"

If the late lamented Woollcott may be said to have had a
successor, it was probably my old friend Burton Rascoe, a
member of the Glauber's-Salts-or-Self-Purgative school,
with further matriculation in the Great-Stuff academy. In
the single season that he substituted on the *World-Telegram* for John Mason Brown, absent in the armed services,
Burton managed to find more great plays and great actors
than even Davies, Hamilton, and Woollcott in their combined long and eager careers. In all kinds of exhibits that
aroused a remarkable lack of enthusiasm elsewhere, he discovered all kinds of rich and notable art, and his tributes to
actors ranging from John Philliber, who had a bit in *Mr.
Sycamore*, to George Coulouris, who in everybody else's
opinion was pretty bad as Richard III, were so voluptuous
that you had to look twice to make sure he was not writing
about someone like Lillian Russell. But the castor oil got
into full operation in the case of the movie actress Geraldine Fitzgerald, whose performance left most of his colleagues constipated. "But let me tell you," he declared,
"that on Saturday afternoon I dropped in at the Morosco
and stood in the back to catch a part of *Sons and Soldiers*
again. I wanted to see if my first impression of Geraldine
Fitzgerald, as she appears in this play, was correct—that
she is one of the greatest actresses of our time. I caught her
in that party scene in which she is the middle-aged mother
getting a little tipsy at the celebration of her son's twenty-
fifth birthday. My physical sensations were these: tinglings

ran up and down my spine; my heart seemed suddenly to fill up and almost to stop; tears trickled down my cheeks. I was in the presence of perfection, of magic, of beauty!"

It was this brand of jive criticism that originally gave birth to movie criticism, with its "epics," "colossals," "supers," "peerless artists," "triumphs," "masterpieces," "director geniuses," and the like. Nevertheless, I somehow still perversely believe, Broadway notwithstanding, that so-called "cold" criticism like Hazlitt's "Miss O'Neill's Lady Teazle appears to us to be a complete failure . . . the only thing that had an air of fashion about her was the feather in her hat," or Shaw's "I think something better could be done with Réjane's talents than this business [*Madame Sans-Gêne*] of playing the washerwoman like a real duchess and the duchess like a stage washerwoman," or, better still, his "Sardou's *Delia Harding* is the worst play I have ever seen; the whole business was so stale, so obviously factitious, so barrenly inept, that at last the gallery broke out into open derision"—nevertheless, as I say, I somehow still perversely believe that such criticism in the long run helps the theatre a thousandfold more than the kind that sounds less as if it were written by reviewers than blown by Louis Prima.

The Theatre Book of the Year, 1948–1949

The Burlesque Show: I

LET US TAKE a look in at the old Olympic Theatre down in Fourteenth Street. Unlike the affectedly tony Columbia Theatre uptown, the Olympic remains true to first principles and devotes itself not, as in the case of the Columbia, to fifth-rate imitations of third-rate Broadway music shows, but to pure, unadulterated, and heart-warming old knock-'em-down-and-drag-'em-out burlesque. Here is rosemary of the palmy days. Not a bustle is safe from the slap slat, not a face is spared from the seltzer siphon, not a wiggle is omitted from the cooch dance, not a bass drum remains whole when the final curtain comes down. Here still is the good old "Casino at Monte Carlo" with the Rocky Mountains appropriately figuring on the backdrop and with Izzy, Pat, and Bozo talking successively into the telephone and receiving, respectively, a spray of flour, a squirt of water, and—ah, Bozo, thou lucky rogue!—a glass of foaming lager. Here still is the good old "Beach at Ostend" with O. U. Kidd and I. M. Woozy coming suddenly, to their horror, upon their wives and fooling the latter by donning aprons and passing themselves off on the ladies as waiters. And here still is the good old "Artist's Studio" with the eight ex-chambermaids arrayed in lobster-colored fleshings, their right arms curved with painstaking grace over their heads and representing—in the elegance of the program—"The Birth of the LePrintemps."

The Burlesque Show: I

Once again, as in the old days, we encounter I. Cheatem ("and he does," confides the program), Willie Takitt ("a live wire"), Lotta Pepp ("full of ginger"), Mary Wise ("and she is"), together with all their old pals, Ima Peach, Izzie Konshuss, Hammond Deggs, M. T. Noodle, G. Howe Smart, Lotta Jazz, Ann Jennue, Miss Taken, Miss Gotrox, Heeza Nutt, Sheeza Pippin, Fuller Bull ("poor but not proud") and his three brothers Fuller Laffs, Fuller Hopps, and Fuller Proons, Otto Mobile, Miss Calla Number, Noah Lott, Helen B. Ware, I. Will B. Goode, Notter Bumm, Gotta Hare Lipp, O. U. Vampire, and, last but not least, A. Kopp. What memories they awaken, these shadow Salvinis and Duses of the dramatic underworld! Who doesn't remember Heinie Dingelbender's "Papa, mama she sess you are some-of-a-peach," with papa Herman's indignant rejoinder: "*What* you sess she called me?" And who doesn't recall the scene wherein Mlle. Fifi, of the Boul' Mich', raises her skirt to insert a bill into her stocking, the while Herman and Heinie at stage left so strain themselves to view the revelation that they lose their balance and fall on top of each other? Then, too, the scene wherein our Heinie strolls drolly among the "Living Pictures," casting significant winks in the direction of the audience, pinching the most corpulent "picture" first on the arm and then, upon no sign of life from the lady, on the youknow—and finally lying down on the floor to achieve a better view of the lovely subjects? What sweetness in the retrospect! What Art, as boyhood knew it!

Well, it is still all here at the Olympic, from the Gas House Quartette to the hoochie dance, from the venerable money-changing act to the floozie with the red necktie—how the exasperated Heinie doth glare at the fellow!—from the drop curtain with the chewing-gum advertisements to the boy who sells boxes of candy in the aisles—

"twenty-five cents—a quarter—a package, and a prize in every box." The grand old smell of stale cigars and cigarettes, of cheap hair tonics and Third Avenue drugstore perfumery, of the hospitably near, frankly unabashed, and doorless "Gent's Walk"—it is present as it was when you and I were boys. The carpetless wooden floor, rich in Homeric expectorations; the orchestra with the squeaky fiddle and indefatigable tapper on the triangle; the drop curtain that goes up like a man pulling an old-fashioned shirt over his head; the girls with no less than three solid gold teeth apiece—they, too, are present as in the dear, bygone days when we and all the world were young. It is all very gay, and just a bit sad. Where the sob-brothers of our American criticism are wont to weep lustily over the touching splendors of John Barrymore, Elsie Janis, Reggie Sheffield, Vincent Serrano, Winifred Lenihan, and Geoffrey Stein, I reserve my soul moisture for this drama of our far-off youth, the wistful echoes of which come down to us in these later and colder years. There is the touch penseroso in its memorable fanning of rears, in its cracking of bladders on pates, in its spacious pants and red under-lingerie and crepe whiskers and pink wigs. It is rapidly being driven from the stage and into the discard by a Puritan censorship, a wave of dull Art, and a reduction in the personnel of the United States Navy. While it is yet here, let us enjoy it and, enjoying it, meditate upon the purple times when Harrison and Grover Cleveland yet held the White House, when the hanging out of the picture of a goat in front of the boulevard inns signalized the great annual dawn of reason, when our coins and currency still bore the faces of noble Indians instead of ignoble politicians, when shoes were polished by grinning, singing black native sons instead of by muttering alien followers of D'Annunzio, when it required an alpenstock to climb into a barber's chair, when no one would eat a sausage because Leutgert had murdered his wife, when John Philip Sousa's hair was still black, when the smallest church in every town was that of the Methodists— when we were still Americans.

Materia Critica, 1923

The Burlesque Show: II

ONE OF THE MOST depressing changes that has come about in the American theatre in our time is the gradual passing out of the old-time burlesque show, erstwhile delight of all connoisseurs of humour in its jockstrap. With the Columbia Wheel presently going in for revivals of *Uncle Tom's Cabin* and productions of such past Broadway successes as *White Cargo*, with police injunctions to managers of such houses as the Chelsea either to behave or to shut up shop, and with the authorities of the Mutual Wheel toning down their exhibitions until they are indistinguishable from so many Epworth League picnics, the burlesque show as we knew it twenty years ago seems doomed to go the way of such other estimable American institutions as cock fights, rye whisky, and liberty.

The signs of the death of burlesque have been in the air these last ten years and more. It was at about that time that the two-hundred-pound blondes whom once we frantically cheered began to send in coupons out of the backs of the magazines asking for free samples of reducing cream, that the sons of the late lamented house managers, succeeding to their fathers' posts after four years at Harvard, began to look askance at the scene in which Ludwig Dinkeplatz besought Hyman Finkelstein to take his feet out of the soup, and that the producers of the shows got rid of the old backdrop representing the Casino at Monte Carlo, a lovable standby since the Civil War, and bought in its place a secondhand set of scenery from the Casino at Broadway and Thirty-ninth Street. It was also at this time that the burlesque entrepreneurs began to feel the first faint symptoms of morality and to wrinkle their brows over the scene in which the Irish comedian inquired ironically of Babe La Gervaise, the prima donna, why she wore her bustle in her shirtwaist, and why she wore two of them.

Up to this period, burlesque had been untrammeled and carefree. It was as left alone as a pretzel in Paris. And it flourished to the delight of all and sundry. Then came the first ripples of the blue waves that were presently to drown it, along with so many other things that once brought happiness to the humble American. Today it is but a ghost of its former self, and that ghost is yearly getting more shadowy. Soon it will vanish completely. On the stage where once we boys applauded the spectacle of the great Al Reeves pointing to a blonde hippopotamus and asking if anyone in the audience would give him a quarter for her, provided he threw in his hat, there will be only a tenth-rate performance of some stale tenth-rate Broadway play. On the stage that once held *Krausmeyer's Alley*, upon which no less than seven Presidents of the United States were fed in their youth, we shall hear nothing but the prayers of Little Eva. On the stage that once gave us, to our eternal joy, the money-changing act, the scene in which the German and Hebrew comedians pretended to be waiters in order to fool their wives, and the scene wherein the Irish comedian got an eyeful of flour when he talked into the telephone, we shall see nothing but a belated copy of the totem-pole number out of *Rose Marie* and an imitation of the Tiller Girls.

Not long ago, in the burlesque house down in Fourteenth Street, I actually saw two sailors and a pickpocket break down and cry like children over the passing of the old order. The Hebrew comedian, instead of stealing up on the cooch dancer and jocosely belaboring her rear with a large bologna sausage, as in the happy days of the McKinley era, simply sidled nervously around her for a moment or two and made his exit. The Irish comique, instead of leaning under the table to get a better view of the soubrette's ample limb and falling on his nose as a result, simply went into a tame song and dance with the lady. And the German funny man, instead of sitting on the elephantine prima donna's lap and dropping nickels down her décolleté, approached the fair creature gingerly and bestowed a peck upon her shoulderblade. To those of us who have the best interests of the native drama at heart and are willing to lay down our lives that the honor and integrity of the American theatre may be preserved, it was all too awful.

Speaking for the generation of the early nineties, I urge upon the burlesque impresarios a reconsideration of their present devastating and highly obnoxious plans. Let them give back to us Billy Watson in all his glory, together with the Heinies and Izzies and Mikes of blessed memory. Let them bring back, without delay, the old fat girls, the old floppy breeches, the old red undershirts, the old suspenders made of rope, the old green vests, the old Limburger-cheese jokes, the old backdrop of Union Square, and the old scene in which the fierce-looking cop who cowed the comedians turned out to be a lizzie. Then again all of us Shakespeare and Ibsen enthusiasts will be happy.

Art of the Night, 1928

Index

i

Index

Index

iii

Index

Index

Index

Index

Index

Index

Index

Index

Index

Index

Index

A NOTE ABOUT THE EDITOR

THOMAS QUINN CURTISS, a friend of George Jean Nathan over many years, is dramatic and film critic for the European edition of the New York Herald Tribune *and Paris theatre correspondent for* Variety.

He was born in New York City and educated there and abroad, attending the University of Vienna and studying the theatre and cinema in France, Italy, Austria, Germany, and Russia. During the Second World War he served in the U.S. Army in Europe.

He has contributed to The New York Times Book Review, *the New York* Herald Tribune Book Review, *the London* Observer, *A. G. Orage's* New Age, Town and Country, *and* Harper's Bazaar, *and writes for the* Encyclopaedia Britannica Book of the Year *on European drama.*

He is now at work on a biography of George Jean Nathan and a study of the Irish drama.

September 1960

A NOTE ON THE TYPE

The text of this book has been set on the Linotype in a type face called "Baskerville." The face is a facsimile reproduction of type cast from molds made for John Baskerville (1706–1775) from his designs. The punches for the revived Linotype Baskerville were cut under the supervision of the English printer George W. Jones.

John Baskerville's original face was one of the forerunners of the type style known as "modern face" to printers: a "modern" of the period A.D. *1800.*

The boldface type used throughout this volume is called "Baskerville Bold"—a modern heavy cutting based on the Baskerville type face.

The book was composed, printed, and bound by Plimpton Press, Norwood, Mass. The paper was manufactured by P. H. Glatfelter Co., Spring Grove, Pa. The typographic scheme and the binding design are by WARREN CHAPPELL.